W9-BWN-328

RELUCTANT PIONEERS

STUDIES OF
THE WEATHERHEAD EAST ASIAN INSTITUTE,
COLUMBIA UNIVERSITY

The East Asian Institute is Columbia
University's center for research, publication,
and teaching on modern East Asia. The
Studies of the East Asian Institute were
inaugurated in 1962 to bring to a wider public
the results of significant new research on
Japan, China, and Korea.

Reluctant Pioneers

*China's Expansion
Northward, 1644–1937*

JAMES REARDON-ANDERSON

STANFORD UNIVERSITY PRESS
STANFORD, CALIFORNIA
2005

Stanford University Press
Stanford, California
www.sup.org

Library of Congress Cataloging-in-Publication Data
Reardon-Anderson, James.
Reluctant pioneers : China's expansion northward, 1644–1937/James
Reardon-Anderson.

MIL   p.   cm.
Includes bibliographical references and index.
ISBN 0-8047-5167-6 (alk. paper)
1. Migrant labor—China—Manchuria.   2. Migration, Internal—China—
Manchuria.   3. China—Economic conditions—1644–1912.   4. China—
Economic conditions—1912–49.   5. China—Territorial expansion.   I. Title.
HD5856.C5R43 2005
951'.803—dc22   2004014667

Printed in the United States of America on acid-free, archival-quality paper.
Original Printing 2005

Last figure below indicates year of this printing:
14   13   12   11   10   09   08   07   06   05

Typeset by G&S Typesetters, Inc. in 10/12.5 Palatino Oldstyle.

To
Peter Dunkley
Robert L. Gallucci
Peter F. Krogh

Contents

Illustrations

Migration   130–31

Transportation   180–81

Commerce   190–91

Tables

Abbreviations

CER   Chinese Eastern Railway
CIGC China, Inspectorate General of Customs
SJTZ *Qinding Shengjing tongzhi*
SMR   South Manchuria Railway

Acknowledgments

IT IS HARD TO IMAGINE that anyone would set out to write a book with the foreknowledge of how long it might take and how many dead ends and U-turns would be met along the way. That is certainly true in this case. I began the project that has resulted in this book in 1990. The plan back then was that I should take the post of director of the Committee on Scholarly Communication with the People's Republic of China (CSC) with the assignment to design and implement programs for the multi-national, multi-disciplinary study of human impacts on the natural environment of China. During my tour of duty (1990–92), the CSC launched two such projects, one dealing with global climate change,[1] and the other with the grassland ecosystem of the Mongolian Steppe.[2] The latter project was the beginning of an adventure that has resulted in this book.

I first made my way onto the steppe in the company of Dr. James E. Ellis, an ecosystem scientist with the Natural Resource Ecology Labora-tory at Colorado State University, who had spent many years studying the grasslands of East Africa and was anxious to expand his work into Asia. Jim Ellis was one of the most engaging scholars and people whom I have known. He viewed his subject—plants, animals, people, the sky above and earth below—as parts of a greater whole and challenged oth-ers to hear his thoughts, while he listened generously to theirs. He was a great scientist, a great traveler, and a great friend. His tragic death in

[1] National Research Council (1992A).
[2] National Research Council (1992B).

an avalanche in Colorado in 2002 leaves many lives and much scholarship incomplete. This book contains the echoes of conversations Jim and I began in Colorado, China, and Mongolia.

The initial stages of my work benefited from a number of individuals and institutions associated with the Committee on Scholarly Communication. President of the National Academy of Sciences, Frank Press, and chair of the CSC and vice president of the Academy, the late James Ebert, did much to defend and promote the conduct of scholarship in China in the years following the Tiananmen Square massacre of 1989. President of the American Council of Learned Societies, Stan Katz, was especially helpful, both personally and professionally, in all of our work. Associate director of the CSC, Bob Geyer, whom many China scholars know as the guiding light of the Committee during its heyday in the 1970s and 1980s, made my time with this enterprise a pleasure and has remained a friend ever since. Program officer Beryl Leach contributed greatly to all of the science projects undertaken by the Committee in the early 1990s. Support for the Grassland Ecosystem of the Mongolian Steppe (GEMS) project was provided by the National Academy of Sciences, the National Science Foundation, and the Johnson Foundation.

Our work in China and Mongolia was made possible by the generous and effective cooperation of many people, including: Chen Zuozhong, Director, Inner Mongolia Grassland Ecosystem Research Station; Chuluun Togtohyn, Mongolian Academy of Sciences; Kou Zhenwu, Director, Wulanaodu Grassland Ecosystem Research Station; Ren Jizhou, Director, Gansu Grassland Ecological Research Institute; Zhang Xinshi (David Chang), Director, Institute of Botany, Chinese Academy of Sciences (CAS); Zhao Shidong, Deputy Director, Shenyang Institute of Applied Ecology, CAS; and Zhu Tingcheng, Director, Institute of Grassland Science, Northeast Normal University.

At various stages, drafts of this book have been read by and profited from the comments of colleagues at Georgetown and elsewhere, including: Carol Benedict, John McNeill, James Millward, Peter Perdue, and Richard Stites. Carol Benedict deserves special praise and thanks for her assiduous and helpful reading. Much of what is good (or, at least, less bad) about this book is the result of her firm and thoughtful intervention. Ethan Schwalbe provided excellent Japanese-to-English translations of Manchurian village histories and proved a pleasure to work with. The students and staff of the Master of Science in Foreign

Service (MSFS) Program, which I now serve as director, have been ever kind and helpful during the final stages of this project.

I take special pleasure in dedicating this book to the three people with whom I have worked most closely and who have made my time at Georgetown University's Edmund A. Walsh School of Foreign Service so rewarding. Peter F. Krogh, the "second founder" of the School of Foreign Service and its dean for 25 years, plucked me from obscurity to join the faculty in 1985 and has protected me from failure ever since. Robert L. Gallucci, dean of the School since 1996, following an illustrious career as one of our nation's finest diplomats, has proven an outstanding leader of the institution and generous partner on the golf course. Peter Dunkley, associate dean for faculty affairs, is my best friend and co-conspirator in the follies of academic administration. I honor all three for the same qualities: their devotion to the vision of the university in which scholarship and education are equally prized, their integrity, and their friendship. No one can have better colleagues than these.

Finally, I take this moment to thank my wife of more than thirty years, Kathleen, and our three children, Jane, Peter, and William, who are the light of my life and my chief reason for being. We are having the greatest of rides together.

JAMES REARDON-ANDERSON
Washington, D.C.
February 2004

Introduction

THIS BOOK DESCRIBES THE SETTLEMENT of Manchuria and the neighboring areas of Inner Mongolia and the incorporation of these territories into China during the Qing (1644–1911) and Republican (1912–37) periods. The account that follows highlights two features of this story and connects it to recent scholarship on the history of modern China. First, is the extraordinary growth of the Middle Kingdom during the Qing Dynasty. Manchuria and Inner Mongolia were among several large territories attached during this period to the ancient core of the empire, doubling its size and creating the immense domain now known as China. Until recently, historians of China, both at home and abroad, have been preoccupied with events that occurred inside the Great Wall. During the past few years, there has been growing interest in China's borderlands and the process by which the empire expanded to reach its present size. This book adds a chapter to that story.

Second, is the question of whether and how China changed in the course of this expansion and during the transition from the late-traditional to early-modern periods. Again, the notion that China may have been changing or developing on its own, before it was forced to respond to the impact of the West, represents a break in the historiography of this subject: away from the view of a stagnant China that dominated scholarship in the 1950s and 1960s, toward a dynamic model, which is supported by evidence from the past and encouraged by realities of the present. To date, most accounts of China's pre-modern development have focused on China proper, while little attention has been paid to the stimulative effects, if any, of the borderlands. A second purpose of this book is to explore the question of whether the spread of

Chinese state and society into Manchuria prompted significant change within this region and in China as a whole. China has grown immensely over the past several centuries, but has this growth been an agent of social and cultural transformation?

A. Growth

The China that now colors so much of the map of Asia is of relatively recent vintage. The core of the empire, or China proper, bounded by oceans on the east and south, the Tibetan Plateau on the west, and the Great Wall on the north, came together more than two millennia ago. Territories of equal size, including Manchuria, Inner and Outer Mongolia, Xinjiang, Tibet, and Taiwan, were attached to this core in the 17th and 18th centuries. Although each of these regions offers its own attractions, by most measures Manchuria, the region the Chinese call *Dongbei* or the Northeast, ranks first. A generous definition of Northeast China might include the fringes of the Mongolian steppe, technically part of Inner Mongolia, which is densely populated, well cultivated and forms a natural extension of the central Manchurian plain. But even in narrow terms, counting only the three provinces of Liaoning, Jilin, and Heilongjiang, this region now accounts for 8% of the area and population, 17% of the cultivated land, 14% of the grain output, and 11% of the gross domestic product of China as a whole.[1] Manchuria is larger than the six states of America's upper Midwest—Michigan, Ohio, Indiana, Illinois, Wisconsin, and Iowa—has twice as many people, and produces nearly 40% as much grain, placing it second among the world's leading corn belts.[2] It is located at the intersection of China, Russia, Korea, and Japan, a neighborhood once called, and perhaps again to become, the "cockpit of Asia." The annexation of this region is the single most important addition of territory to China, since the unification of the empire in the 3rd century B.C.

The expansion of China is of both historical and contemporary significance. Historically, China is one of a handful of agrarian empires—the others are Russia, India, and the Ottomans—that took control of the Eurasian steppe during the 17th and 18th centuries, putting an end to the long reign of nomadic power and preparing the way for the

---

[1] *Zhongguo tongji nianjian* (2000).

[2] U.S. Census Bureau, *Statistical Abstract of the United States*, 2001; and U.S. Department of Agriculture Web site. U.S. grain includes corn, wheat, and soybeans. Chinese grain includes corn, wheat, soybeans, and rice.

competition with the nation-states of Europe that followed. Today, the three great empires that dominate global politics—China, Russia, and the United States—all grew to their present size from the 17th to the 19th century, displacing the small, compact, coastal powers that shaped history during the preceding ages of exploration and imperialism. No textbook on American history is complete without a reference to the "Manifest Destiny" that drove this nation across the continent. Similarly, Russian history, as a leading scholar in this field, V. O. Kliuchevsky observes, "is the history of a country undergoing colonization. . . . Migration, colonization constituted the basic feature of our history, to which all other features were more or less directly related."[3] Until recently, historians of China paid less attention to territorial expansion and its effects on the development of China. Now, that too is beginning to change.

B. Change?

The growth of China during the Qing and Republican periods is a fact. Whether and how this growth fostered change in Manchuria and in China as a whole remain questions. Expansion and change have been so intertwined in the history of the West that historians who approach these questions from the Western perspective may be excused for assuming that the connection between the two is universal. Students of frontier history, which examines migration, settlement, and the incorporation of new territories into existing regimes, have been especially susceptible to this view. But does the equation of expansion and change also apply to China?

Since 1893, when Frederick Jackson Turner delivered his now famous essay, "The Significance of the Frontier in American History," historians have enjoyed a lively and illuminating debate over the nature of the frontier and its role in history. One aspect of this discussion, which is especially important for our study of Manchuria, is the role of the frontier as the locus of historical change. In Turner's account, the frontier, the expanding edge of conquest and settlement, generated the values, practices, and patterns that transformed society and drove history forward. In the American case, the subject of his study, Turner rejected the "germ" theory, which explained American history as an outgrowth

[3] V. O. Kliuchevsky, *Kurs russkoi istorii* (Moscow, 1937), v, 20–21, cited in Donald Treadgold (1957), 14.

of European culture and institutions, and argued instead that it was man's engagement with nature on the frontier that created and defined the American character. This process occurred not once, but repeatedly as each generation of Americans took the next step across the line that separated wilderness from civilization and helped to transform the former into the latter. In Turner's own words: "American development has exhibited not merely advance along a single line, but a return to primitive conditions on a continually advancing frontier line, and a new development for that area. American social development has been continually beginning over again on the frontier."[4]

Turner has been and remains a controversial figure, whose work has attracted critics in each succeeding generation. The latest crop of anti-Turnerians, the so-called "new Western historians," have identified many of his shortcomings and offered remedies for each. Among the chief targets of their attack is Turner's basic model, in which a "core" empire or civilization expands outward along an advancing edge or "frontier" to conquer and eventually consume a "periphery" of wilderness. The critics challenge this model on several grounds: that it is racist, because the core is dominated by whites and the periphery by coloreds; sexist, because the expansion is the work of men to the exclusion of women; anti-environmentalist, because it overlooks the destruction wrought by conquest; and most of all, because it rests on the false assumption that the "manifest destiny" of the core civilization or nation is the proper course of history, whereas the periphery or wilderness is without history until it is conquered and consumed by the core. In the current revisionist view, to identify the frontier as the locus of historical change is to accept the entire model and the assumptions on which it rests. If the frontier is where history is being made, then its makers are civilized white men who are bringing order out of chaos and imposing their culture and institutions on the blank sheet of the wilderness. And that, according to the new Western historians, denies all other ways of understanding the history of those landscapes and people who, inadvertently and inconsequentially, just happen to be in the way.

One antidote offered by the new Western historians is "the middle ground." In a book by this title, Richard White treats his subject, the Great Lakes region of the 17th and 18th centuries, not as a wilderness waiting to be cut down by an advancing frontier and incorporated into the expanding American nation, but as a place "in between cultures,

[4]Frederick Jackson Turner (1963), 28.

peoples, and in between empires and the non-state world."[5] While Turner described history as a process of change along a steadily moving line, the "middle grounders" study distinct places, each with its own environments and peoples, that have made and continue to remake their own stories. "Turner's frontier was a process, not a place," explains Patricia Limerick, a leader of the new Western historians. "In rethinking Western history, we gain the freedom to think of the West as a place—as many complicated environments occupied by natives who considered their homelands to be the center, not the edge."[6] Unlike pioneers on the frontier, whose role is to transform the wilderness and add the digested product to an expanding core, the people of the "middle ground" work out their own history, shaping their land and themselves without regard for the pretensions of their more civilized (?) neighbors.

Given current trends in scholarship, it is hardly surprising that younger scholars should gravitate to the model proposed by White and the theories of the new Western historians. In the field of East Asian history, Brett Walker's book on the Ainu lands (or Ezo), islands and peoples that lie off the mainland of Asia and now form part of Japanese Hokkaido, Sakhalin, and the Kurils, does just that. Walker describes the transition of this region during the 17th and 18th centuries from a "middle ground," where the native Ainu interacted with Japanese and other peoples, to their present status as an administrative territory of Japan. Walker declines to label this region a "frontier," because doing so would peripheralize it in relation to the process of state formation in Japan, and because the period of interaction between the Ainu and their neighbors—that is, their experience as a "middle ground"—is what accounts for the fate of both groups. "The point," Walker explains, "is that the Ainu culture that emerged in the seventeenth and eighteenth centuries was in some respects a product of interaction on the middle ground, as was much of Japanese behavior in Ezo. . . ."[7] Walker's use of this model blows a fresh breeze through the study of Japanese history, reminding us that the framing of history around the nation can reduce peripheral territories and peoples to the status of losers, waiting to be gobbled up by the inevitable march toward someone else's destiny. Given the success of this approach, one might ask, why not apply the same model to the study of other complex and unbounded areas that

---

[5] Richard White (1991), x.
[6] Patricia Nelson Limerick (1987), 26.
[7] Brett L. Walker (2001), 12.

lay outside the borders of traditional Asian empires? Why not treat Manchuria in this way?

It is, of course, possible to think of Manchuria during the Qing and Republican periods as an area transformed by an advancing "frontier," as the site of a "middle ground," or both. Robert Lee, whose book *The Manchurian Frontier in Ch'ing History* remains after more than thirty years the principal study of this subject in English, says that one of his major aims is "to trace the process of sinicization of the Manchurian frontier."[8] Without making reference to Turner, Lee nonetheless embraces the essence of his frontier thesis. A recent study by Burton Pasternak and Janet W. Salaff (1993) of Chinese and Mongol settlements on the border between Manchuria and the Mongolian steppe, points in a different direction. By showing how ecology, society, and culture interact to produce communities that are distinct from their parent bodies in both China and Mongolia and generate new identities all their own, Pasternak and Salaff favor an open-ended history of place which is akin to the "middle ground." To extend either of these accounts backward in time, one could turn to the Russian naturalists and ethnographers of the early-20th century, who describe the tribal minorities of Manchuria and their interactions with Chinese settlers along the Amur, Sungari, and Ussuri Rivers.[9] Reports by Chinese exiles in the 17th century[10] and Manchu officials in Jilin and Heilongjiang in the early 19th century,[11] surveys conducted during the 1950s and 1960s of surviving Manchu communities in Manchuria,[12] and other scholarship published in China[13] offer additional information that can be used to reconstruct the interplay among Chinese, Manchus, and other tribal groups. In sum, the foundations for either a "frontier" or "middle ground" study of Manchuria have been established and could be elaborated here.

But this book follows neither of these lines. For discussion of the merits of the "frontier" versus the "middle ground," like other historical debates, tends to highlight the differences between these alternatives, while ignoring their underlying similarities. And in the present study,

[8] Robert Lee (1970), 1–2.

[9] V. K. Arseniev (1941), S. M. Shirokogoroff (1924) and (1926).

[10] Three works by exiled officials Fang Gongqian (1894), Wu Zhenchen (1894), and Yang Bin (1894) are discussed in Xie Guozhen (1948), 16–33, 40–60, and in Robert Lee (1970), 9–14.

[11] Works by Xiqing [Hsi Ch'ing] (1894) and Saying'e (1894) are discussed in Robert Lee (1970).

[12] *Manzu shehui lishi diaocha* (1985), and Jin Qicong (1981).

[13] See, for example, a local history of Manchus in Xiuyan by Zhang Qizhuo (1984).

the similarities are more telling. The difference between Turner and White lies in the locus and method of change: for Turner, change is produced on the edge of an expanding core and by the transformation of wilderness into civilization, whereas for White, change occurs in a place where various peoples and landscapes interact to produce their own history. Each of these models highlights different players, processes, and outcomes. Yet Turner and White share the assumption that societies and cultures are formed or changed by a dynamic that occurs *outside* the dominant empires, civilizations, or nations. Whether the source of change is a "frontier" process or a "middle ground" place, the action occurs on the edge or in the spaces in between. In both cases, history is made and the shape of things to come is set by events that proceed from the outside in.

This study of Chinese expansion into the territories north of the Great Wall supports a different model or explanation: namely, that Chinese migration to, settlement in, and eventual incorporation of this region into the empire occurred by the reproduction or transplantation of institutions and practices previously established in China proper, rather than by the creation or invention of new forms in the wilderness or on the frontier. There was in Manchuria a Chinese frontier—a line of demarcation between areas that were more populated, cultivated, and integrated on one side than on the other—and a middle ground— where Chinese and other ethnic groups interacted and worked out common solutions to common problems. But these edges and places played only a marginal role in defining the emerging Manchuria, compared to the wholesale importation of an essentially Chinese society, economy, and culture. Modern Manchuria, according to the argument presented below, was made less from the outside in, than from the inside out.

C. Growth Without Change

The case for this thesis—growth without change—is made in three parts, which are both thematic and chronological. Part One, "Land," covers the Qing Dynasty and focuses on the role of the state in trying, and failing, to establish a new system of landownership and land tenure in Manchuria and Inner Mongolia. The Qing experiment, by which land grants and enforced labor were given in trust to the dynasty's Manchu and Mongol allies in exchange for military and other forms of service, could neither stem the tide of migration nor limit its impact. With grow-ing speed and scope, Chinese migrants moved to, settled in, farmed on, and ultimately took over land above the Great Wall. And their signal success—as attested to by millions of people, producing millions of tons of grain, on millions of hectares of prime farmland—was unsup-ported by the invention of new technologies, practices, organizations, or patterns of behavior. The expansion of China northward occurred as Chinese moved forward and kept on doing more of the same old thing.

Part Two, "People," focuses on the Chinese migrants who left their homes in China proper to move at first temporarily and then gradually to settle in areas above the Great Wall. The title of this book, "Reluctant Pioneers," derives from Part Two and is frankly ironic. Pioneers are supposed to take risks, explore frontiers, open new vistas, and create new worlds. They are not supposed to be timid, halting, or indecisive. But the men and women who established a social and political order in China's northern territories backed into this role, extending or trans-planting the way of life they had known in China proper, rather than in-venting new techniques and behaviors to fit the environment and cir-cumstances beyond the Great Wall. These pioneers were reluctant to move in the first place, those who moved were reluctant to stay, and those who stayed were reluctant to change the world around them or their own ways of adapting to it. They expanded the realm of China more by replication than by device.

Part Three, "Economy," describes the development of Manchuria—or the lack thereof—during the late-19th and early-20th centuries. Re-cent scholarship on Chinese economic history has produced both a new consensus and an ongoing debate. The consensus is that the economy of late-traditional China was growing in total output and becoming more commercialized. The debate is between those who, following the "clas-sical" model of Adam Smith, see these changes as leading to develop-ment in the form of higher productivity (output per unit of labor) and transformation of socioeconomic structures, on one side, and those who see growth and commercialization without development, on the other. The former school, proponents of "early modern" development led by Thomas Rawski (1989) and Loren Brandt (1989), argue that during the period 1870–1930 China achieved higher productivity in agriculture by increasing specialization in cash crops, selecting crops to suit different environments, and extending the application of the best available tech-niques—all measures that could be and were applied in Manchuria. The latter, who make the case for "growth without development," explain China's stagnation by pointing either to material conditions—the unfavorable balance between population and resources, which leads in the term made popular by Philip Huang (1985, 1990, 1991) to "involution"—or to social factors—the dominance of a small producer economy, that Sucheta Mazumdar (1998) cites in her analysis of "property relations." To show how the case of Manchuria contributes to this debate, the following account will address these two questions: First, whether the growth in China's territory and production was accompanied by development? And second, if not, whether this was due to social, material or some other cause(s)? The answers offered in this book are that development did *not* occur, and that the most important reason for this outcome was the persistence of past practices, even under circumstances that favored the introduction of new patterns of behavior and new techniques.

D. Note on Geography

Details regarding the land and climate of Manchuria will be introduced in Chapter 4 and elsewhere in the text, as appropriate. Meanwhile, three overarching features, which are central to this story, deserve a few comments. These features are: the enormous natural wealth and potential of Manchuria; the imbalance between the densely populated, land-short north China plain and the sparsely populated, land-rich Manchuria; and the seasonal or monsoon climate that gives Manchuria its warm, wet summers and cold, dry winters.

First, Manchuria enjoys extraordinary natural endowments, far beyond those of any other region adjacent to China proper. The topography of Manchuria is defined by a broad central plain surrounded by a horseshoe of mountains that contain abundant and valuable timber, furs, medicinal plants, minerals, and other natural resources. Two major river systems, the Liao in the south and the Sungari-Nenjiang (Map 1) in the center and north, provide access to the mountains, water and recharge the plains with their sediment, and facilitate transportation throughout the region. The soils of the plain, aeolian in the west and alluvial in the south and east, are fertile and relatively free of stone. The Manchurian summer is sufficiently warm and long to support a single crop as far north as the Amur River on the Russian border, while ample precipitation during the growing season ensures maximum plant response. Recent history and current conditions confirm that

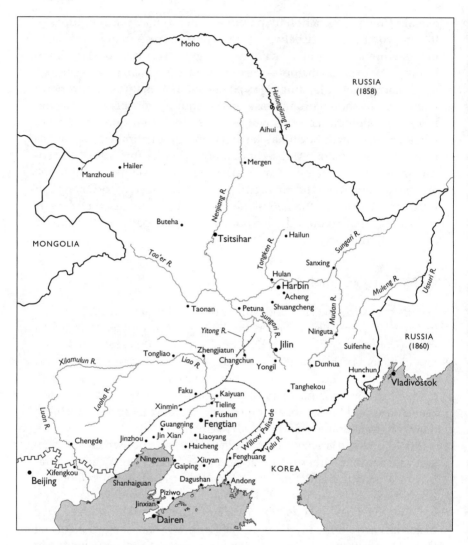

MAP 1. Manchuria, Select Cities

Manchuria has the wherewithal to support a dense population and productive economy of the sort that has existed for thousands of years in China proper.

Second, throughout the period covered in this study there was a steep man-to-land gradient, running from the densely populated north China plain, where virtually all arable land was under cultivation and the continuous growth of population reduced the area of farmland per capita, to the sparsely populated and richly endowed Northeast, where both cultivated and arable land per capita increased steadily, proceeding from south to north. Despite the changes that occurred from the 17th to the 20th centuries, this gradient remained sharp, the distances to be covered short, and thus the gravitational pull on farmers in the south to exploit the land and other resources of the north persistent, powerful, and compelling. Whatever government officials and other actors in this story might have done, not done, or done differently, there was nothing that could have dampened the urge for land or stemmed the tide of migration northward.

Finally, there is the peculiar effect of the monsoon, or seasonal, climate. The concentration of rainfall during the warm growing season made Manchuria, along with the rest of eastern China, particularly well suited for agriculture. Farmers who were familiar with this pattern on the north China plain found it easy to adapt their techniques above the Great Wall. Conversely, the cold, dry winters, while unsuitable for agriculture, were favorable to travel over the frozen earth. This alternation encouraged the seasonal migration of farmworkers: northward for spring planting in Manchuria, and southward after the harvest in time to celebrate the New Year's Festival back home in China proper. This rhythm made a strong imprint on a society dominated by families whose branches extended above and below the Great Wall.

These three factors—the natural wealth of Manchuria, the gravitational pull on people in the south toward land in the north, and the seasonality of climate and hence migration—drove Chinese across the Great Wall and into a new chapter in their history. This story begins with the conquest of the Qing Dynasty and the quest for "land," which is the subject of Part One.

PART ONE

Land

Introduction to Part One

PART ONE DESCRIBES HOW THE QING DYNASTY sought to create its own system of land tenure in the territories north of the Great Wall and how Chinese migrants in these territories transformed the Qing system to conform to practices previously adopted in China proper. During the first century of Qing rule, the Manchus established banners, banner-lands, and estates, which were designed to ensure the control of the dynasty and its allies over land, labor, and agricultural production in Manchuria and the neighboring areas of Inner Mongolia and to preclude the Chinese from taking over this region and incorporating it into the society and economy that existed below the Great Wall. But this effort failed. By the early-19th century, Chinese migrants had spread throughout southern and central Manchuria, while the banners, banner-lands, and estates were replaced by free markets in land and labor, dominated by peasant households practicing intensive agriculture on the model common in China proper. At the close of the century, the government in Beijing accelerated this process by selling land and encouraging Chinese settlement in Manchuria as a way of raising additional revenue and denying this region to the Russians. By the end of the dynasty in 1911, the Sinification of the Manchurian land tenure system was essentially complete.

The traditional system of land tenure practiced in north China, which was based on free markets in land, private ownership by households, and partible inheritance or the partition of land in equal shares among the male heirs of the succeeding generation, was challenged when the Qing Dynasty confiscated or laid claim to large tracts of land

and distributed this land to Manchu nobles and bannermen and Mongol banners. The novelty of the Qing system was *not* that the Manchus seized land from the vanquished and shared it among the victors, for previous dynasties had pursued the same strategy. Rather, it was that the recipients of land grants during the Qing, while allowed to pass the right of ownership on to their heirs, were prohibited from buying, selling, trading, or alienating the land from the commonweal—and especially prohibited from selling it to Chinese. Meanwhile, the trustees of this land oversaw a workforce composed of enforced laborers. The system of "manors"—large landholdings, governed by hereditary elites who held the land in trust and exercised control over unfree labor—described in Chapter One, was established wherever there were Manchu nobles or bannermen. Official or noble estates and bannerlands held a near monopoly on land in Manchuria, while a variant form, also called a "banner," prevailed in Inner Mongolia.

The breakdown of the manorial system and its replacement with free markets in land and labor, the subject of Chapter Two, followed the spread of population and the agrarian economy from China proper to the territories above the Great Wall. During the 18th and 19th centuries, migrants arrived in growing numbers, bringing with them the requisite skills in agriculture and commerce and the presumption that the land and its products should belong to themselves. And they overwhelmed the Manchus, Mongols, and other native peoples of this region, who lacked both the will and the way to resist. The decline of the manors was exacerbated, moreover, by the growing inequality within these domains, as Manchu and Mongol elites used their control over land and other resources for personal gain, while their poor relatives sold off their assets and abandoned their posts. Finally, the dynasty, which had originally designed the manors to support a service class that would perform military or administrative duties on behalf of the state, gradually shifted toward the commercialization of this enterprise, extracting the surplus production first in kind and later in cash. The effects of inequality and commercialization further unraveled the manors and hastened the transition to competitive markets in land, labor, and produce.

This system of corporate ownership, after declining gradually during most of the Qing era, came to a rapid collapse at the end of that period, as the Qing rulers abandoned their earlier ambivalence and adopted a policy of promoting Chinese settlement north of the Great Wall. The dual crisis facing China in the late-19th and early-20th centuries—the debt and the threat—prompted the dynasty to set aside all other concerns in an effort to raise money and strengthen the national defense. Land previously held in imperial reserves or tied up in banners, bannerlands, and estates was sold to raise cash and expand the area of taxable farmland. In Manchuria, where arable land lay near a vulnerable border, settlement and cultivation also helped to fend off foreign rivals, first the Russians and later the Japanese. Chapter Three shows how the balance began to tilt in the middle of the 19th century, when the combination of wars abroad and rebellion at home brought on the problems in security and finance, while the full-blown crisis was announced in the "New Policies" of 1902. From then until the end of the dynasty in 1911, the Manchu system of collective ownership and management of land was in headlong retreat.

CHAPTER 1

The Manorial Experiment (1644–1740)

WHILE THE INSTITUTION OF THE "MANOR," including banners, bannerlands, and estates, had roots in the 16th century, before there was a Qing Dynasty or even a "Manchu" people, the decision to fasten on this form of organization in the region above the Great Wall evolved gradually and in response to conflicting pressures that followed the Qing conquest of China in 1644. At first, the Qing welcomed the movement of independent Chinese farmers into the northern territories: migration would relieve pressure on north China and reduce the potential for disorder, help restore the economy of southern Manchuria which had been destroyed and depopulated during the Ming-Qing wars, create a stronger presence in an area that was vulnerable to external attack, spur the development of agriculture and commerce in regions vital to the dynasty and its allies, and help supply the capital in Beijing. At the same time, the Manchu rulers feared the Chinese: a tide of migration could overwhelm the small native populations north of the Great Wall, undermine the control of Manchus and Mongols over these territories, and ultimately weaken the dynasty's hold on a region vital to the ruling house and to the defense of the empire. The Manchus depended upon Manchuria for their identity, security, and long-term welfare, and they depended upon the Mongols to sustain the rule of the small Manchu minority over a vastly greater Chinese empire. The Qing wanted to see the northern territories developed and thriving, not lost in a sea of Chinese.

Qing policies toward this region were as conflicted and changing as their interests. At first, the Manchu rulers spurred the movement of Chinese northward to restore production in the war-torn areas of the Liaodong, just above the Great Wall, and support the deployment of forces against the Russians on the distant Heilongjiang (or Amur) and Sungari rivers (Map 1). Then, alarmed by the number of migrants, Beijing tried to pull back, limit the pace of migration, and restrict its impact. Finally, the Qing fastened on a solution, which was to allow (indeed, they could not stop) the flow of Chinese northward, but fit them into institutions that would ensure the control of Manchus and Mongols over land, labor, and production throughout the territories above the Great Wall. Chapter One describes these institutions—bannerlands of the Eight Banners, Mongol banners (a different organization with the same name), and official or noble estates, which we will refer to collectively as "manors"—and shows how Chinese migrants occupied the roles and spaces made available to them within the manorial system.

A. The Challenge (1644–81)

One challenge facing policy makers of the early Qing was how to move the right number and kind of Chinese into Manchuria and how to organize them after they arrived. The migrants could be neither too many nor too few, and they could be neither too free nor too tightly constrained. The problem, moreover, was different in the south than the north. In the south, along the Liao River, Beijing needed to repair the damage done during the war of conquest, restore production, and to achieve these goals resettle refugees within this region or import them from below the Great Wall. The latter measure would have the added benefit of relieving pressure on the overcrowded north China plain. Here, the migrants could be attracted with carrots, and when their number grew too large, the carrots could be withdrawn. The problem in the north was different: namely, to mount a defense against the Russians who were entering Manchuria along the Heilongjiang and Sungari Rivers, just as the preponderance of Manchu troops were leaving this region to join the invasion of China proper. For this purpose, the Qing sent banner forces, supported by Chinese farmworkers, to meet the Russians, while the only way to persuade these parties to accept the hardship of frontier life was to use forced labor—criminals, convicts, and exiles—and the threat of harsh punishment for those who sought to escape. But this practice could be counterproductive, for the harder the rod was applied to keep workers in place, the less likely others were to join them. In both locations, south and north, the goal of the Qing was to strike the right balance, regulate the number of workers, and keep them on task. In the end, however, both the carrot of free land and the stick of slavery met their limits. The system of "manors," the subject of the following section, was the Qing response to these competing concerns, which are described below.

1. The South

Southern Manchuria suffered badly in the course of the Ming-Qing war. The Liao River plain, which spread out before the Manchu capital of Shengjing (later called Fengtian, Mukden, and now Shenyang) and served as the breadbasket of the preconquest Qing, was depopulated and its cities destroyed. The departure of Qing armies for the south unraveled the economy and left the whole region in disarray. Refugees fled in despair. As late as 1661, the Governor of Fengtian reported that all of the cities east of the Liao had become "abandoned fields."

Only Fengtian City, Liaoyang, and Haicheng have any sort of administrative order; and Liaoyang and Haicheng still do not have moats. Cities like Gaizhou [Gaiping], Fenghuangcheng, and [Jinxian] have only a few hundred people. Tieling and Fushun have only a few vagrants. They cannot cultivate the land and do not have any means of livelihood. Most single able-bodied people have fled. Those who have families just grow old and die here. . . .There are more walled cities west of the River, but people are few. Only Ningyuan, Jinzhou, and Guangning have any concentration of people.[1]

The Jesuit missionary Ferdinand Verbiest, who visited this region in 1682, found that the towns and villages of the Liaodong, which had been "sedulously destroyed" during the transition from Ming to Qing, remained "completely ruined."[2] A half-century later, another Jesuit chronicler, Jean-Baptiste Du Halde, confirmed that, except for Fengtian, "the other towns of this province are of little note, thinly peopled, ill-built, and without any defence, except a wall either half-ruined, or made of earth. . . ."[3]

The initial response of the Qing, here as elsewhere, was to resettle refugees and restore production. In 1653, Beijing promulgated the

[1] Zhang Shangxian, "Genben xingshi shu" [A description of the form of our dynasty's roots], *Huangchao Qingshi wenbian* [Collected essays on statecraft under the reigning dynasty], comp. He Changling, zhuan 80, cited in Richard Edmonds (1979), 613; and Richard Edmonds (1985), 74. Ningyuan, which does not appear on contemporary maps, was located near the present-day city of Xingcheng. Jinzhou is the city located on the Xiaoling River. Jinxian is the city located at the tip of the Liaodong Peninsula. The original text incorrectly refers to both as "Jinzhou." I have modified the text using the current names of these cities. Note that neither should be confused with Jin Xian, which is located on the Daling River. See Map 1.
[2] Père d'Orleans (1971), 105–6.
[3] Jean-Baptiste Du Halde (1741), 90–92.

"Regulations on Recruitment and Reclamation in Liaodong," which offered food, seed, draft animals, and other incentives to peasants who
would settle in designated areas of the lower Liao. Taxes on reclaimed
land were deferred for up to six years, and government agents combed
the northern provinces to recruit settlers.[4] A number of villages in the
Liaodong region later surveyed by Japanese scholars were founded by
Chinese migrants who came to this area following the 1653 edict.[5]

The lure of free land and other benefits undoubtedly "pulled" many
migrants into the Liao, while pressures from north China provided a
persistent "push" outward. The outlines of the story—the rapid rise in
China's population during the 18th and early 19th centuries, the much
slower increase in land under cultivation, the intensification of farming,
higher inputs of labor and fertilizer, double and triple cropping, and the
squeezing of people into marginal areas and migration to the periphery
of Taiwan, Manchuria, and Southwest China or further abroad—are
well known.[6] Within the four provinces of northern China—Shandong,
Zhili [Hebei], Shanxi, and Shaanxi—which provided the bulk of migrants to the north, the balance between population and farmland
worsened to a degree equal to or greater than for China as a whole.
Dwight Perkins estimates that the population of these provinces grew
from 54.1 million in 1749 to 84.5 million in 1851, an increase of only
56%, which was well below the national average (and is explained in
part by the fact that these provinces experienced a net outflow of migration). During the same period, however, Perkins found *no* growth in
the land under cultivation in these provinces, which means that the area
of farmland per capita declined by around 35%.[7]

Against this backdrop of growing population and shrinking resources was the episodic force of natural disaster—drought, flood,
pestilence, and disease. The Yellow River made the north China plain
enormously attractive to farmers, hence the continuous intensive cultivation of this region for two millennia, and risky, since the region is susceptible to both drought when the monsoons fail and flood when the
river breaks through its dikes. In the great famines of 1743 and 1876,
this region suffered unbearably. At their worst, according to an 1840
gazetteer from one county in Shandong, conditions were "so bad and

[4]For a discussion of Qing policies toward the north during the period 1644–68, see:
Xu Shuming (1990), 90–92; Guo Songyi (1990), 15; Zhang Xuanru (1983), 186; and Sun
Zhanwen and Wu Wenxian (1982), 65.
[5]For examples of migration to Liaodong during the 1650s and 1660s, see especially
Kotoku sannendo, sites 11, 12, 13, 14.
[6]See: Dwight Perkins (1969), 207–16, 233–40; Gao Wangling (1992), 61–66.
[7]Dwight Perkins (1969), 207, 212, 234–36.

people so poor that no matter how hard one worked he could not make a living through agriculture. Things were so bad that if crops failed, people would leave their village and cross the northern border into Liaodong."[8] The surveys of Manchurian villages conducted by Japanese scholars in the 1930s show that the original settlers were more often driven from their homes in China proper by hardship than they were drawn by the prospects for a better life above the Great Wall.[9]

Finally, the Ming-Qing transition fell especially hard on the northern provinces, which were subject to persistent rebellion, banditry, and war. The Manchus, after replacing the Chinese rebels who overthrew the Ming, took nearly four decades to bring all of China proper under control, extending the conflict and its effects from north to south. Once in Beijing, the new rulers seized the holdings of Ming nobles in and around the capital, enclosed neighboring farmlands to form landed estates, which were turned over to members of the Manchu nobility, and distributed smaller plots to bannermen, who formed the backbone of the Qing army and remained in China after the conquest to garrison the empire. Over a quarter century, from 1644 to 1669, all of the prime farmland within 250 kilometers of Beijing was expropriated and redistributed in this way.[10] According to one estimate, the enclosures covered 17 million *mu*, or one-seventh of the cultivated area of Zhili, the province surrounding the capital. In some counties as much as 70 to 80 percent of the farmland was seized and the dispossessed farmers forced to work for Manchu overlords.[11]

The steady deterioration in the balance between population and resources and the episodes of man-made and natural disasters produced pulsations of migrants and refugees out of the villages of north China. Not all headed north. Most probably went to live with relatives in nearby villages. Others flocked to the cities. Many went south, where the climate was warmer and wetter, the society more familiar, and

[8]*Rongcheng xianzhi* [Rongcheng county gazetteer] (1840), cited in Richard Edmonds (1979), 614.
[9]A detailed discussion of this point, based on statistical data from the *Kotoku* surveys, appears in Part Two.
[10]Zhang Xuanru (1983), 187; Frederic Wakeman (1985), 69–70, 471–74; Pamela Crossley (1990), 48–49.
[11]Yang Xuechen (1963), 176. There are no figures for the area of cultivated land in China during the late 17th century, so it is impossible to be precise about the impact of these enclosures on the Beijing area. However, Dwight Perkins (1969), 234, provides an upwardly adjusted estimate of 120 million *mu* for Hebei (Zhili) Province in 1766. Taking this inflated figure, covering the entire province, at a later date, as the base, the enclosure of 17 million *mu* would still represent a hefty 14% of the available farmland.

farmland could still be carved out of hillsides, lakes, and forests.[12] Still, this left a significant number who crossed the Great Wall and the Gulf of Bohai to Manchuria and Inner Mongolia. They provided both an opportunity and a challenge to the new rulers of the Qing.

Soon after they began encouraging migration northward, the Qing rulers became concerned about the large Chinese population in what remained of the Manchu homeland, and began to apply the brakes on the forward policy. In 1668, the edict on "Recruitment and Reclamation" was rescinded along with the incentives to attract settlers to the Liaodong. Similarly, over a period of several years ending in 1681, Beijing erected the Willow Palisade [*liutiaobian*], a barrier beyond which the Chinese were prohibited from encroaching on Manchu and Mongol lands. The main branch of the Palisade ran 700 km, from the Great Wall to the Sungari River, marking the western boundary of Chinese settlement, while a second branch from a point north of Kaiyuan to the Korean border marked the eastern limit (Map 1). The Palisade was constructed of two parallel levees, each slightly more than 1 meter (3 *chi*) high and a meter wide, separated by a trench, 3.5 meters wide, and topped with Chinese (yellow) willows, large bushes about 2–3 meters high. While properly maintained, it provided a clear line of demarcation between the separate populations and modes of production on opposite sides.[13]

The construction of the Willow Palisade represents less a decision by the Qing to block or "close" [*fengjin*] Manchuria to Chinese migration than ambivalence about what its policy was or should be. The Qing rulers could never quite make up their minds about whether to open or close the gates to the north. Or rather they wanted to have it both ways: to relieve pressure on the labor-surplus provinces of China proper and supply workers to the land-surplus areas of Manchuria and Inner Mongolia, while at the same time maintaining control over these areas in the hands of their Manchu and Mongol allies. When Beijing withdrew the incentives to entice farmers into the Liaodong in 1668, they were replaced *not* by a prohibition on entry into this region, but by a system for registering migrants so that the regime could track their flow. The Willow Palisade was a flimsy barrier, more suitable for demarcating and supervising a boundary than for obstructing the movement of anyone determined to cross it. Qing pronouncements of the late-17th and early-18th centuries included periodic calls to "close"

---

[12] For an account of migration and settlement in Hunan during the early Qing, see Peter Perdue (1987), chapter 3.

[13] Willow Palisade: Richard Edmonds (1979); and Richard Edmonds (1985), 55–82. Other details: Xu Shuming (1990), 94–95; Guo Songyi (1990), 15.

Manchuria and Inner Mongolia to Chinese, alternating with encouragement for migration and the reclamation of land in these territories.[14] In sum, the Qing wanted to control rather than restrict the movement of Chinese—which explains why they sought to channel migrant workers into banners, bannerlands and estates.

2. *The North*

In the absence of willing migrants, the settlement of northern Manchuria during the first century of the Qing was an act of state, made in response to a foreign military threat and carried out with a generous use of force. The threat came from the Russians, who entered the Heilongjiang River Valley in 1643, and during the next half century challenged the Manchus for control of the Heilongjiang and the Sungari. In 1652, Beijing ordered 2,000 horsemen, armed with bows, matchlocks, and iron cannons, to establish a garrison at Ninguta on the Mudan River, a tributary of the Sungari—the first deployment of Qing forces beyond the Willow Palisade. In 1676, the military command at Ninguta moved to the "Dockyard" [*chuanchang*], the center of shipbuilding on the upper Sungari and a site better situated to supply troops in the north. From then on, this city, later known as Jilin, became the headquarters of the Jilin Military Region. As fighting spread, the Manchus established garrisons at Aihui (also called Aigun or Heilongjiangcheng, 1683), Mergen (or Nenjiang, 1686), and Bukui, later Tsitsihar (1693), the last of which became the headquarters of the Heilongjiang Military Region. The settlements at Petuna (Fuyu), Alachuke (Acheng), Sanxing, and Hunchun, all in Jilin, also began as military garrisons.[15]

Following clashes with Russian forces on the Heilongjiang and Mudan rivers, the Manchus discovered how difficult it was to support forces far from home and moved to create "military-agricultural colonies" [*tuntian*] alongside the garrisons or in strategic locations nearby.[16] In addition to the garrisons, which established their own farmlands, the cities of Buteha, Shuangcheng, Hulan, and Hailar all got their start as military-agricultural colonies.[17] Each *tuntian* colony was composed of

[14]Zhang Xuanru (1983), 187–88. For another view of the "closure" policy, see Ma Yueshan (1986).

[15]Joseph Sebes (1961), 67–70; Xu Shuming (1988), 17–20. For details on the general [*jiangjun*] of Heilongjiang, 1683–99, see Joseph Sebes (1961), 200n, 223n.

[16]Diao Shuren (1993), 108–9; Jean-Baptiste Du Halde (1741), 94. For a general discussion of *tuntian* in the early-Qing, see Ma Dongyu (1985).

[17]Owen Lattimore (1934), 198–99; Sun Zhanwen (1981), 90–92; Xu Shuming (1988), 17.

hundreds of men, 70 to 80 percent of whom farmed land assigned to them by the state, allowing the remaining 20 to 30 percent to devote their time to military training, patrol, or warfare. In Manchuria, Manchus commanded the armies and provided most of the military forces, while Chinese, many of whom were convicts or forced laborers assigned to the colonies, made up the bulk of the workforce.[18] Most *tuntian* colonies in Jilin and Heilongjiang took the form of bannerlands or estates.[19] By 1736, there were 69 estates in the Jilin Military Region, and 61 in Heilongjiang.[20] Courier stations, which were built to connect these settlements and facilitate travel between Beijing and the borders, also opened land to cultivation.[21]

Having committed to this system, the Manchus soon discovered how difficult it was to attract Chinese farmers to distant frontiers. The history of a village near Aihui, which was established in 1684 as an agricultural colony to support the Aihui garrison on the Heilongjiang River, demonstrates the problem. Owing to the cold climate, resistant soil, and periodic attacks from Russian forces on the far side of the river, it was difficult to make a living in this area, much less produce a surplus large enough to support the garrison. Reclamation of land using traditional hand tools was extremely difficult. Even as late as the 1930s, cultivated land in this village had little value, since it was surrounded by wasteland waiting to be reclaimed by whoever cared to try.[22] Only after 1949, when a much larger population was squeezed onto China's periphery, and more draft animals and heavy equipment were brought to bear, was this area able (or forced) to support numerous farms and villages. Surveys conducted during the 1950s and 1960s of surviving Manchu communities in Heilongjiang produced evidence showing how difficult it was to establish and support military bases in this region during the 17th century.[23]

Faced with this reality, the Qing fell back on convicts, prisoners of war, exiles, and slaves to man the agricultural colonies on the northern border. Coerced workers came from three sources:[24] First, there were ordinary criminals who had been exiled or banished, often with their wives, children, and other family members. Owing to the difficulty of recruiting workers, in 1647, 500 exiled households were rounded up

[18] Jean-Baptiste Du Halde (1741), 94, 110, 147, 327; Xu Shuming (1988), 20.
[19] Sun Zhanwen (1981), 90, 97–98.
[20] *SJTZ* (1736), zhuan 24:1234–37.
[21] Owen Lattimore (1934), 198–99; Sun Zhanwen (1981), 90–92; Xu Shuming (1988), 17.
[22] *Kotoku sannendo*, site 1.
[23] Jin Qicong (1981), 23–33; and *Manzu shehui lishi diaocha* (1985), 211–13.
[24] Diao Shuren (1993), 72, 111–13.

and put to work on an estate near Kaiyuan.[25] The experiment worked, and in 1660, these and other convicts were moved from Kaiyuan and Petuna to Ninguta. A second source was rebels, captured in the rebellions against Qing rule in southern China and banished to the north. One group of rebels were sent to Ninguta in 1661, and others followed.[26] Third, were slaves [*nupu*] who were assigned to or purchased by bannermen or estates and operated under the direction of the banner chief or estate head. "The families of criminals may be registered as slaves and assigned as workers on the various estates," read an imperial proclamation of 1645, while another edict of 1779 explained: "Estate workers will be selected from among the sons, daughters, and heirs of convicts who have been banished to Heilongjiang or from the household slaves of bannermen. They will be assigned to the official estates of Tsitsihar and Mergen and will be required to deliver grain each year according to the regulations."[27]

The Jesuit missionary Jean-Baptiste Du Halde found few Chinese settlers, when he passed through Jilin in the 1730s. There were only three cities in this region, Du Halde noted, all "wretchedly built, and surrounded with Walls of Earth." Jilin City, the headquarters of the military government, seemed the best of the lot. Petuna was "of much less note and almost wholly inhabited by Tartarian Soldiers and Exiles." Only Ninguta had a bustle of Chinese merchants, trading in furs and ginseng, and thriving agriculture, which depended on convict labor: "The Emperor has also taken care to repeople the Country, by sending hither all the Tartars and Chinese condemned to Banishment by the Law, so that when we were at a great Distance from Ningouta we met with good entertainment, for they are in no want of Provisions." Although lacking the bustle of Ninguta, Du Halde found a similar cast of characters in Tsitsihar, where "the Garrison chiefly consists of Tartars, but the merchants, artificers, and working people are mostly Chinese, either drawn thither by traffick, or exiled by the Law. . . ."[28]

In contrast to the banners and estates of southern Manchuria, which worked in large measure on the basis of contracts between labor and management and had to attract wage-workers and tenants to farm existing or reclaim additional land, the banners and estates of Jilin and Heilongjiang were prison camps. In the north, authority had to be centralized and absolute. The harsher the terms, the greater the temptation

[25] Wang Yuquan (1991), 327.
[26] Diao Shuren (1993), 108–9.
[27] *Da Qing huidian shili*, zhuan 1219, cited in Sun Zhanwen (1981), 98.
[28] Jean-Baptiste Du Halde (1741), 94, 110.

forced workers had to flee, and thus even harsher controls had to be imposed to keep them in place. It was a vicious cycle: on one turn, encouraged by the fact that Chinese migrants would not move voluntarily to these distant locations, and on the next turn, discouraging them from doing so. The result was to keep the migrants where they were most inclined to settle, which was near home. Only later, as Chinese gradually expanded the perimeter of their settlement and Jilin and Heilongjiang began to fill in with tightly packed villages and fields, did the banners in the northern territories abandoned their reliance on forced labor, which was never very efficient, and recruit wage-workers and tenants on the open market.[29]

B. The Manorial System

The system of "manors" established by the Qing Dynasty in Manchuria and Inner Mongolia (as well as in China proper, which lies outside the scope of this book) took different forms: first, "bannermen," or members of the Eight Banners, exercised control over "bannerlands" principally in Manchuria; second, Mongol princes or "chiefs" played a similar role in governing the Mongol "banners" (same name, different institution) of Inner Mongolia; and third, government officials, Manchu nobles, and members of the imperial household managed "official," "noble," and "imperial estates" in both areas. In all three cases, the essentials of the manors and the manorial system were the same: first, the power to dispose of land and manage labor within a designated area lay in the hands of agents (bannermen, Mongol banner chiefs, estate heads) who owed their appointment to authorities in Beijing; second, land (bannerland, land of the Mongol banners, estate land) was assigned to groups or individuals in perpetual trust, and could *not* be bought, sold, traded, or alienated by any of the parties to the arrangement; third, labor was supplied by the trustees of this land themselves or by tenants, wage-workers, bond servants, slaves, or convicts, who provided rent, tax, labor, military service, or a share of the crop in exchange for food or wages or for temporary use of the land, but who could in no case lay permanent claim to the property; and finally, the parent body responsible for each manor (a government agency, military command, imperial, or noble household) took a share of production in the form of taxes, goods, or services.

[29] Diao Shuren (1993), 111–13; Xu Shuming (1988), 18–19; and Sun Zhanwen (1981), 97–98.

The idea underlying the manorial system was that reliable allies of the Qing, especially Manchus and Mongols, would manage the agricultural economy of the northern territories, on land entrusted to them by the state, using labor that would have no rights of landownership and only temporary rights to its use, and that they would dispose of the output in a manner suitable to Beijing. The goal was to ensure development *with* control. Since the population of the northern territories was too small and unskilled to achieve the desired results, the manors would recruit workers, principally from China proper, and fit them into this structure of control. In some ways, the Qing was simply continuing Ming practices, transferring land and other assets from the vanquished to the victors, while substituting one group of masters for another. But in some respects the manorial system of the Qing was without precedent: land granted to the manors was inalienable, much of it lay outside the Great Wall, and control fell disproportionately to non-Chinese elites.

1. The Eight Banners

The Eight Banners [*Baqi*] were the military units that carried the Manchus to power and garrisoned the empire of the Qing.[30] The first "banners" [*qi*, in Chinese] were established in 1601 by the founder of what became the Qing Dynasty, Nurhaci (1559–1626). Once assigned to a banner, the "bannerman" [*qiren*] joined a hereditary military caste, which carried both rights and responsibilities that were passed on from father to son. Even before the formation of the banners, Nurhaci had initiated the practice of rewarding his followers with grants of land to which were attached bond servants taken as booty in raids or as prisoners of war. Over time, bannermen acquired "bannerlands" [*qidi*] and "bond servants" [*booi* in Manchu, *baoyi* in Chinese] to support their livelihood and as a reward for service. Initially, the Jurchen and other peoples who followed Nurhaci lacked clear ethnic identities, so that assignment to a banner united people of various races and cultures, giving a sense of belonging to its members and a defining character to the movement as a whole. In 1635, the name "Manchu" was applied by imperial fiat to the members of the Eight Banners that had been established up to that time. During the following decade, the groups that

[30] The following account of the development of banners and bannerlands is based on: Xu Shuming (1990), 89–90; Pamela Crossley (1990), 5–6, 13–14; Pamela Crossley (1997), 40–43; Evelyn Rawski (1998), 62–63; Edward Rhoads (2000), 18–24; Gertraude Roth (1979), 6, 15–27; Preston Torbert (1977), 15–19, 53–56; Frederic Wakeman (1985), 45–47, 53–55, 69–71, 161.

made up the Eight Banners were sorted out, and Manchus, Mongols, and Chinese [*Hanjun*] were organized into separate divisions of Eight Banners each. Thus, the term "Eight Banners" actually refers to the full slate of 24 banners. Although the number and distribution of the bannermen and their households was never precisely recorded, Mark Elliott estimates that in the course of the conquest, most of the 260,000–500,000 bannermen moved with the dynasty to China proper, leaving 50,000–100,000 in the Northeast, and that by 1720 the numbers in both areas had tripled. He also estimates that the total membership of the banner households, including dependents and bond servants, was three to five times the number of actual bannermen.[31]

The practice of making land grants to bannermen served at least three purposes: First, it rewarded the military forces who had carried the Qing to power and had the greatest capacity for keeping them in power or, if neglected, causing them trouble in the future. Second, it was a means of ensuring that the banners would remain viable and intact, so that banner forces would be available when needed for military service. Finally, and of special importance for this study, bannerlands formed the basis of agrarian domains under the direction of parties loyal to the Qing, who would oversee the development of agriculture on sensitive frontiers and forestall the expansion of markets in land, labor, and produce that might attract Chinese farmers and merchants and enable them to gain the upper hand over the Manchus and their Mongol allies.

The terms governing bannerlands were designed to benefit members of this privileged military caste. In Manchuria, where the population was relatively sparse and land less valuable than in China proper, the standard allotment was a generous 6 *shang* (36 *mu*) to each ordinary bannerman and larger amounts to banner officials, who might also have a number of bond servants or coerced workers under their control.[32] At first, bannermen paid a modest rent, but no tax on the official allotment and were allowed to reclaim and cultivate wasteland, which also remained untaxed. With the rise of foreign threats and the need to supply troops on the northern and western borders, in 1693, Beijing imposed the first tax on bannerlands. Still, the tax rate on bannerlands was much

[31] Mark Elliott (2001), 17, 363–64.

[32] Diao Shuren (1993), 49. This study uses the following conversion rates: in Shengjing (Fengtian), 1 *shang* = 6 *mu*; in Jilin, Heilongjiang, and Mongol territories, 1 *shang* = 10 *mu*. Most Chinese sources, such as Kong Jingwei (1990), 128, give the former conversion for Fengtian, but provide no figure for Jilin and Heilongjiang. *Sihai* (Taibei: Taiwan zhonghua shuju, 1979), Vol. 2, p. 2153, gives the following numbers of *mu* per *shang*: Southern Liaoning, 6; Northern Liaoning, 10; Jilin, 12; Heilongjiang, 12. CER (1924), 48, and C. Walter Young (1932), 346, both give 1 *shang* = 10 *mu* for northern Manchuria.

lower than that levied on common land in Manchuria: only about 3% of the common land rate during the Kangxi era (until 1723), rising to 20% under Yongzheng (1723–35). Additional land, privately reclaimed by bannermen and known as "banner surplus land" [*qiyudi*], was taxed at a slightly higher, but still favorable rate.[33]

At the same time, the banners, which formed the backbone of the Qing armies, were subject to strict discipline. Controlling the bannermen began with controlling the bannerland, which was a principal source of their income and wealth. Bannerland was given in trust to individual bannermen for use during their lifetimes and eventually to pass on to their heirs. If a bannerman could no longer work his land, he was required to return it to the banner or banner chief. The initial prohibition, promulgated in 1670, stated simply: "The land of officials and soldiers must not be traded outside the banner." As the bannermen sought various ways around this rule, more elaborate pronouncements followed. The purpose of bannerland was to produce income for members of a military caste who would be ready to serve when called. To sell or alienate the land would remove the foundation from beneath the forces that were needed to defend the dynasty and the state.[34]

Besides prohibiting trade in land, Qing laws restricted the movement and other rights of the bannermen themselves. Each ordinary bannerman was identified as either a soldier [*bing*] or worker [*ding*] and assigned to a particular "company" ["niru" in Manchu, *niulu* in Chinese], a unit composed of some scores of households, which was responsible for organizing agricultural production, military service and corvée labor. Only higher authorities could appoint bannermen, and once assigned to a company, a bannerman could not move his residence, change or leave his post, or withdraw from the banner without permission. The company commander or "banner chief" [*qizhu*] had absolute authority over his men. Any bannerman who "fled the banner" [*taoqi*] without permission was subject to severe penalties. To ensure that such infractions did not go unnoticed, Beijing carried out a triennial "screening" [*bianshen*], at which each banner soldier or worker had to be present and accounted for. Absentees were subject to punishment, including fines, floggings, or exile.[35]

[33] These tax rates were applied to land distributed to bannermen and included in the "Red Register" [*hongce*], the official tax roll specifying the landholdings of each banner household that was created following the land survey of 1726, and so named because it was deposited in Beijing and marked with a red thread. See: Diao Shuren (1993), 119–22; 142.

[34] *Da Qing huidian*, zhuan 84, 159, cited in Diao Shuren (1993), 50, 127.

[35] Diao Shuren (1993), 52–53, 138; and Yang Xuechen (1963), 181. For different views of the status of bonded workers and changes in the number and status of these workers over

2. Estates

The "imperial" [*huangzhuang*], "noble" [*wangzhuang*], and "official estates" [*guanzhuang*] established by the Qing Dynasty in Manchuria and some parts of Inner Mongolia share some of the "manorial" features of bannerlands under the Eight Banners. The estates, like the banners, were designed to develop agriculture under the management of corporate bodies that held land in trust, controlled labor, and were in the end dependent upon the state. There was a difference, however: Bannerlands were established to serve the bannermen, to reward them for their previous contributions, provide for their livelihood, and ensure their commitment, when needed, for military service. Imperial or official estates were production units, created for the benefit of the imperial family, Manchu noblemen, or government agencies, and manned by workers who paid heavy rents and taxes or worked under some degree of coercion and duress. Bannerlands were to reward, estates were to exploit. The models for both were established by Nurhaci, in the early 17th century, and the practices continued following the conquest of China in 1644.[36]

The standard estate was composed of 10 members, one of whom served as the "head" [*zhuangtou*], the other 9 as ordinary "workers" [*zhuangding*], and an allocation of land that might range between 120 *shang* (720 *mu*) in Shengjing to 200 *shang* (2,000 *mu*) in Jilin or Heilongjiang. The estate head managed the day-to-day affairs of the estate, conducted periodic "screenings" to assure that the estate workers were fulfilling their duties, and collected rents and taxes, which were turned over to the parent body. Most estates were required to produce grain, although some specialized in cotton, fruit, vegetables, or salt, and all had to deliver a specified quota of their output each year. The largest number of estates were located in Shengjing, managed by the Imperial Household Department [*Neiwufu*], Board of Revenue [*Hubu*], or Board of Rites [*Libu*], and devoted to supplying the dynasty or government agencies with their abundant requirements. Estates (and bannerlands) were also established in Jilin and Heilongjiang to grow grain for Manchu forces that were sent north to meet the Russian threat.[37]

---

time, see: Preston Torbert (1977), 16–17; Frederic Wakeman (1985), 69–71; and Gertraude Roth (1979), 15–27.

[36] Xu Shuming (1990), 89–90.

[37] Diao Shuren (1993), 59, 68, 78–107, 111. For details on the Imperial Household Department, see: Beatrice Bartlett (1991), 23–24, 30.

The land of each estate was divided into plots that were assigned to the estate head or individual estate workers in trust. Estate land, like bannerlands, could not be alienated, although fully vested estate workers enjoyed permanent and hereditary rights to use the land assigned to them and could expand their holdings by reclaiming wasteland. Bannermen, estate workers, or anyone who engaged in the misappropriation or sale of land belonging to a banner or an estate were subject to severe penalties. According to the Qing legal code, "Any person who sells one *mu* of land will be given 50 strokes with a bamboo cane. For every 5 *mu* the punishment will be increased by one degree, up to 80 strokes and 2 years of banishment. If the case involves the sale of official land, the punishment will be raised two degrees."[38]

Estate workers, like bannermen, were bound to their land, had no right to travel, relocate or abandon their posts, and faced stiff penalties if they fled or were found absent without leave. Under Qing law, the punishments for attempting to flee from an estate were, "On the first instance, 100 lashes; on the second instance, 100 lashes plus 40 days in shackles; on the third instance, 100 lashes plus two months in shackles; and on the fourth instance, exile to hard labor in a distant and forbidding place."[39] The law also covered such personal behavior as marriage: If the daughter or widow of an estate worker was married without official approval, "the bride, father, mother, and groom will all be subject to trial and punishment, and maidens or widows who have been married in this fashion will be forced into slavery."[40] Estate workers of all ranks were required to pay onerous rents, taxes, and other exactions, were excluded from the civil service examinations for three generations, and were subject to severe punishments for any violation of these terms.[41] The status of estate workers was hereditary, which ensured that the rights and obligations of service would remain unchanged from generation to generation and left them with no choice but to remain on the land of their fathers.

The status and conditions of workers and others employed on the estates varied according to the time, location, and circumstances under which they entered service. Some of the earliest estate workers were

---

[38] *Da Qing lu: hulu* [Qing Legal Code: Household Laws], cited in Diao Shuren (1993), 162. For other similar legal provisions, see *ibid.*, 156.

[39] *Dubu zeli* [Laws on supervision and arrest], cited in Diao Shuren (1993), 159. In 1737, as conditions on the estates worsened and estate workers [*zhuangding*] demanded better treatment, the Qing was forced to rescind the restrictions on marriage and allow the estate workers to choose their own mates. See Diao Shuren (1993), 160.

[40] *Heitudang* [Black file] (1666), cited in Diao Shuren (1993), 160.

[41] Diao Shuren (1993), 77–78.

criminals or prisoners of war, captured in the campaign against Ming loyalists, and sent to Manchuria as slave labor. Others were more fortunate: Chinese farmers, some of whom had lived in the Liaodong region for generations, and others who arrived with the wave of immigrants in the early Qing, "surrendered with their land" [*daidi touchong*] to an estate. Under this arrangement, the smallholder gave up his status as a commoner and right of ownership in exchange for protection for himself and his land, which now belonged to the estate and was thus exempt from taxation. Many early settlers provided the farmland that formed the estates under the Imperial Household Department and in this process gained favorable terms for themselves and their heirs.[42] Conditions were quite different for migrants who arrived later after the estates were established, "surrendered with only their bodies" [*danshen touchong*], and as a consequence enjoyed none of the rights of the founding members.[43] Most unfortunate were peasants from the area surrounding Beijing, whose land had been seized and turned over to Manchu nobles and bannermen, after which they were sent as forced workers to estates in Shengjing.[44]

The same inequities applied to tenants. Those who were present at the creation of the estate and helped reclaim the original estate lands enjoyed "long-rent" [*changzu*] agreements, which guaranteed permanent and hereditary tenancy rights. Those who arrived later, during the 18th century, when southern Manchuria began to fill up and the competition for farmland grew more intense, had to accept "short-rent" [*duanzu*] agreements, which normally ran for 3–5 years, carried no permanent right of renewal, and could not be passed on to their heirs.[45]

Labor conditions on the estates in southern Manchuria were relatively good. The bannermen, estate heads, or estate workers who held land in trust were generally unable or unwilling to farm the land themselves and preferred to recruit wage-workers or tenants from a mobile labor pool composed primarily of migrants from China proper. Meanwhile, migrant farmers had to find land or work and preferred established communities near their homes in north China. Most were inclined to accept the conditions offered on estates or bannerlands in southern Manchuria or the adjacent steppe, rather than take their chances in the unsettled north. The layout of the southern estates

[42] Diao Shuren (1993), 71–73; *Manzu shehui lishi diaocha* (1985), 205–8.
[43] Kong Jingwei (1990), 113.
[44] Yang Xuechen (1963), 177.
[45] Diao Shuren (1993), 167–68.

favored a fluid labor market. Most estates were patched together from existing settlements, the fields were scattered across more than one department or county, and workers lived intermixed among the plots and strips of different estates, banners, or common lands that belonged to different jurisdictions. Production was carried out by separate households, each of which worked its own land. In sum, the estate was not so much a centrally managed production unit, as it was a group of separate farms, held together by the collection of levies.[46] Under these conditions, estate workers, as well as their hired laborers or tenants, enjoyed considerable freedom.

Conditions in the north were exactly the opposite. Migrant farmers were unwilling to travel beyond the limits of dense settlement in southern Manchuria, and if they had done so would have found it difficult to return to their homes in China proper. There were Chinese who went to the distant frontiers—fur trappers, ginseng gatherers, gold miners, and bandits who dealt in these and other high-value, light-weight, and often proscribed products—but not peasants, nor indeed anyone who considered settlement in faraway places a desirable way of life. In the absence of a mobile labor force, estates and bannerlands in Jilin and Heilongjiang had to rely on convicts, exiles, slaves, and other coerced workers, resembled prison camps, and were unlikely to attract migrants who would join these units on a voluntary basis.[47]

3. Mongol Banners

The problem of understanding organization of the northern territories is complicated by the fact that the Qing applied the same term, "banner" [*qi*], to two different institutions. In several essential ways, the "Eight Banners" (discussed above) were similar to the "Mongol banners" (described below), for they share the manorial character through which the Qing rulers sought to control migration and development in the regions above the Great Wall. However, the history, setting, and operation of the Mongol banners were quite different from the Manchurian institutions of the same name.

In the early-17th century, as the Manchus expanded outward from their base in central Manchuria, they came into contact with the Mongols of the eastern steppe. At this time, the eastern tribes were themselves threatened by the Chahar Mongols further west, who were seeking,

---

[46] Diao Shuren (1993), 64.
[47] Diao Shuren (1993), 71–73.

under the leadership of Ligdan Khan (d. 1634), to reunify the steppe nomads and revive the empire of Genghis Khan. In 1628, the Keerqin
(Khorchin), one of the leading tribes of eastern Mongols, chose to side
with the rising Manchu power against the Chahar, after which the neighboring tribes of Zhaowuda [Jo-Oda], Zhelimu [Jerim], and Zhuosuotu
[Josoto] Leagues followed suit.[48] Support of the eastern Mongols was
crucial as the Manchus turned south to conquer and occupy China
proper. Throughout its subsequent history, the Qing considered the
Mongol alliance and control of the eastern steppe essential for the defense of the Manchu homeland and the empire as a whole.

To incorporate the Mongols into the Qing system and ensure that
they would remain loyal to the new regime, the Manchus adapted a traditional Mongol organization—the *hoshun* or *khoshun*—and gave it a
new twist. The *hoshun* was an intermediate unit, larger than the household, smaller than the tribe, which was governed by a hereditary no-
bleman, who might be a "prince" [*wang*] or "duke" [*gong*] or go by another noble title, such as *beile* or *taiji*. The chief functions of the reigning
prince included assigning pastures to the herding households that
made up his *hoshun*, negotiating with neighboring *hoshun* for the use
of common pasturelands, and enforcing these and other arrangements
bearing on the life of the community within and without. The *hoshun*
had no fixed territory, but fit into a system of nomadic pastoralism,
which was governed by the opportunity or need to move in search of
greener pastures, rather than devotion to a particular space. Members
of the *hoshun*, both hereditary princes and ordinary herders, considered
land a collective good, whose value might vary with the season, the
year, or the movement of the herds, and might be assigned temporarily
to a particular household, but which was not "owned" by anyone and
could not be separated, sold, or permanently alienated from the common endowment.[49]

After the eastern tribes accepted Manchu rule, the Qing, in order to
assure that Mongols and Mongol territories remained under their control, incorporated the *hoshun*, renamed "banners" [*qi*], into an administrative system that was governed by a new set of rules: First, the territory and membership of each banner were fixed, and the movement of
people and livestock into and out of a given banner prohibited—in contrast to the open and fluid nature of the *hoshun*, which had no territorial

[48] Evelyn Rawski (1998), 67.
[49] Sechin Jagchid and Paul Hyer (1979), 274–82.

boundaries or restrictions on movement. Second, consistent with previous practice, land was considered a collective good, which could not be alienated, although it could be assigned to an individual or household or rented to someone outside the banner, such as a migrant farmer. Third, the hereditary prince, who had traditionally been chosen by informal processes sanctioned by the *hoshun* itself, was replaced by a banner "chief" [*jasagh*], who was drawn from the native nobility, but was appointed by Qing officials and might be replaced if he violated his trust or fell out of favor with Beijing. Following this model, the eastern Mongols were organized into 49 banners, whose chiefs reported through the *Lifanyuan* [Mongol Superintendency] and could be rewarded, punished, promoted, or dismissed by the authorities in Beijing. The purpose of the banner system was to divide the Mongols into manageable units, bind each unit directly to the state, and prevent them from forming alliances among themselves or with outsiders, particularly Chinese, so that each banner would remain dependent upon and loyal to the Qing Dynasty. The banners paid no tax, but were expected to provide military service in time of war.[50]

Although the Mongols relied primarily on animal products for food and other needs, they also consumed grain, vegetables, and other agricultural goods, some of which could be grown on the well-watered land of the banners themselves. The Qing authorities, as noted, were ambivalent on the question of who might farm within the Mongol territories. All things being equal, Beijing preferred that the Mongols remain separate and dependent on the Qing state, rather than on one another or on Chinese merchants and workers. "Commoners [*minren*] from China proper are not permitted to go outside the passes to open land for agriculture in the Mongol areas," stated one of many government edicts on this subject. "Violators who privately reclaim pasturelands will be prosecuted."[51] Meanwhile, Beijing sent agents to the Mongol banners to teach farming techniques, hoping to preempt the development of ties between the Mongols and Chinese merchants and farmers. But there were also pressures working in the opposite direction: Chinese migrants and refugees came to the Mongol areas in search of land. Mongol banner chiefs could profit handsomely by renting out portions of the banner to Chinese tenants.[52] And when disaster struck, Beijing might relieve the pressure on northern China by opening the passes

[50] Lu Minghui (1994), 1–3.
[51] *Da Qing huidian shili*, zhuan 979, cited in Kong Jingwei (1990), 96.
[52] Ma Yongshan and Zhao Yi (1992), 86–87.

through the Great Wall and urging Mongol authorities to let the refugees "borrow land to nourish the people" [*jiedi yangmin*].[53]

C. The Settlement of Manchuria and Inner Mongolia

During the first century of Qing rule, most Chinese who made their way from north China across the Great Wall in search of land or work had to settle for positions as workers or tenants on a banner, bannerland, or estate. Information on the identity, character, and motivation of these early migrants is limited, so we will postpone our examination of these issues until a later period, when the evidence is more abundant. It is clear, however, that the pattern of settlement and cultivation during the early Qing favored areas adjacent to the Great Wall or in southern Manchuria over the north. At the beginning of the Qing, most farmland in southern Manchuria was allocated to banners or estates, while Chinese migrants who arrived in the 17th and 18th centuries initially served as tenants or wage-workers on these manors. Those who arrived first and proved the most resourceful might rise to become the "head" of an estate or member of a banner and exercise the powers of foreman or sublandlord over friends, relatives, and fellow-provincials whom they recruited from back home.[54] Later arrivals were forced to take less desirable land and less exalted positions under increasingly crowded conditions. Unless they were willing to move beyond the boundaries of previous settlement and take their chances on a distant frontier, migrant farmers had to work for someone else and had little hope of gaining land of their own.

The "Imperial Shengjing Gazetteer" [*Qinding Shengjing tongzhi*], which was published in five editions between 1684 and 1784, provides the most complete statistics on landownership and land use in Manchuria during the early Qing.[55] These figures show: first, the imbalance

[53] Ma Ruheng and Cheng Chongde (1990), 10–11. Mongol agriculture: Ma Yongshan and Zhao Yi (1992), 86–87; Wang Yuhai (1990), 194.

[54] See, for example, village histories in *Kotoku sannendo*, sites 13 and 14.

[55] Reports on the area of land in various categories and regions appear in the following sources: Bannerland, Shengjing: *SJTZ* (1736), zhuan 24. Bannerland, Jilin: *Baqi tongzhi* (*BQTJ*), zhuan 21. Estates, Shengjing: *SJTZ* (1736), zhuan 24:1220–27; *SJTZ* (1784), zhuan 38:7–8, 20–21; Diao Shuren (1993), 84, 87; Yang Xuechen (1963), 177. Estates, Jilin and Heilongjiang: Calculated by multiplying the number of estates, listed in *SJTZ* (1736), zhuan 24:1234–37, times 200 *shang*, which, according to Diao Shuren (1993), 111, was the standard size of an estate in Jilin. Courier Stations: *BQTJ*, zhuan 21. Common land: *SJTZ* (1784), zhuan 37:4, 23. Different conversion rates are used for Shengjing (1 *shang* = 6 *mu*), and Jilin and Heilongjiang (1 *shang* = 10 *mu*).

between the heavily cultivated south and sparsely cultivated north; and, second, the substantial amount of privately owned common land in Shengjing compared to the paucity of such land in Jilin and Heilongjiang. By 1735, the total area of cultivated land in Shengjing was over 18 million *mu*, which was more than one-third of the cultivated area of Liaoning Province at the end of the Qing, and nearly one-quarter of the area of cultivation in Liaoning in 1933, indicating that by the early 18th century a substantial start had been made, while there was still room for further growth.[56] By contrast, in 1735 Jilin and Heilongjiang had less than 3 million *mu* of cultivated land: this, despite the fact that these two regions were nearly five times as large as Shengjing and today have more than three times as much land under cultivation.[57] The area of common land—2.6 million *mu* in Shengjing versus only 29,000 *mu* in Jilin and none in Heilongjiang—is especially interesting, because it is a strong indicator of Chinese migration. Manchus had no incentive to enter land onto the tax rolls. On the contrary, if a Manchu bannerman, his tenant, or servant reclaimed wasteland, they invariably found ways to incorporate the land into the banner and thus avoid paying tax on it. The only people interested in registering land with the tax office were Chinese commoners who wanted to establish ownership of the land and protect it against seizure by a banner or estate. Although most immigrants had no choice but to work for wages or rent land from banners and estates,[58] the abundance of taxable common land in Shengjing shows that by the first half of the 18th century a substantial minority were making the transition to land ownership.

Studies of banners in the Shengjing region during the early Qing show that the area of land assigned to these units increased along with the number of Chinese farmworkers. For example, a banner garrison was first established in Xiuyan, located midway between the Liao River and the Korean border, in 1633. During the following century, as more Manchus came out of the mountains and settled on the plains, many were given land grants, and the area of bannerland in Xiuyan tripled from around 12,000 *shang* in 1693 to 36,000 *shang* in 1727. Some

[56] Dwight Perkins (1969), 234–36, reports the following figures (in million *mu*) for the cultivated area of Liaoning Province: 1766, 19; 1873, 22; 1893, 30; 1913, 47; 1933, 74; 1957, 71.

[57] According to *Agricultural Statistics of the PRC, 1949–1990*, Table 6, in 1990, the area of cultivated land (1,000 hectares) of the three northeastern provinces was: Liaoning, 3,470; Jilin, 3,936; Heilongjiang, 8,827.

[58] According to the *Gaozong shilu*, zhuan 127, cited in Kong Jingwei (1990), 140, a survey of the bannerlands of Shengjing conducted in 1679 found that most "hire commoners to cultivate the land."

Manchus farmed their own land, but most depended upon Chinese immigrants who moved to Xiuyan with the acquiescence and even encouragement of the government in Beijing.[59] The story was similar in Ningyuan (now Xingcheng), located along the Shengjing-Shanhaiguan road, the route taken by Qing forces on their invasion of China and thus thick with settlements of Manchu bannermen. In 1958, over 60,000 Manchus remained in Xingcheng County, although only about 2,000 were descendants of true "Manchu bannermen" who had made up the original Qing armies, whereas the rest, over 90%, were "Chinese bannermen" who joined the movement after 1644, either inhabitants of the Liaodong region who "surrendered with their land" or migrants from China proper who saw membership in a banner as the best option for newcomers with limited assets and opportunities.[60]

Another indicator of agricultural development and the presence of Chinese is the establishment of government offices on the model used in China proper to administer and collect taxes on privately owned farmland. John Shepherd has argued that Qing policy makers viewed the establishment of these offices in another border area, Taiwan, as an investment that could be justified only if the income from taxes offset the costs of administration and security, and that the dynasty was reluctant to take on the burdens of a larger bureaucracy.[61] If Shepherd is correct, then we can read the opening (and closing) of tax offices in Manchuria as a sign of how much development had occurred or how much Beijing expected to occur in these regions. Again, the evidence points to strong, rapid development in Shengjing and late, halting moves further north. Between 1653 and 1665, two prefectures [*fu*], Jinzhou and Fengtian, and under them nine counties [*xian*] or departments [*zhou*]—Jin Xian, Guangning, and Ningyuan in Jinzhou, and Kaiyuan, Tieling, Liaoyang, Haicheng, Gaiping, and Chengde in Fengtian[62]—were established along both sides of the Liao River inside the Willow Palisade (Map 2). All these offices continued to operate without interruption—in fact, they did a booming business—into the 20th century. Compare this with the history of tax collection further north: Three offices were established in Jilin in 1727: at Yongji Zhou near Jilin City, Changning Xian near Petuna, and Taining Xian near Ninguta. In the absence of taxable farmland—the total reached only 29,000 *mu* in 1735—the two counties,

[59] Zhang Qizhuo (1984), 6–14, 20.
[60] *Manzu shehui lishi diaocha* (1985), 204–7.
[61] John Shepherd (1993), 198–208, 215–26.
[62] Establishment of government agencies: Zhang Xuanru (1983), 186–87.

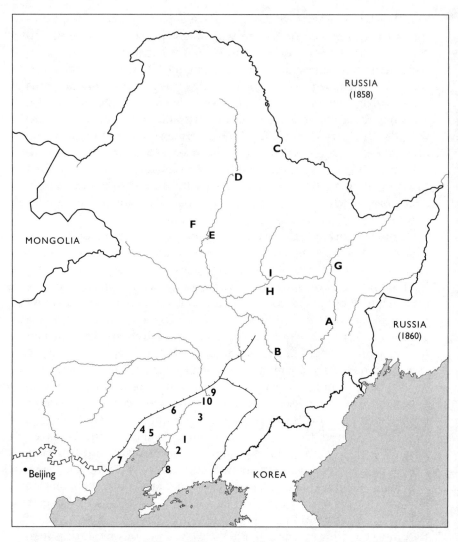

MAP 2. Government Offices, Military Garrisons, and Agricultural Colonies, Northeast China, 1653–65

Map 2 Legend

Map No.	Est. Date	Place	Status
1	1653	Liaoyang	Prefecture
	1653	Liaoyang	County
2	1653	Haicheng	County
3	1657	Fengtian	Prefecture
4	1665	Jinzhou	Prefecture
5	1665	Jin Xian	County
6	1665	Guangning	County
7	1665	Ningyuan	County
	1665	Chengde	County
8	1665	Gaiping	County
9	1665	Kaiyuan	County
10	1665	Tieling	County

Military Garrisons and Agricultural Colonies
[*tuntian*], 1652–1700

A	1652	Ninguta
B	1676	Jilin
C	1683	Aihui
D	1686	Mergen
E	1691	Tsitsihar
F	1691	Buteha
G	c. 1700	Sanxing
H	c. 1700	Alachuke
I	c. 1700	Hulan

SOURCES: Sun Zhanwen (1981), 90–92; Xu Shuming (1988), 17–20.

Taining and Changning, had to be closed, in 1729 and 1736 respectively, leaving Yongji as the only tax office in Jilin, until the creation of a sub-prefecture at Changchun in 1802 (Map 3).[63] The first government office in Heilongjiang opened in Hulan in 1875.[64]

The evidence on population and land under cultivation in the Mongol areas is less complete than for Manchuria, because Mongol banners lacked a regular system of collecting or reporting data. Still, scattered reports reveal conditions consistent with the picture drawn above: that is, settlement and cultivation were much heavier in the south than in the north. Most development took place under the auspices of banners, bannerlands, and estates, although there was also some private reclamation and the formation of taxable common land. And in most cases, farmwork was done by Chinese migrants who served as workers or

[63] *SJTZ* (1784), zhuan 37, 33–34.
[64] Robert Lee (1970), 73–74; Richard Edmonds (1985), 116.

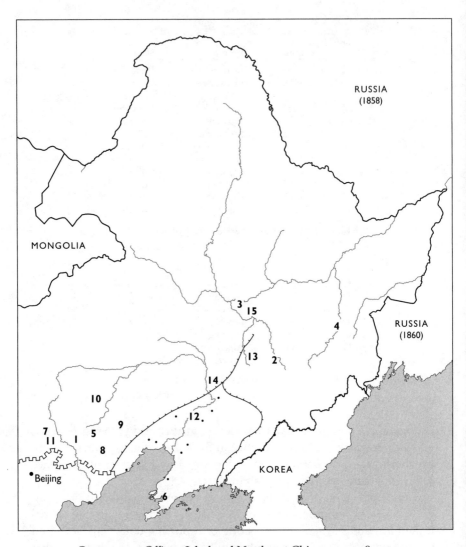

MAP 3. Government Offices, Jehol and Northeast China, 1723–1810

Map 3 Legend

Map No.	Est. Date	Place	Current Name of Location	Status
1	1723	Jehol	Chengde	Subprefecture
2	1727	Yongji		Department
3*	1727	Changning		County
4*	1727	Taining		County
5	1729	Bagou	Pingquan	Subprefecture
6	1734	Fu Zhou		Department
7	1736	Siqi	Fengning	Subprefecture
8	1738	Tazigou	Jianchang	Subprefecture
9	1738	Sanzuota	Chaoyang	Subprefecture
10	1738	Wulanhada	Chifeng	Subprefecture
11	1738	Kalahetun	Luanping	Subprefecture
12	1798	Xinmin		Subprefecture
13	1802	Changchun		Prefecture
14	1806	Changtu		Subprefecture
15	1810	Petuna	Fuyu	Subprefecture

*These two offices closed within 8 years. After 1735, Yongji Zhou remained the only office in Jilin until Changchun Prefecture was established in 1802.

SOURCES: Guo Songyi (1990), 21; Alexander Hosie (1904), 162–63.

tenants in one of the manorial institutions or, as these opportunities were exhausted, reclaimed land on their own.

During the Ming Dynasty, Chinese farmers had begun to spread into the hills, valleys, and flatlands directly north of the Great Wall, which enjoys a relatively warm, moist climate (compared to the cooler, drier north), and a mountainous topography that forms watersheds and protected valleys. But their progress was limited by the unfriendly Mongol tribes that dominated this region and the reluctance of the Ming to bear the costs of defending and taxing a contested area. The Qing subdued these tribes, established banners and estates along the Great Wall and encouraged Chinese farmers to serve on these manors as tenants or seasonal farmworkers. In the course of the 17th and 18th centuries, growing numbers of Chinese migrated and eventually settled in the Kalaqin [Kharchin][65] and Tumote [Tumet][66] banners of Zhuosuotu League (Map 4), and, following the establishment of the Imperial Hunting Grounds [Mulan Weichang] and Summer Palace, in Jehol [also called

[65] For details on Kalaqin Banner, see: Cheng Chongde (1990), 174–76; Guo Songyi (1990), 21–22; Yuan Senpo (1986), 28–29; Wang Yuhai (1990), 193–95; Jean Baptiste Du Halde (1741), 116–17; and Owen Lattimore (1934), 71–72, 237–38; 247–49.

[66] For details on Tumet Banner, see: Ma Ruheng and Cheng Chongde (1990), 12; and Owen Lattimore (1934), 237–40, 249–53.

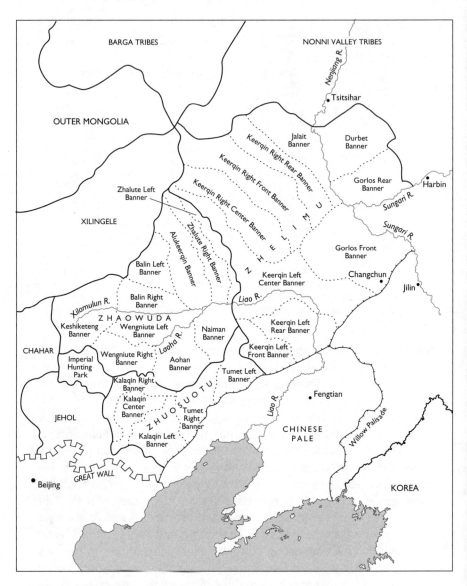

MAP 4. Mongol Leagues and Banners

Chengde].[67] During the period 1723–38, eight government tax offices were established in this area (Map 3), indicating the density of settlement and cultivation.

Finally, developments on the border between China proper and the steppe along the Great Wall west of Beijing, although outside the scope of this book, fit with the picture drawn above. In this region, the Qing faced the same tension between a desire to relieve pressure in the south, expand cultivation in the north, and thus tolerate the movement of peasants and merchants from the former to the latter, and the fear that this might produce an unhealthy partnership between Mongols and Chinese and thereby undermine the dynasty's control. They pursued the same shifting and sometimes conflicting policies of restricting migration to protect the status quo and opening the border to relieve pressure within or combat threats from without. And as a result, Chinese migrants pressed their muddled, but steady expansion north.[68]

D. Conclusion

The Qing Dynasty ended its first century with the conflicts and ambiguities of its policy toward the northern territories still unresolved. The threat from the Russians had been repulsed, and a network of military forts, supplied by agricultural colonies, had been established on the Heilongjiang and Sungari rivers. The system of banners, bannerlands, and estates functioned successfully in Manchuria and the neighboring areas of Inner Mongolia. And migrant farmers from north China played their appointed roles as workers or tenants in the various manors. But the balance among these policies and forces depended on the size, scope, and character of the Chinese presence. The following chapter will show how, as the numbers of Chinese increased, the area of their settlement expanded, and the nature of their involvement deepened, the ability of the Qing to sustain the manors and the system of control over land at first eroded and then came undone.

[67] For details on Jehol, see: Yuan Senpo (1986), 26–28; *Weichang Manzu Mengguzu zizhixian zhi* (1997), 128–29, 138–39, 140–47; Guo Songyi (1990), 20–21; Wang Yuquan (1991), 324–25; and Cheng Chongde (1990), 176.

[68] The abundant Chinese scholarship on this subject includes: Chen Yuning (1986), 77–78; Cheng Chongde (1990), 173–76; Cheng Chongde (1991), 29–31; *Chifeng shi* (1991), 181; Diao Shuren (1993), 130; Guo Songyi (1985), 118; Guo Songyi (1990), 20; Kuang Hao-lin (1985), 46; Liang Bing (1991), 42–51, 151–53; Ma Ruheng and Cheng Chongde (1990), 12, 19; Wang Bingming (1990), 61–62; Wang Shangyi (n.d.), 21–22; and Zhao Yongfu (1981), 39; Zhang Zhihua (1987), 85–87. For additional information in English, see: Rene Grousset (1970), 519–31; and Sechin Jagchid and Paul Hyer (1979), 279.

CHAPTER 2

From Manor to Market (1740–1850)

DURING THE SECOND CENTURY of the Qing, the system of manors, which had spread throughout the areas just above the Great Wall, gave way to free markets in land and labor on the model previously practiced in China proper. In the preceding century, Chinese migrants had moved into these areas, reclaimed land, and had taken their places as workers or tenants under Mongol banners, Manchu bannerlands, or noble, official, or imperial estates. The heirs to these early settlers oversaw the dissolution of the estates. By the middle of the 19th century, the territories north of the Wall were dominated by densely populated walled villages, surrounded by intensely cultivated fields, owned or rented and farmed by Chinese households—that is, a society and economy much like the one these settlers had known in Shandong, Hebei, or elsewhere on the north China plain. Finally, as the Liao River plain was incorporated into the expanding circle of China, this perimeter was itself sending out migrants who would begin the next cycle of settlement in central Manchuria and on the eastern steppe.

The disintegration of the manors and the creation in their place of a system of markets in land and labor was primarily the work of migrant farmers and merchants. During the 18th and early 19th centuries, migration swelled the ranks of Chinese in Manchuria and Inner Mongolia, overflowing the barricades erected to contain them, and creating a growing surplus of wage-workers, tenants, and eventually landowners, who undersold, outproduced, and in the end overwhelmed the Manchus and Mongols who had been entrusted with managing the banners, bannerlands, and estates. Whatever measures the Qing might have tried to protect the manorial system, an army of hardworking, skilled, and entrepreneurial Chinese found ways to take control of the land and turn it to their own purposes.

The pressure of the Chinese workforce accelerated a second trend, which was the growing inequality within the manors themselves. The divide between rich and powerful Manchu and Mongol elites and poor and powerless bannermen, herders, and workers eroded the corporate strength of banners, bannerlands, and estates and created incentives among both high and low to sell the land for personal gain. The manors broke up, because the people who had been entrusted with the management of collective wealth chose, by legal or illegal means, to expropriate and liquidate their assets. Finally, these pressures bore on the Qing, prompting the government to make the best of a losing hand by commercializing the manors, which Beijing came to view less as a means of controlling development, as had been their original intent, than as an instrument for raising revenue for the dynasty and the state. The shift from labor service to taxation, and from taxation in kind to taxation in cash turned the banners, bannerlands, and estates into sources of revenue whose performance was judged by how much they could deliver. The pressure of growing Chinese migration and the secondary effects of inequality and commercialization contributed to the breakdown of the manorial system and its replacement first by a system of rent-tenancy and eventually the transfer of land to new owners.

A. The Breakdown of the Manorial System

Three developments contributed to the breakdown of the manorial system and its eventual replacement by competitive markets in land, labor, and other resources: first, the growing number of immigrants from China proper; second, the growing inequality in status and wealth among Manchu and Mongol members of the banners and estates; and third, changes in Qing policy regarding the extraction of resources from the manors, from military service and corvée labor to taxation, and from taxation in kind to taxation in cash. The first factor, the increase in population, had an additional effect: Besides contributing to the breakdown of the manorial system, crowding and the corresponding shortage of farmland in southern Manchuria triggered a second stage of migration to regions further north.

1. Increases in Migration and Cultivation

The factor that had the greatest impact on the breakdown of the manorial system and the rise of a market economy was the tremendous increase during the 18th and early 19th centuries in the migration and settlement of Chinese in areas north of the Great Wall. The flood of skilled,
hardworking, entrepreneurial Chinese farmers offered the banners and
estates a more economical, productive, and profitable workforce than
they could find elsewhere. Once engaged, migrants advanced from
wage-workers to tenants, creditors, and finally owners of former banner
and estate lands and freeholders of land reclaimed on their own. This
transformation was accelerated by Chinese merchants, who sold goods
manufactured in China, provided credit, took advantage of their Manchu and Mongol debtors, and in the end seized control of the land. The
foundations of the manorial system were in the first instance washed
away by a tide of Chinese.

It is ironic that a discussion of Manchuria during the Qianlong era
(1736–96) should focus on migration, because this period began on the
opposite note: namely, the announcement of the "closure" policy, which
was designed to restrict the access of Chinese to areas north of the Great
Wall. Qianlong was not the first to impose this ban. The first two Qing
emperors, Shunzhi (1644–61) and Kangxi (1662–1722), had forbade
Chinese to cross the Wall and ordered those already in Manchuria to
return home.[1] But these regimes were ambivalent or inconsistent on this
subject, and one can point to as many edicts from the 17th and early
18th centuries that *en*couraged as *dis*couraged the move north. The
turning point in the declaratory policy occurred in 1740, when the
throne pronounced against the movement of people across the Wall and
all forms of contact between parties on the two sides. Officials in Fengtian were ordered to "dispatch additional military forces to carry out in-
vestigations, prohibit people from China proper from moving beyond
the passes [i.e. the Great Wall] and close Shanhaiguan, Xifengkou, and
the Nine Gates [of the Wall]."[2] "It is strictly prohibited," said another
edict of 1749, "to harbor people in residence or to increase the cultivation
of land [beyond the Great Wall]. It is also strictly prohibited to 'pledge'
or reclaim land for cultivation in the [Mongol] banners of Wengniute,

---

[1] See, for example, the edicts of 1704 and 1714, from the *Da Qing huidian shili*, zhuan 58,
cited in Richard Edmonds (1979), 614.

[2] *Gaozong shilu*, zhuan 115, cited in Kong Jingwei (1990), 151.

Balin, Keshiketeng, Alukeerqin, and Aohan or the eight banners of Chahar."[3] In 1750, these prohibitions were extended to cover sea travel, as Beijing ordered coastal provinces as far south as Guangdong and Guangxi to stop merchant ships from carrying migrants to or calling on ports in the Northeast and told officials on the coast of Fengtian to block illegal landings and arrest would-be immigrants.[4] In the final analysis, however, these statements had little effect, for they were overwhelmed by more powerful, spontaneous forces of nature and man.

The data on population and land under cultivation in Manchuria reveal significant changes during the 18th and early 19th centuries. The population of the Shengjing Military Region, already the most densely populated area of Manchuria at the beginning of the Qing, increased nearly fivefold, from 360,000 in 1741 to almost 1.8 million in 1820.[5] Meanwhile, the total area of cultivated land in Shengjing failed to keep pace with the growth of population, with the result that the availability of farmland per capita reported declined from nearly 50 mu per person in 1735 to 22 mu in 1780.[6] There can be little doubt that during this period southern Manchuria was getting more crowded and that the crowds were having a harder time finding land to work, rent, or reclaim.

Before the middle of the 18th century, both the population and land under cultivation in the northern territories of Jilin and Heilongjiang trailed far behind the south. Prior to 1740, Chinese went to these territories as fur trappers, gold diggers, ginseng hunters, or loggers, rather than farmers or settlers. In the absence of volunteers, the Qing had to send soldiers to defend the borders and convicts, exiles, and slaves to

---

[3] *Qing Gaozong shilu*, zhuan 348 (1749), cited in Ma Ruheng and Cheng Chongde (1990), 15. Ma and Cheng, 14–15, provide a detailed description of the "closure" policy and the various edicts proclaiming it.

[4] *Da Qing huidian shili*, zhuan 158, cited in Kong Jingwei (1990), 152.

[5] For data on population for all three military regions of the Northeast during the period 1741–1820, see: 1741–81: *SJTZ* (1784), zhuan 36:1–13. 1808–12: *Xuanzong shilu*, zhuan 250, and *Heilongjiang waiji*, zhuan 3, cited in Kong Jingwei (1990), 157. 1820: *Zhongguo lidai hukou tudi tianfu tongji* [Historical statistics on population, land and taxes of China], 401, cited in Kong Jingwei (1990), 166.

[6] According to figures for bannerland, estate land, courier stations, and common land, the area of cultivated land in Shengjing declined slightly between 1735 (17.9 million *mu*) and 1780 (17.4 million *mu*). Although these figures exclude reclaimed land that was kept off the tax rolls, still the increase in cultivated land in southern Manchuria almost certainly failed to keep pace with the growth of population. For figures on each type of cultivated land, see: Bannerland: *SJTZ* (1736), zhuan 24:1233–34; *Baqi tongzhi*, zhuan 21:393–94; and *SJTZ* (1784), zhuan 38:13–25. Estate land: Diao Shuren (1993), 62–63, 84–87, 112; *SJTZ* (1736), zhuan 24:1234–37; *SJTZ* (1784), zhuan 38:6–8, 20–24. Common land: *SJTZ* (1784), zhuan 37:4–6, 23, 34–35; *Zhongguo lidai hukou tudi tianfu tongji* [Historical statistics on the population, land and taxes of China], 401, cited in Kong Jingwei (1990), 166.

raise the food needed by the troops. Even the soft and fertile valleys of central Manchuria attracted few pioneers. Then, after the middle of the 18th century, the tide of migration and the reclamation of land for farming began to flow northward. In 1771, when figures for Jilin and Heilongjiang become available, there were reportedly 92,000 people in these two regions, while by 1820, their number reached 725,000, or nearly 30% of the population in Manchuria as a whole.[7] Similarly, the area of land under cultivation in these territories increased from 1.5 million *mu* in 1735 to nearly 7 million *mu* in 1780.[8] Farmland was also more plentiful in the north: 37 *mu* per capita in Jilin, and 55 *mu* in Heilongjiang, compared with only 22 *mu* in Shengjing. As southern Manchuria and the areas adjacent to the Great Wall filled up with settlers, later arrivals had to crowd into already populated villages or move on to open spaces further north.

The pattern of migration, settlement and cultivation in Manchuria also characterized the movement of Chinese into the neighboring areas of Inner Mongolia. Under pressure from growing numbers of migrants, the Mongols lost control of their land, while Chinese farms and villages took over an expanding portion of the steppe. One line of advance was from the south, through the Kalaqin and Tumet banners of Zhuosuotu League and the mountains of Jehol.[9] After the middle of the 18th century, virtually all of the arable land in the Kalaqin was under cultivation, with the result, according to one report, that the "Mongol herders had no place to graze their herds."[10] A second line was from the central Manchurian plain west, into Zhelimu.[11] One of the signal events in this move was the decision in 1802, to allow the Mongol prince of Gorlos Front Banner to "recruit farmers and reclaim land for cultivation" in this region and to establish the subprefecture at Changchun, which soon emerged as the center of commerce and governance in central Manchuria.[12] These two lines converged by the early 19th century in the Xilamulun River basin of Zhaowuda, which also came to support a

---

[7]See footnote 5, for population figures in Jilin and Heilongjiang.

[8]See footnote 6, for various categories of cultivated land in Jilin and Heilongjiang.

[9]Guo Songyi (1990), 21; Wang Yuhai (1990), 193; Wang Yuquan (1991), 315; Yuan Senpo (1986), 29.

[10]Ma Ruheng and Cheng Chongde (1990), 16; Wang Yuhai (1990), 195–97.

[11]Ma Ruheng and Cheng Chongde (1990), 17; Kuang Haolin (1985), 47; Hu Zhiyu (1984), 67; Tian Zhihe (1982), 187–88; Tian Zhihe (1984A), 88; Ma Yongshan and Zhao Yi (1992), 89; Wang Yuquan (1991), 315; and Owen Lattimore (1934), 202–3.

[12]Tian Zhihe (1982), 187–88; Tian Zhihe (1984A), 88. Ma Ruheng and Cheng Chongde (1990), 17; Sun Zhanwen (1981), 100; Guo Songyi (1990), 19.

large Chinese population.[13] Meanwhile, a similar advance was occurring northward, across the Great Wall west of Beijing.[14]

Several reports indicate that intensive settlement and cultivation of these regions led to deforestation, soil degradation, and other forms of environmental damage. Members of the British Macartney mission who visited Chengde [Jehol] in 1793, reported that on the hills surrounding the Summer Palace, which had once been heavily forested, "nothing now remained that was not stunted [and] timber was scarce."[15] The removal of tree cover increased runoff from the mountains, silted up the Luan River and its tributaries, and caused severe flooding. By the early 19th century, the number of animal species in Jehol had declined, tigers, bears, and leopards had disappeared, and even deer were becoming scarce.[16] The palaces of Chengde fell into disrepair and the imperial reserve was overrun by hunters, woodsmen and squatters.[17] North of the mountains, in the Xilamulun River basin, conditions were also in decline. For centuries, the Abbé Huc reported, this region had been covered with "fine forests" and "rich pasturage," whereas at the time of his arrival in 1840, "the country became entirely changed. All the trees were grubbed up, the forests disappeared from the hills, the prairies were cleared by means of fire, and the new cultivators set busily to work in exhausting the fecundity of the soil. Almost the entire region is now in the hands of the Chinese. . . ."[18]

2. Inequality

The increase in the number of Chinese migrants and settlers, the reclamation of land, and the intensification of agriculture in southern Manchuria and the Mongol banners adjacent to the Great Wall had two effects. The first, already noted, was to cast the next generation of migrants onto more distant frontiers. The second was to weaken the banners, bannerlands, and estates of southern Manchuria and Inner

[13] Wang Yuquan (1991), 313–15; Ma Ruheng and Cheng Chongde (1990), 16–17; Kuang Haolin (1985), 47; Hu Zhiyu (1984), 67; Cheng Chongde (1990), 173–74; Owen Lattimore (1934), 239–40.
[14] Cheng Chongde (1990), 174; Kuang Haolin (1985), 46–47; Liang Bing (1991), 48, 151–53; Ma Ruheng and Cheng Chongde (1990), 12, 17; Wang Yuquan (1991), 311, 317; Zhao Yongfu (1981), 39; Zhang Zhihua (1987), 87–89; George Timkowski (1827), 276; Evariste-Regis Huc and Joseph Gabet (1987), 119,159.
[15] Sir George Staunton (1797), 216.
[16] Yuan Senpo (1986), 29–30.
[17] Evariste-Regis Huc and Joseph Gabet (1987), 19.
[18] Evariste-Regis Huc and Joseph Gabet (1987), 4.

Agriculture in Manchuria. These photos show four stages of farming by Chinese peasants in Manchuria: plowing to prepare a field for planting soybeans, *top left* (1); harvesting sorghum [*gaoliang*], *bottom left* (2); threshing sorghum by bamboo flail and stone roller pulled by mules, *top right* (3); and grinding grain by mill-stone pulled by a horse, *bottom right* (4). All of these devices and techniques were

widely used in China proper prior to the 17th century.[1] With the exception of the heavy plow drawn by large teams of draft animals, which was introduced from Russia and used to break the thick sod of the Mongolian Steppe, there is no evidence to suggest the invention of new tools or innovation of new practices by Chinese peasants north of the Great Wall.

SOURCES: Nos. 1–3: Adachi Kinnosuke (1925), 140, 166. No. 4: SMR, 4th Report (1934), 14.23.

[1] For illustrations of similar devices used in China proper in much earlier times, see Francesca Bray (1984), 130–378, and Sung Ying-Hsing (1966), 3–34. John Lossing Buck

Mongolia, which were destroyed or transformed to make way for an economy based on free markets in land and labor such as practiced in China proper. The unraveling of the manors was caused by the widening gap between rich and poor, which is the subject of this section, and by changes in Qing policies for extracting resources from the manors, which will be dealt with in the next. Under the best of circumstances, most Manchus and Mongols were ill-prepared to compete with Chinese farmers, merchants, or craftsmen or to manage the complex organizations of a commercial economy. This disadvantage was magnified when the initial egalitarian and collective character of the manors gave way to differences in status and wealth. Rich and powerful Manchus and Mongols came to control large tracts of land, which they could dispose of for their own benefit, while impoverished members of both groups were forced to sell off whatever assets they had just to get by.

When the Qing rulers, or their Manchu or Jurchen predecessors, set up the first banners and estates, they had conflicting views on how wealth and power should be distributed within these units. On one hand, inequality was imbedded in the manorial structures. The Eight Banners and the imperial or official estates were directed by nobles and officials, who owned slaves and exercised control over convicts and bonded servants and who by virtue of their elevated status received land grants larger than those given to ordinary bannermen or estate workers.[19] A survey of the bannerlands of Shengjing conducted in 1679 found that, even at this early date, much of the land was being farmed by Chinese commoners, working for wages, paid by whoever controlled the land.[20] In similar fashion, Mongol banner chiefs disposed of collectively owned land in ways that benefited themselves at the expense of the ordinary herders. Inequality was part of the original set-up. At the same time, the manors were designed to ensure that hierarchy was held in check by the collective ownership of land and other measures that froze social and economic relationships: land grants assigned to ordinary bannermen or estate workers were of equal size, land and other assets were collectively owned and managed and could not be sold or alienated, and higher levels of authority had to approve the actions of manorial elites, enabling them to block attempts to misappropriate resources or act against the commonweal. In short,

---

(1930), 62, pictures a plow and harrow used in Shandong in the 1920s, which are identical to the same implements used in Manchuria.

[19] Yang Xuechen (1963), 176, 180.

[20] *Gaozong shilu*, zhuan 127, cited in Kong Jingwei (1990), 140.

while banners and estates required a governing hierarchy, the corporate nature of these structures was supposed to protect the livelihood and maintain the welfare of all.

Over time, however, the collective and egalitarian features of the manorial system could not be sustained. Instead, the gap between the top and bottom widened. The life of an ordinary bannerman was hard: Unskilled in agriculture, he had to support his household on 6 *shang* of previously undeveloped land and could be called away at any time for military service. The life of an estate worker was even harder: His freedom was narrowly restricted, he paid heavy rents and taxes, and he had to perform services of various kinds. The life of the slave or convict was the hardest of all: He was effectively owned by his master and could be put to work without recourse. As a result, large numbers of rural laborers in all categories slid into poverty, those with access to land were obliged to rent or sell their rights, and many risked cruel punishment to flee the banner or estate in desperation.[21] Nor were those who stayed behind content with their lot, for throughout the mid-Qing "anti-rent struggles" joined poor bannermen and commoners, Manchu and Chinese, in acts of violence.[22]

At the other end of the spectrum were officials, nobles, estate heads, and the particularly skillful or lucky bannermen and estate workers who found ways—some legal, some illegal—of exploiting their advantages. Enterprising workers at all levels rented, mortgaged, or transferred land and succeeded in changing their legal status so that they could own and protect their property. Some became landlords, moved to the cities where they could enjoy a more comfortable lifestyle, and lived off income from rents and the interest on loans.[23] A few Manchu princes wielded control over hundreds or even thousands of *shang* of farmland, all of which was cultivated by tenants under registered contract.[24] Court cases from the 17th and 18th centuries show how estate heads and local officials held up the delivery of grain, concealed population (who might otherwise be called for corvée labor service), and diverted public property for private use. Six estate heads, tried in 1691 for failing to make the required deliveries of grain, claimed that two years earlier they had been unable to collect enough grain and had to borrow to meet their obligations. "This year, we used the harvest to repay our

---

[21] Diao Shuren (1993), 154–55.

[22] Yang Xuechen (1963), 189–92.

[23] Yang Xuechen (1963), 184–86.

[24] *Manzu lishi ziliao xuanji* [Selected materials on Manchu history], cited in Xu Shuming (1990), 107–8.

creditors and do not have enough left to make ends meet," they explained. "How are we supposed to make our payments?" The court rejected their plea, sentenced them to 100 strokes of the bamboo, and dismissed them from office.[25]

The flood of Chinese into the Manchu and Mongol areas widened the gap between rich and poor. This occurred, first, because Chinese labor was plentiful and cheap, and anyone with access to land could earn more by hiring Chinese workers or renting to Chinese tenants, than by restricting the land for use by members of the manors. One illustration of the wage gap comes from the case of Shuangchengbao, Jilin, where an attempt was made in 1812 to reclaim land for the benefit of impoverished bannermen. In this project, the authorities reserved land for bannermen from nearby locations who they thought would welcome they thought would welcome the opportunity to make a fresh start, while prohibiting Chinese from entering the area. Almost immediately, however, Chinese rushed in and took control of the land. A follow-up study found that the effective cost of labor for each bannerman had been 47 taels, whereas the Chinese performed the same work for about 5 taels.[26]

Chinese merchants also played a role in exacerbating the differences among Manchus and Mongols. The merchants supplied goods imported from China proper on credit to Manchu and Mongol elites, who took this opportunity to borrow heavily, using collectively owned land under their control as collateral, consumed beyond their means, and plunged deeply into debt. The deeper the debt, the more the manor officials borrowed, and the more they borrowed, the more they used land to secure the loans and eventually repay their creditors. The heads of banners, bannerlands, and estates got the goods, the Chinese merchants got the land, and the ordinary bannermen and herders got nothing. This process, repeated with numbing regularity, stretched the fabric of Manchu and Mongol society to the breaking point.

The inequalities increased with the passage of time. According to one report, by the middle of the 18th century, the vast majority of bannermen in the Shengjing Military Region had lost the land originally assigned to them by the Qing. Two out of three banner officials and 7 of 8 ordinary banner soldiers or workers held no land at all. A separate study of land tenure in an estate/village of Liaoyang County traces the widening gap in landownership over time. Starting from an equal allotment of 6 *shang*

[25] *Heitudang* [Black chart file] (1691), cited in Kong Jingwei (1990), 119.
[26] Diao Shuren (1993), 206–13. For further details, see: Xu Shuming (1990), 104; Sun Zhanwen (1981), 94; and *Manzu jianshi* (1979), 112.

per household, by 1843, one-third of the households in this village had lost all of their land, although most still had modest holdings of between 1–5 *shang*. By the beginning of the 20th century, however, more than four-fifths of the land was concentrated in a few very large holdings, while most households had little or none.[27] The same trend was evident in the Mongol territories, where the banner chiefs enriched themselves by disposing of collectively owned land at the expense of the ordinary herders. Beijing repeatedly intervened to redress this imbalance, but the illness was generally more powerful than the cure.[28]

One effect of this growing inequality was to drive the poorest members out of the banners and estates. By the early 18th century, the illegal flight of bannermen and estate workers had reached epidemic proportions, triggering a downward spiral that threatened the entire system. Since each worker was responsible for paying a "duty," which helped cover the expenses of the manor and contributed to the surplus it owed to its parent body or noble patron, when a worker fled, his share of the payments was lost, and the remaining members had to rent out his land to make up the difference. As more workers fled, those left behind were under more pressure to meet the required payments, persuading more of these workers to leave, and making it even more compelling to rent out land to cover the decline in income. The result was to transform the estates from collectives that extracted a surplus by the use of forced labor to intermediaries that raised money by the rental of land.[29]

After efforts to enforce the "escapee law" [*taorenfa*] proved ineffective, the decision to excuse some violations and reduce the punishments for those who were caught made matters even worse. Under the legal reforms, slaves were allowed to purchase their freedom and bannermen and estate workers to adopt the status of "commoner," which meant that they could buy, own, and sell land and move to a location where they could reclaim land and become freeholders on their own. These measures encouraged bannermen and estate workers to dispose of their land, reducing the labor available to the banners and estates, while increasing the pool of commoners who became mobile wage-workers, tenants, or landowners. In sum, measures adopted to deal with the growing inequality served to reinforce that trend, removing both land

[27] Diao Shuren (1993), 147–50, 173.

[28] *Da Qing huidian shili*, zhuan 979, cited in Kong Jingwei (1990), 96.

[29] There are numerous examples of this change in the role of the estates. For one example, from the archives of Faku County in 1803, see Diao Shuren (1993), 154–55.

and labor from the banners and estates, and leaving the manorial system less able to meet the challenges of an increasingly commercial economy.[30]

3. Commercialization of Rents and Taxes

The pressures of migration, settlement, and cultivation in southern Manchuria also triggered changes in the methods by which the Qing extracted resources from the banners and estates: first, from labor service to taxation, and second, from taxation in kind to taxation in cash. The commercialization of relations between producers and the state acted as a solvent, loosening the bonds of authority that had been set up to govern the development of territories north of the Great Wall. In the process, the banners and estates gradually dissolved and a market economy filled the vacant space.

In managing the agrarian empire of China, the Qing Dynasty faced the same challenge and adopted the same fiscal strategy as its predecessor: that is, it had to make each part of the empire pay *as best it could* for its share of the costs, while at the same time shifting the burdens *as much as possible* from the poorer to the richer provinces. Both principles applied to Manchuria and Inner Mongolia. At the height of the Qing, in 1780, the total area of taxable common land in the Northeast was less than 4 million *mu*, compared to 351 million *mu* in the four adjacent provinces of North China.[31] Meanwhile, the tax rates in the Northeast were significantly lower than in China proper.[32] The network of government offices and personnel was not so dense in Manchuria as in north China, but the cost of maintaining military forces and civil administration on the distant borders was high. Thus, both Jilin and Heilongjiang were ranked among the "deficit" provinces that received annual "silver transfers" [*xiexiang*] from the "surplus" provinces in the more richly endowed areas of China proper. During the first half of the 19th century, 80% of the budget of Jilin and virtually the entire budget of Heilongjiang was paid for by these subsidies.[33] From a fiscal point of

[30] Kong Jingwei (1990), 121–22; Diao Shuren (1993), 138–39, 160; Yang Xuechen (1963), 186–88.

[31] *SJTZ* (1784), zhuan 37, gives figures for taxable common land (million *mu*): Fengtian, 2.7; Jilin 1.2; Heilongjiang, 0. Dwight Perkins (1969), 234, gives figures for cultivated area of north China provinces.

[32] Kong Jingwei (1990), 158, shows that between 1661–1724, tax rates in Fengtian were 62–77% of the average for the empire as a whole.

[33] James Millward (1998), 58–63, 235–38; Yeh-chien Wang (1973), 18; Robert Lee (1970), 75–76.

view, this was an unhealthy situation, and it would prove disastrous when rebellion struck the wealthy provinces of Lower Yangzi in the 19th century. Thus, it is not surprising that Beijing should look increasingly to the banners and estates of Manchuria as a source of income.

In the beginning, the policy of the Qing had been to exempt bannermen and bannerlands from rent, tax, and corvée labor. The purpose of the land grants to bannermen was to reward the dynasty's servants and ensure that the banner forces remained economically viable and intact. To tax bannerlands would have been counterproductive. By the 1690s, however, two factors caused the Qing to reconsider this approach: First, the successful reclamation of wasteland by bannermen, or those working for them, enabled bannermen in Manchuria to make a greater contribution to the public coffer (in contrast to bannermen in China proper, who grew increasingly destitute and dependent upon government stipends). Second, the rise of military threats in the north (the Russians) and west (the Dzungars) created a demand for grain and other products to supply Qing forces on the frontier. In sum, the Manchurian bannermen could afford to pay, and Beijing needed their contributions. In 1690, the Qing called on banner troops from Manchuria to put down the Dzungar rebellion in Inner Mongolia and bought food for these troops using a portion of the land tax collected in Fengtian. Then, following a survey of the Fengtian bannerlands in 1693, Beijing imposed the first tax on the bannerlands of the Northeast (but *not* on those in China proper), which was levied on the area of cultivated land and collected in kind—beans and grass. After a second survey, carried out in 1726, the government regularized the system for taxing bannerlands, which was recorded in the so-called "Red Register" [*hongce*]—tax records that were distinguished by the use of a red thread in the binding. Finally, in the course of the 18th century, rent on Manchurian bannerlands was increasingly collected in cash rather than kind. Still, the tax rate on bannerland remained well below that on common land—about 3% of the common land rate during the Kangxi period (1662–1723), rising to 20% during Yongzheng (1723–36)—demonstrating the privilege accorded to bannermen over commoners.[34]

In the following years, the system for extracting resources from imperial and official estates shifted from taxation in kind to taxation in cash. Unlike the bannerlands, the estates had been created to produce

---

[34] 1693 tax: *Baqi tongzhi*, zhuan 18:329. Other details: Diao Shuren (1993), 119–22, 127–28, 142–43.

goods for the royal family, its agencies and allies, and were viewed as a source of revenue, pure and simple. Diao Shuren estimates that in the early 18th century, the effective tax rate on the Shengjing imperial estates was 3–4 times as high as that on common land (in contrast to bannerland, which was taxed at a fraction of the common land rate). Indeed, the taxes on estates were so high that almost none ever met its quota. At the beginning of the Qing, taxes (or rents) were paid by individual estate workers and collected in kind. Finally, in 1759, the grain estates of Shengjing and Jinzhou prefectures began to collect taxes in cash. With this change, the relationship between the government, the estate, and the estate workers or tenants became fully commercialized.[35]

These changes in the treatment of the banners and estates undermined the corporate nature of both institutions. The banners and estates set up at the beginning of the Qing were designed to ensure that the development of Manchuria would be managed and controlled by the dynasty or its agents and to preclude the growth of markets in land and labor, which might fall prey to Chinese peasants and merchants. But the flood of cheap Chinese labor into southern Manchuria persuaded the banners and estates to hire workers or rent out land, which helped to commercialize the agrarian economy. The Qing, which was under growing pressure to meet expenses, opted to join this trend and extract its share of the proceeds in cash, rather than agricultural products, military service, or political support. In this way, the banners and estates became middlemen between tenants, who farmed the land and paid the rents, and government tax collectors, who extracted the profits and viewed the producers as a source of income, rather than objects of social and economic control.

B. From Manor to Market

Under the pressure of migration from without and growing inequality and commercialization from within, the manorial structures erected at the beginning of the Qing broke down and were replaced by a system of free markets in land and labor. The market system included a mixture of practices that varied from time to time and place to place. The earliest and most modest change was to rent-tenancy, in which the land remained within the collective ownership of the manor, but was let out to individuals in exchange for a fixed rent or share of the crop. Meanwhile,

[35] Diao Shuren (1993), 64, 74–75, 169–72.

the area of privately owned land increased as a result of reclamation by bannermen, estate workers, or their agents, who were allowed to keep whatever they wrested from nature. Finally, a variety of practices were invented to evade the prohibition on the sale of manor land and transfer effective ownership to outsiders in exchange for payments in cash. All these measures gradually eroded the power of the bannerlands, the Mongol banners, and imperial estates and made both land and labor marketable commodities.

1. Rent-tenancy

Unlike the sale of banner or estate lands, which was prohibited under Qing law, the rental of land to outsiders including commoners was never specifically forbidden. However, the Qing considered tenancy a threat to the manorial system and discouraged the practice. One edict warned that "The farmland assigned to bannermen must not be entirely rented out to commoners, and [the bannermen] must make every effort to band together to work the land," and encouraged officials to investigate cases of bannermen who abandoned farming.[36] Unable to stop the rental of bannerland to commoners in 1780 the Qing accepted the practice, while limiting tenancy arrangements to three years and threatening to confiscate rents collected after this period had expired. But these admonitions had little effect, and the practice of rent-tenancy spread from the 18th century on.[37] In addition, Chinese farmers who reclaimed land in the vicinity of a banner or estate were required, and in fact proved quite willing, to turn the land over to the parent body, in exchange for which they received permanent tenancy rights and a fixed rent. This arrangement, which suited all of the parties, increased the holdings of the banners and estates, while changing their character from collective units using captive labor to meet production goals, to landlords bidding to attract the most enterprising and productive tenants.[38]

Estate lands were rented on "long-rent" or "short-rent" terms. "Long-rent" tenants were generally those who had been present at the time the estate was established, took part in the original reclamation of land, and were rewarded with the permanent right of tenancy, which could be passed on to their heirs. "Short-rent" tenants, who had been recruited after the establishment of the estate, held leases of 3 to 5 and

---

[36] *Qing Gaozong shilu*, zhuan 127, cited in Diao Shuren (1993), 139.
[37] Kong Jingwei (1990), 141; Diao Shuren (1993), 139–40.
[38] *Manzu shehui lishi diaocha* (1985), 208.

never more than 10 years, which had to be renewed at the end of the term and did not convey to their heirs. Despite the tough terms, there were always more landless peasants anxious to sign tenancy agreements, including migrants from China proper and estate workers who fled the estates and sought to change their status to commoner. Owing to the escape of their workers, most estates were forced to adopt aggressive campaigns to recruit tenants, often among the very workers who had left the estate just a few months before.[39]

2. *Reclamation and Privatization of Land*

Rent-tenancy was a step toward the commercialization of agriculture, because it converted the land from a restricted asset that was assigned to bannermen and estate workers for their own use into a commodity that the estate or its individual members could let out in exchange for cash or grain. The more radical step toward creating and trading in privately owned land was hastened by the reclamation of land outside the banner or estate. Once the original banner and estate lands had been assigned, all other unattached wasteland became the property of whoever reclaimed and cultivated it. This process brought large tracts of land into the market.

The establishment in southern Manchuria and Inner Mongolia of "common land" [*mindi*], privately owned farmland that was registered with a government office and taxed on the model practiced in China proper, predated the Qing and expanded after the conquest in 1644. The "Regulations on Recruitment and Reclamation in Liaodong," promulgated in 1653, encouraged the creation of more taxable common land, which increased to around 2.6 million *mu* in 1735. Bannermen or their agents in Manchuria had always been allowed to reclaim land outside their official allotments.[40] In 1727, one year after the census of bannerlands and creation of the "Red Register," which recorded the holdings of each banner household, a new category known as "banner surplus land" [*qiyudi*] was introduced.[41] "Surplus land" was land outside the banner that was reclaimed by a bannerman and became his private property. It was *not* entered onto the Red Register and was subject to tax at a rate higher than Red Register land, but still lower than common land. Data from the period 1766–80, show that between 9–12% of the land

---

[39]Diao Shuren (1993), 165–72.
[40]*Baqi tongzhi*, zhuan 18, 326.
[41]*SJTZ* (1784), zhuan 24, cited in Diao Shuren (1993), 186.

held by bannermen in Fengtian was reclaimed "surplus land," while the percentage of this type of land owned by Chinese commoners was on the rise.[42]

3. Transfer of Land

The final step in the transformation of the land system occurred with the transfer of land ostensibly held in trust by the banners or estates to outside parties. Since such transactions were illegal, the forms adopted by the two parties provided in theory for the rental or temporary use of the land, although in substance they resembled a sale. Often, the sale was disguised as a "rental agreement," "deposit," "loan," "pledge," or other device that would escape attention and (the parties to the contract hoped) withstand scrutiny if brought before the law. But the result was effectively the same—to break up the manors into individual proper-ties, which were traded on the open market and over time gravitated into the hands of Chinese.

There is some evidence from the 17th and 18th centuries for the un-varnished "sale" [*mai*] of bannerlands in Manchuria.[43] The scale of these transactions varied: Some were for the sale of one or two *shang* by a Manchu soldier, who might have been forced to dispose of his last bit of goods. Others involved thousands of *mu* from the private estate of a wealthy family that could have been pressed by creditors or was seeking to raise capital for some other purpose.[44] In most of the cases that sur-vive in court records, however, use of the term "sale" was restricted to deals between bannermen, which kept the land within the privileged category. Transactions involving commoners posed a more serious legal problem and thus had to be covered up in some way.

The most widespread, and from the perspective of the Qing, per-nicious practice was the "pledge" [*dian*] or "pledge-sale" [*dianmai*] of land. Under this arrangement, a commoner or other individual (in the-ory the tenant, but in practice the buyer) would pay a cash pledge to

[42] 1766: Report by the commanding general of Shengjing, *Qingchao wenxian tongkao*, zhuan 5, cited in Diao Shuren (1993), 187. 1780: *Dong sansheng zhenglue* [Administrative records of the three eastern provinces], zhuan 8, and Guangxu, *Da Qing huidian*, zhuan 11, cited in Diao Shuren (1993), 117, 133.

[43] *Shengjing neiwufu dimu gaodang* [Land records of the Shengjing Imperial Household Department], 1772, cited in Diao Shuren (1993), 134.

[44] Diao Shuren (1993), 134, citing cases from the *Shengjing neiwufu dimu gaodang* [Land Records of the Shengjing Imperial Household Department], 1772; the *Heitu dang* [Black Chart File], 1730; and the *Hubu dimu dangce* [Board of Revenue Land Records], volume 3.

a bannerman, estate head, or estate worker (in theory the landlord, but in practice the seller), in exchange for which the party that made the pledge would gain permanent right to rent the parcel of land at a nominal fee and to continue or renew the arrangement, which could not be dissolved unilaterally by either party. Ostensibly, and especially if subjected to examination by agents of the state, the parties could claim that the agreement was for the rental, rather than sale, of the land, and that the pledge was simply a portion of the rental fee that was paid up front. In fact, however, the party that made the pledge gained the right to use the land himself or rent it to a third party and to maintain or renew this arrangement indefinitely—although he could not sell the land, which could not be sold to him in the first place. Thus, the pledge represents a transition from the system of manors, in which land was held in trust and could not be traded, to markets, in which land could be freely bought and sold.

As more and more land was transferred under the pretense of the pledge from banners and estates to private hands, Qing policy makers retreated and in so doing gave legal cover to the trend toward markets. The "Law on Commoner Pledge of Bannerland" of 1727, which tried to outlaw the practice, proved ineffective.[45] There is abundant evidence, beginning early as 1665 and increasing over the next two centuries, for the growing pledge-sale of manorial property to commoners.[46] In 1735, the Board of Revenue admitted that despite the prohibition, "secret exchanges between individuals have been going on for generations."[47] Unable to stop this practice, Beijing tried the next best thing, which was to redeem the land that had been illegally separated from the banner or estate. Under the "Law on the Redemption of Pledge-sold Bannerlands" promulgated in 1740, the government bought back several million *mu* of land that had been pledge-sold over the previous decades and returned this land to the Red Register, which listed the official holdings of the banners. It is worth noting that this law also confirmed the rights of those who had paid a pledge to continue to rent land on the terms provided in the original pledge agreement. In other words, the state stepped in to pick up the bannermen after they had fallen down, buy back their lost land, return it to the banner

---

[45] The "Law on commoners pledging bannerland" [*Mindian qidi fa*], cited in Kong Jingwei (1990), 142.

[46] Kong Jingwei (1990), 122, 142–47; Diao Shuren (1993), 136–37, 176; Yang Xuechen (1988), 166.

[47] *Qingchao wenxian tongkao*, zhuan 5, cited in Diao Shuren (1993), 156.

endowment, and thus restore the economic base of the bannerlands, but at the same time decreed that the bannermen would *not* be allowed to renege on their rental agreements, raise the rents, or reclaim control over the land in question.[48] Rather than revive the manorial system, which had proven impractical, the Qing reaffirmed the standing rental arrangements, and thus took an important step toward establishing permanent tenancy rights and eventually a system of markets.

Finally, in the face of widespread violations, Beijing abandoned efforts to enforce the prohibition on pledges or to redeem pledged land.[49] In 1804, the throne issued an edict permitting commoners to pledge bannerland, provided that both parties report the arrangement to the authorities. During the next year and a half, officials in Shengjing received more than two thousand applications to register transactions of this type.[50] Even the emperor had to admit that, despite the prohibitions against this practice, the pledge-sale of land to commoners had been going on for "a very long time," and the government would have to ignore "violations of proper legal procedures."[51] A report by the commanding general [*jiangjun*] of Shengjing, submitted in 1816, explained that it was difficult to police the relations between bannermen and commoners, who lived in mixed communities and came under the jurisdiction of different authorities. "Our investigation of the Shengjing bannerlands," the Shengjing general reported,

shows that less than half [of the bannermen] cultivate their own land, whereas the majority rent to commoners who do the actual farming. Over time, it is inevitable that borrowers and lenders should come together and in the end make the transition from renting to pledging [land]. In this way, our problems have mounted, and the property of the banners no longer belongs to the banners.[52]

One study, based on evidence from three villages in the vicinity of Tieling, Shenyang, and Liaoyang in 1822, demonstrates the widespread and profound effects of the pledging of estate land. In these villages a majority of the estate heads and estate workers accepted pledges on all or some of the land under their control. In all, more than 70% of the land in these estates was pledged out, leaving less than 30% to support the remaining members. The effect was to disperse the land from the

---

[48] Yang Xuechen (1963), 186–87, 192. For a discussion of this practice in Guihuacheng region, see Wang Yuquan (1991), 318.

[49] Diao Shuren (1993), 137.

[50] Xu Shuming (1990), 105–6.

[51] Guangxu, *Da Qing huidian shili*, zhuan 1117, cited in Diao Shuren (1993), 137.

[52] *Junji lufu* [Military records], (1816), cited in Diao Shuren (1993), 177.

relatively large holdings of the estates into small parcels, in the range of 2–4 *shang* each, held by individual households that either pledged the land directly from the estate or rented it from landlords who served as middlemen, obtaining the land by pledge and letting it out to tenants. The result was to break up the estates and create in their place a system of rent-tenancy. The bulk of the land came into the hands of small pledge-paying or rent-paying farmers, while the balance was insufficient to support the surviving estates and estate workers, who were forced to take in pledges on the remaining land or simply flee the estate and seek their fortunes as fugitive workers or tenants.[53]

In addition to the pledge, other devices were used to disguise the transfer of land from banners and estates to commoners: the former could "relinquish control" [*tuiling*] of land to the latter, let the land out in exchange for a cash "deposit" [*yaqian*], or use it as collateral to "borrow money backed by land" [*zhidi jieqian*].[54] In each case, the trustee on a banner or estate accepted a cash payment, ostensibly to rent, lease, or permit the temporary use of the land by a lender, depositor, or tenant, although in fact the right to use the land was transferred on a permanent basis to an outside party. In form, both buyer and seller tried to maintain the appearance that the deal was temporary, contingent and therefore legal, whereas in substance it was permanent, and thus a violation of Qing law.[55]

Often such deals were verbal, so that if discovered, there would be no record to present in court. In some cases, however, the terms were written down, and from these contracts and court cases we can see the true intentions of the two parties. The text of the following agreement, dated 1849, shows how such arrangements worked:

This is a loan agreement between Cai Fuyou and Jin Youshu of the Bordered Blue Banner, who, unable to make ends meet, willingly assign 7 *shang* of registered land to Zhang Yifu, in exchange for a loan of 1,760 cash [*diao*], which must be paid in full. The land is transferred to Zhang Yifu to cultivate as though he were the owner. It is clearly stated that the money will be held without interest, and the land will be used without rent. After the agreement has been consummated, it cannot be rescinded. In case of conflict [regarding implementation of

[53] Yang Xuechen (1988), 167–68.

[54] Diao Shuren (1993), 135–36, 162–64, and 178; Kong Jingwei (1990), 142.

[55] According to official statistics, by 1780, nearly 1.2 million *mu* of bannerland was either rented or pledged to commoners or jointly cultivated by commoners and bannermen. See: *SJTZ* (1784), zhuan 37, citing figures for: "land removed from the enclosure and jointly cultivated by bannermen and commoners," 772,405 *mu*; "surplus land rented by commoners," 264,467 *mu*; and "banner surplus land pledged by commoners," 154,093 *mu*.

the agreement], it will be resolved by the guarantor. Oral statements will have no standing, and the text of this written agreement will serve as the evidence.[56]

This agreement provides that in exchange for his loan, Zhang Yifu is allowed "to cultivate [the land] as though he were the owner" (because, of course, he is the owner). It states that "the money will be held without interest" (because it is a purchase price, not a loan), and "the land will be used without rent" (because the new owner has already paid for it). The agreement, once complete, "cannot be rescinded," disputes that arise will be "resolved by the guarantor," and in such cases, "oral statements will have no standing, and the text of the written agreement will serve as the evidence"—all for the reason that the parties to the agreement, knowing that it was illegal, wanted to keep it out of the courts.

Perhaps the strongest evidence for the success of the Chinese in taking over manorial land comes from cases in which the authorities did their best to prevent this outcome. For example, during the 18th and early 19th centuries, the Qing sponsored a series of projects to relocate bannermen from the capital of Beijing to sites in Jilin.[57] Following the consolidation of Manchu power, Beijing had been overrun by bannermen, who served no useful purpose and spent, or misspent, the government stipends that were their chief means of support. Projects to relocate these "Capital banners" [*Jingqi*] to agricultural colonies in Manchuria were designed to reduce the drain on the treasury, give the bannermen useful employment, and strengthen the dynasty's hold on this strategic locale. At first, bannermen from Beijing were expected to reclaim land on their own. When this failed, unemployed bannermen in Jilin, who had previous experience with farming, were brought in to reclaim land, after which the Capital banners would take over the land already under cultivation. When this failed, Chinese migrants were recruited to carry out the initial reclamation, then step aside. In each case, the guiding principle was to protect the interests of the bannermen, minimize the role of the Chinese, and ensure that the bannermen maintained control over the land. And in each case, the bannermen failed to show up, or came and left, while Chinese migrants reclaimed, farmed, and in the end owned the land. "The unemployed migrants began as hired farm workers, essentially selling their labor, and have gradually

[56]Source: *Manzhou jiuguan diaocha baogao*, cited in Diao Shuren (1993), 136. Other similar cases are described in *ibid.*, 135 and 164.

[57]Three attempts to relocate Capital banners to Lalin and Alachuke (1744), Shuangchengbao (1812), and Petuna (1824) are described in Diao Shuren (1993), 202–16, and Xu Shuming (1990), 102–5.

become tenants," explained an edict of 1826, which ordered the expulsion of the Chinese. "Now that these tenants are so numerous, the bannermen are content to take their leisure, do not know how to work, and their livelihood is becoming progressively more tenuous."[58] A survey conducted in 1877 of the area surrounding Petuna, which had been the site of one major project, found only Chinese farmers, heirs of the original homesteaders who did not even know that they were on land once designated for bannermen.[59]

The mechanisms used to transfer land in Manchuria were also adopted in the Mongol territories and with the same results. Mongol princes used the "pledge" or "deposit" to extract cash from willing migrant farmers and merchants in exchange for land that belonged to the banner. The government in Beijing condemned these practices, redeemed the pledged land, confirmed the tenancy rights of the Chinese partners, and when these efforts failed, effectively condoned the practice by specifying the forms the agreements should take and requiring that they be registered with government agents.[60] Over time, customary land rights began to congeal into a system of effective ownership, which was first sanctioned in practice and later recognized by government authorities. By the 1860s, private ownership had become the most common form of landholding in the Kalaqin region.[61] A similar process occurred along the Great Wall west of Beijing, where efforts to deal with the problems of inequality and hardship among the Mongols only accelerated the trend toward privatization.[62]

The types of land contracts used in Manchuria and Inner Mongolia, most notably the "pledge," were borrowed directly from practices familiar in north China. Studies of rural Shandong and Hebei during the 19th and early 20th century describe many examples that are identical in substance and often in name.[63] This underlines the main point of

[58] *Qing Xuanzong shilu*, zhuan 102, cited in Diao Shuren (1993), 212.

[59] *Manzu jianshi* (1979), 111–12.

[60] Pledge: The *Qing Xuanzong shilu*, zhuan 215, cited in Xu Shuming (1990), 106, describes the 1832 edict for redeeming pledged land. For other details on pledges in Mongol territories, see: Wang Yuquan (1991), 313–14, 317–18; Kong Jingwei (1990), 96–97; and Kuang Haolin (1985), 49–50. Deposit: Tian Zhihe (1984B), 85, cites the 1832 "Regulations of the Superintendent of Trade" [*Lifanyuan zeli*], describing the system of deposits as practiced in the Mongol banners. For other details on deposits in Mongol areas, see: ibid. 85–86, and Kong Jingwei (1990), 98–99.

[61] Wang Yuhai (1990), 197–209. See especially 199–202 for details on Mongol nobles, monasteries, and priests, and 202–3 on livelihood lands.

[62] Liang Bing (1991), 49–50.

[63] Sidney Gamble (1954), 156–57, 257–58; Martin C. Yang (1965), 133; Ramon Myers (1970), 52–53, 77, 93–94, 111–14; Philip Huang (1985), 176. Gamble, Yang, and Myers refer to the arrangement described in this section—the *dian*—as a "mortgage." But this is a

this chapter, which is that Chinese settlers in Manchuria and Inner Mongolia were taking over and effectively reproducing the society and culture they had known in China proper—a theme that will be developed further in Part Two.

C. Conclusion

By the middle of the 19th century, attempts by the Qing Dynasty to establish unique forms of land tenure and land use on the northern frontier had been tried and had failed. The Qing accepted and in fact encouraged modest levels of Chinese migration, settlement, and cultivation in this region, in order to secure the empire against enemies without, stabilize it against disorder within, and increase production for the benefit of both society and the state. Meanwhile, the Qing hoped by means of the manors to preserve the welfare and dominance of Manchu bannermen and their Mongol allies.

The experiment failed for three reasons: First, the parties responsible for managing the manorial institutions were not up to the task. The Manchus and Mongols, upon whom the Qing relied to oversee and control the banners and estates, lacked experience in and a taste for farming and preferred to live (sometimes quite well) off loans and rents. Second, the small, ineffective (at least, in this context) native population was overwhelmed by large numbers of competent, hardworking, and entrepreneurial Chinese. Wherever the Chinese appeared, they outperformed all rivals in reclaiming and farming the land, and eventually in setting the terms by which the land was owned and used. Finally, the Qing could never quite decide what it wanted or, when it did decide, enforce its will. On one hand, the Manchu rulers tried to protect their homeland and their Manchu and Mongol allies by imposing limits on the Chinese and their ability to own and use the land. On the other hand, the Qing, which was responsible for the empire as a whole, sought ways to relieve hardship in impoverished and volatile regions, secure the borders against foreign threats, and increase agricultural production and revenues—which sometimes required that they permit or even encourage migration to and changes in practices in the northern

---

misnomer, because in a mortgage the borrower retains control of the collateral property and pays interest on the loan, whereas under a "pledge" [*dian*] the collateral property is transferred to the lender, while the borrower pays no interest. Huang calls it a "pawn," which is closer to the mark. I prefer "pledge," because it indicates that the active agent, or buyer, is putting up the money.

territories. The result of these conflicting pressures was that Beijing shifted back and forth, lacked commitment to any single goal, and in the end was unable or unwilling to check the more powerful forces that controlled events above the Great Wall.

By the middle of the 19th century, the first phase of expansion was complete. Chinese migrants had infiltrated and transformed southern Manchuria and Jehol and by these means succeeded in moving the boundaries of China northward. The formation of this tier of settlement was also the beginning of the next phase of migration, for the newly established communities sent out their own migrants, who eventually became settlers on a yet more distant frontier. In the final round, which is described in the following chapter, the Qing would play a more positive role, for rather than restraining migration in order to protect the interests of Manchus and Mongols, the dynasty was driven by economic and military crises to propel the move north.

CHAPTER 3

The Advance of the Qing (1850–1911)

IN THE MIDDLE OF THE 19TH CENTURY, the ambivalence that had marked Qing attitudes and policies toward Manchuria was replaced by a decisive and eventually overpowering commitment to change. For two centuries, the Manchus had wavered between insulating their homeland against outsiders and tolerating or even encouraging the movement of migrants north. Despite their many proclamations and edicts on this subject, the Qing never effectively "closed" the boundary between China proper and the Manchu and Mongol areas, and the flow of Chinese never ceased. Beginning around 1850, and until the end of the dynasty in 1911, however, they began to promote the migration and settlement of people and the reclamation and cultivation of land throughout the northern territories. To achieve these goals, the Qing rulers abandoned the manorial system and put land in the Northeast up for sale, removing the last obstacles to the takeover of this region by the Chinese.

The orientation and behavior of the Qing changed for two reasons, the debt and the threat, and at two points, which punctuated the downward spiral of the empire and hastened the Chinese advance. The change began in the middle of the 19th century, when domestic rebellions and foreign wars prompted Beijing to adopt measures aimed at raising revenue and strengthening the empire's defenses. In the Northeast, these measures included renting, selling, and taxing public lands and "moving people to strengthen the border." The second change, much sharper and better defined than the first, came at the turn of the century, when another wave of foreign wars and domestic conflicts triggered even more serious fiscal and security crises, leading to a sweeping reassessment of the imperial order. The "New Policies," introduced in 1902, extended to every aspect of government and every corner of the empire, including land ownership and land use in the areas above the Great Wall. At both points, the pressures for change were the same: to raise money by the sale of land and the expansion of taxable farmland; and to strengthen the nation's defense by establishing a larger and more permanent population on or near the borders. The process unfolded in two stages, which at first hastened the movement and then unleashed a tide of Chinese migration, settlement, and cultivation that flowed to the Russian border.

A. "Moving People to Strengthen the Border" (1850–1902)

The change in the attitude of the Qing Dynasty, from skepticism to enthusiasm toward northward migration, was prompted by two factors—the debt and the threat—which affected all aspects of Chinese state and society from the middle of the 19th century on. After 1840, rebellion and war shook the Middle Kingdom and sent ripples onto the frontiers. The Taiping (1853–64), Nian (1853–68), and Moslem (1862–73) Rebellions and the Opium Wars (1839–42 and 1856–58) weakened the empire, making it more vulnerable to enemies at home and abroad and prompting changes in policy on all fronts. The earliest and hardest blows fell on the southern coast and the lower Yangzi, far from Manchuria and Inner Mongolia. But the secondary shocks reverberated on the distant frontiers.

The first factor that shook the empire was the debt: The 19th century rebellions, especially the Taiping, drained the imperial treasury and reduced funds available for transfer to the poorest regions, including Jilin and Heilongjiang. To keep taxes low and at the same time support the most backward areas—two principles of Confucian statecraft—the Qing required the "surplus" provinces of the Lower Yangzi, whose tax receipts exceeded their expenditures, to make annual "silver transfers" to the "deficit" provinces of the northwest and frontier regions, including Jilin and Heilongjiang, that perforce spent more than they could collect.[1] During the first half of the 19th century, the annual deficits of Jilin and Heilongjiang exceeded 1 million taels,[2] or around one-quarter of the total silver transfers of 4 million taels, so that any reduction in subsidies would surely affect the Northeast. Beginning in the 1850s, the outbreak

---

[1] Yeh-chien Wang (1973), 17–19.
[2] Robert Lee (1970), 75–76, cites reports from the Jiaqing (1796–1820) and Daoguang (1821–50) periods, that show annual deficits of around 500,000 taels for both Heilongjiang and Jilin combined.

of the Taiping Rebellion disrupted financial accounting, the surplus provinces failed to meet their obligations, and in the absence of silver transfers, the military governors of Jilin and Heilongjiang had to look for new sources of revenue. The only significant asset available to them was land that could be sold or taxed to help balance the books.[3]

The second factor weighing on the government in Beijing and its agents in Manchuria was the threat. Most military action during the mid-19th century was in southern China, site of the Opium wars and the Taiping Rebellion. But the Russians, seeing a chance to recoup the losses they had suffered in the 17th century, demanded and in the treaties of Aigun (1858) and Beijing (1860) obtained a redrawing of the borders of Manchuria that returned to Russia all of the territory north of the Heilongjiang and east of the Ussuri Rivers, which had been lost in the Treaty of Nerchinsk (1689). From 1860 on, the Russians pressed for a larger role throughout the Far East and especially in Manchuria.

Facing for the first time in two centuries a powerful, aggressive enemy on its northern border and with fewer resources to meet this challenge, Beijing recognized (or rather recalled) the value of a productive population on the frontier. The early Qing had encouraged the settlement and cultivation of the Liaodong region and sent soldiers and farmers to form "military-agricultural colonies" on the northern and western borders, creating a self-supporting bulwark against foreign aggression. These policies worked so well, or at least the initial Russian threat melted so quickly, that the Manchu rulers apparently forgot about the importance of facts-on-the-ground, and during the 18th and early 19th centuries viewed migrants and settlers in the northern territories as a nuisance rather than an asset. Now, with the outbreak of the financial crisis and the return of the Russians, the old strategy was revived under the slogan of "moving people to strengthen the border" [*yimin shibian*].

From 1860 on, Qing policies in the northern territories were dominated by financial and strategic concerns. Passively, Beijing accepted the privatization of the bannerlands and estates of southern Manchuria. As the estates declined and control over bannerland gravitated to Chinese commoners, the authorities could lay claim to more taxable farmland. Actively, the Qing "opened" to reclamation, rental, or the transfer to private hands what had previously been "closed" or protected territories, such as horse farms and hunting reserves or general wastelands in the undeveloped regions of the north and east. The military governments of Fengtian, Jilin, and Heilongjiang leased or sold plots of land to

[3] James Millward (1998), 58–63, 235–38.

Chinese commoners, and once the land had been reclaimed, taxed it as farmland. Finally, civil administration—county-level offices that collected taxes on farmland as part of the nationwide system of revenue— was expanded in Fengtian, Jilin, Heilongjiang, and the neighboring Mongol banners. None of these practices was new, but all of them accelerated after the middle of the 19th century and expanded onto the northern, eastern, and western frontiers.

The late Qing benefited from the transfer of land from official estates and banners to Chinese commoners, trends that preceded the change in Qing policies and were caused by forces outside of government control. Beginning in the late-18th century, the number and size of the official estates in Manchuria declined, as the land originally assigned to these units was taken over by Chinese. In some cases, estate land became vacant when estate workers failed to pay their dues. In other cases, estate workers abandoned their posts to assume the status of "commoner," preferring to take their chances as farmworkers or tenants and in hopes of becoming independent landowners. As bonded laborers left the estates, those who stayed behind could not work all of the land themselves and rented out the surplus or transferred ownership to others. Meanwhile, estate workers or commoners acting in the name of estate workers reclaimed wasteland in areas surrounding the estate. As a result, from the end of the 18th to the early 20th century, the number of grain estates operated by the Imperial Household Department in Fengtian declined from 300 to 219 and the area of these estates from 688,305 to 490,000 *mu*.[4] Land removed from the estates was susceptible to taxation by the counties and departments that were established for this purpose.

In contrast to the estates, which shrank in number and size, the area of bannerlands in Jilin and other parts of Manchuria increased, although in reality the actual control of land was changing hands. The bannerlands grew because the bannermen succeeded in adding land that had been reclaimed or rented by commoners. Under the practice known as "commoner recognizing the banner landlord" [*min ren qi dongdi*], migrant farmers who reclaimed wasteland in the vicinity of a banner paid a bannerman to pose as the titular landlord, so that the land could be registered under the banner, subject to lower tax rates and protected from confiscation by the state. In the same way, Chinese farmers entered into pledges and other arrangements that gave them effective control over land that remained technically part of the banner. Conversely, Qing officials sought to remove land from the banners and

---

[4] Kong Jingwei (1990), 122, 223–27.

make it taxable "common land." That explains why, for example, in 1852, the Board of Revenue relaxed the prohibition on the transfer of bannerland to commoners. By the end of the century, most bannerland in Fengtian had been "entered onto the tax rolls" either directly [*qi shengke di*] or as "surplus land." During the last decade of Manchu rule, nearly 9 million *mu* of bannerland in Jilin also lost its privileged status and began to be taxed.[5]

Qing tax collectors could sit by and wait for the banners and estates to sell or transfer land to commoners. Meanwhile the military governments in Manchuria, in need of immediate income, moved aggressively on another target—the sale of public lands. At the beginning of the Qing, large tracts of land were set aside for use by the imperial cavalry as "horse farms" [*machang*] or "rangelands" [*muchang*] or by the Manchu nobles as "reserves" [*weichang*] for hunting and extracting timber, ginseng, and other forest products. The commanding generals of Fengtian and Jilin were charged with protecting these enclosed areas against hunters, loggers, and squatters. After the middle of the 19th century, however, the generals received permission to tax farmers already in the enclosures or to "survey and release" [*zhangfang*] this land for sale.[6] Even larger than the reserves were the "official wastelands" [*guanhuang*] that lay beyond the areas of settlement and administration. In theory, unclaimed wasteland was the property of the dynasty or the state. In practice, it was occupied and used by whoever got there first. Once they decided to enforce their rights, however, Qing authorities did not hesitate to sell the land and to tax it from that point on.

During the latter half of the 19th century, vast tracts of land carved out of former reserves, unoccupied wasteland, and areas that had been settled but not registered as part of a banner or estate or as taxable common land, were surveyed, assessed, and put up for sale. Much of this land lay outside the densely populated central Manchurian plain, in eastern Fengtian,[7] especially around the city of Fenghuang, and eastern

[5] Kong Jingwei (1990), 235–45. See especially: 235, area of bannerlands in Jilin increased from 365,092 *shang* during Daoguang (1821–51) to 885,353 *shang* in Guangxu (1875–1908); and 240–41, area of bannerland entered onto the tax rolls in Jilin increased from 60,833 *shang* (0.6 million *mu*) in 1905 to 837,400 *shang* (8.4 million *mu*) in 1911.

[6] The compound *zhangfang*, which I have translated "survey and release" combines the term for "survey," to measure the area of land, *zhangliang*, or "comprehensive survey" [*qingzhang*] and an expression meaning "release" or "let go" [*kaifang* or *fangchu*]. In this context, it means that the authorities removed the land from a protected status, such as under a banner, estate, reserve, or public wasteland, and made it available for sale to commoners and eventual taxation as farmland.

[7] For the operation of land bureaux in Fengtian, see: *Kotoku sannendo*, sites 6, 16, and 17. Sales of land in eastern Fengtian are described in: *Fengtian tongzhi* [Fengtian gazetteer], zhuan 41, cited in Kong Jingwei (1990), 252–53; and *Manzu shehui lishi diaocha* (1985), 51.

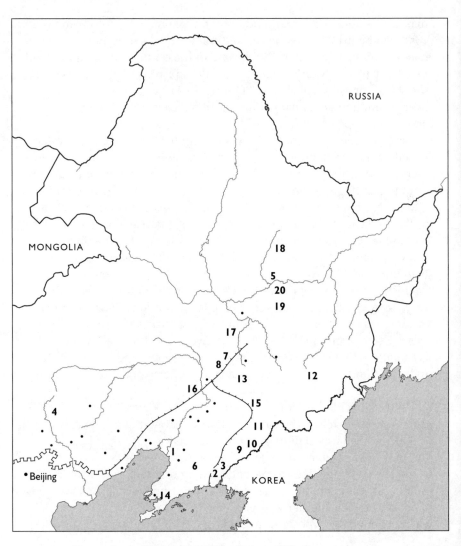

RUSSIA

MONGOLIA

18

5

20

19

17

7

8

13

12

16

4

15

11

9 10

1

6

3

2

• Beijing

14

KOREA

MAP 5. Government Offices, Northeast China, 1868–85

Map 5 Legend

Map No.	Est. Date	Place	Status
1	1866	Yingkou	Subprefecture
2	1868	Andong	County
3	1868	Fenghuang	Subprefecture
4	1875	Weichang	County
5	1875	Hulan	County
6	1876	Xiuyan	Department
7	1877	Huaide	County
8	1877	Fenghua	County
9	1877	Kuandian	County
10	1877	Huanren	County
11	1877	Tonghua	County
12	1877	Dunhua	County
13	1877	Yitong	Department
14	1877	Xingjing	Subprefecture
15	1877	Hailong	Subprefecture
16	1880	Kangping	County
17	1882	Nong'an	County
18	1885	Suihua	Prefecture
19		Wuchang	Subprefecture
20		Binzhou	Subprefecture

SOURCES: Kong Jingwei (1990), 253–55; Alexander Hosie (1904), 162–63.

Jilin,[8] along the arc running from Sanxing through Ninguta to Hunchun (Map 1). Heilongjiang, which had been too far from China proper to serve as a hunting or logging reserve or to attract settlers during the first two centuries of the Qing, now came into range, with the greatest development along the Tongken River to the north and the Sungari to the east of Hulan.[9] Mongol banners in the west also had land that could be surveyed and sold and thus came within the purview of official land bureaux.[10] The creation of tax offices during this period (Map 5) testifies to the expansion of settlement and cultivation on the northern, eastern, and western frontiers.

[8]*Jilin tongzhi* [Jilin Gazetteer], cited in Kong Jingwei (1990), 251–57; and Xu Shuming (1990), 113, 120. Note: 12 of the 14 reclamation sites listed by Xu, lay east of the axis running through Harbin, Changchun, and Fengtian, while only two were located in the western Mongol areas. For examples of the sale and settlement of public lands in eastern Jilin around Dunhua and Yanji and on the lower Sungari near Huachuan and Fujin, see *Kotoku sannendo*, sites 5, 8, 3, and 4, respectively.

[9]Xu Shuming (1990), 109, 114; Kong Jingwei (1990), 259–60; Robert Lee (1970), 127–29. Most of the 16 sites included in the *Kotoku gannendo* surveys lie in the region between the lower Sungari and Nenjiang Rivers (see Map 7). See especially the histories of villages in Suihua (site 3), Hulan (5), and Bayan (6), mentioned here.

[10]Kong Jingwei (1990), 249–50; Hu Zhiyu (1984), 67–68; Owen Lattimore (1934), 202, 221–23.

B. The "New Policy" on Land (1902–12)

The "New Policies" adopted in 1902 were Beijing's response to the intensification of those problems—the debt and the threat—that it had faced during the previous half-century. What had changed was the locus and scale of these problems. The financial crisis of the mid-19th century was a domestic affair: triggered by internal rebellions and requiring underdeveloped regions, like Jilin and Heilongjiang, to make up for the loss of silver transfers from the surplus provinces of the Lower Yangzi. The financial crisis of the early-20th century stemmed from international causes: the need to pay indemnities imposed on China by the foreign powers following wars and unequal treaties, especially the 200 million taels owed for the loss to Japan (1895), and a staggering 450 million taels for damages caused by the Boxer Rebellion (1901). Meanwhile, threats to China's security became more severe. Lacking confidence that Beijing could enforce the treaties that protected their special rights, after 1895 the imperialist powers shifted to a strategy of carving out separate "spheres of interest" surrounding coastal cities and along routes of access into the interior. In Manchuria, the Russians won the right to build railroads and occupy ports and expanded their presence throughout this region. To defend the empire, pay off the debt, and preserve the dynasty, the Qing adopted a radically new approach to government, which called for direct intervention into all areas of public life—including the ownership, sale, and taxation of land in Manchuria and the Mongol banners.

The implementation of this policy began with the establishment of an official "land reclamation bureau" [*kenwuju*], which directed local authorities to "report [land for] reclamation" [*baoken*], "surveyed" or "assessed" [*zhangkan*] the land to establish the size, grade, and value of each plot, and "released" [*kaifang, chufang,* or *fang*] the plots for sale.[11] In principle, the sale should go to the highest bidder, although it was common to offer local landowners the right of first refusal, and perhaps even more common for officials to collude with local power holders to transfer land at below market prices.[12] Land treated in this way might be undeveloped wasteland, which would have to be reclaimed before it could be cultivated and taxed, or land that was already under cultivation

---

[11] The following account is based on Kong Jingwei (1990), 273, 277. For a discussion of the terms used in this process, see Flemming Christiansen (1992), 23–32. And for individual examples see: *Kotoku gannendo,* sites 13 and 14, and *Kotoku sannendo,* site 4, all of which were subject to government land sales after 1902.

[12] For an example of the sale of land to estate heads involving alleged bribes and kickbacks, see: *Manzu shehui lishi diaocha* (1985), 208–9.

and had been rented out to a tenant or transferred to a third party under a deposit, pledge, or other device. The sale of unused wasteland generally proceeded without incident, because the profits could be shared among all interested parties. But attempts to confiscate and resell land that was already claimed could trigger violent reactions.[13]

The "buyer" [*jialing huzhu*] of land from a government bureau enjoyed greater control over his purchase than the tenant who had paid a pledge or deposit under the former system, for the buyer could "sell" [*duimai*], "pledge" [*dianya*], or "transfer tenancy" [*zhuandian*] of the land to a third party. There were generally strict guidelines for the distribution of income derived from the sale: First, a small amount was set aside for the military expenses of the land bureau. (Given the number of parties who stood to lose as the Qing stepped in to extract a share of the proceeds, the land bureaus often needed protection!) After deducting these expenses, the balance was divided equally between the provincial government and, if appropriate, the banner or estate that had jurisdiction over the land. In the latter case, the portion returned to the original owners was divided among the banner or estate heads, subheads, and perhaps the public granary, which supported the ordinary bannermen, estate workers, or herders in times of need. This final provision, which was designed to protect those who lost out when land was sold or transferred to outsiders, was often honored in the breach and became the source of conflict among the bureau, the local elites, and the lower classes.

It is difficult to say how much land changed hands in this way, how much wasteland was reclaimed for agriculture, or how rapidly these changes occurred, for data on landownership and use in Manchuria and Inner Mongolia during the late Qing remains scattered and imprecise. But the evidence suggests that the scope and speed of land reclamation and cultivation in these regions were considerably greater after 1902 than before, and that the changes were brought about by a government determined to achieve its ends. During the last decade of the Qing, tens of millions of *mu* of farmland throughout the Northeast were surveyed and released for sale or simply added to the tax rolls. The creation during the period 1902–10 of new administrative offices in the eastern half of Manchuria—from the Willow Palisade to the Korean Border, along the Mudan, Muleng, and Ussuri Rivers, and throughout the Tongken and Lower Sungari systems—attests to the aggressive program to survey, sell, and add farmland to the tax rolls (Map 6).[14]

---

[13] Kong Jingwei (1990), 265.

[14] Kong Jingwei (1990), 249–63. Kong, 262, cites evidence that by 1908, 15 million *mu* of cultivated land had been added to the tax rolls in Heilongjiang.

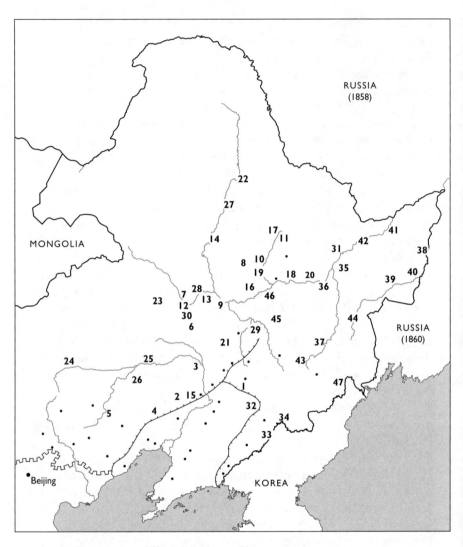

MAP 6. Government Offices, Northeast China, 1902–10

Map 6 Legend

Map No.	Est. Date	Place	Status
1	1902	Liaoyuan	County
2	1902	Zhangwu	County
3	1902	Zhengjiatun	County
4	1903	Fuxin	County
5	1903	Jianping	County
6	1904	Kaitong	County
7	1904	Tao'an	County
8	1904	Anda	Subprefecture
9	1904	Dalai	Subprefecture
10	1904	Qinggang	County
11	1904	Hailun	Subprefecture
12	1905	Taonan	Prefecture
13	1905	Anguang	County
14	1905	Tsitsihar	
15	1906	Faku	County
16	1906	Zhaozhou	County
17	1906	Baiquan	County
18	1906	Bayan	Department
19	1906	Lanxi	County
20	1906	Mulan	County
21	1907	Changling	County
22	1908	Mergen	County
23	1908	Liquan	County
24	1908	Linxi	County
25	1908	Kailu	County
26	1908	Suidong	County
27	1909	Nahe	County
28	1910	Zhendong	County
29	1910	Dehui	County

The following offices were established in eastern Fengtian and Jilin during or shortly before this period, although the exact date is uncertain.

Map No.	Place	Status
30	Heishui	Subprefecture
31	Tangyuan	County
32	Liuhe	County
33	Ji'an	County
34	Linjiang	County
35	Yilan	Prefecture
36	Fangzheng	County
37	Ning'an	County
38	Raohe	County
39	Mishan	Prefecture
40	Hulin	Subprefecture
41	Fujin	County
42	Huachuan	County
43	Emu	County
44	Muleng	County
45	Yushu	County
46	Shuangcheng	Subprefecture
47	Yanji	Subprefecture

SOURCE: Kong Jingwei (1990), 163, 253–58.

TABLE 1

Population and cultivated land, by province, Northeast China, 1820–1910

Province	1820	1909–1910	Increase, 1820–1910 (x)
Fengtian			
Population (1,000)	1,757	11,019	6.3
Cultivated land (1,000 *mu*)	4,137	41,803	10.1
Jilin			
Population (1,000)	567	5,538	9.8
Cultivated land (1,000 *mu*)	1,560	38,867	24.9
Heilongjiang			
Population (1,000)	168	1,859	11.1
Cultivated land (1,000 *mu*)	1,509	21,588	14.3
All Provinces			
Population (1,000)	2,491	18,416	7.4
Cultivated land (1,000 *mu*)	7,207	102,258	14.2

SOURCES: Population: 1820: *Zhongguo lidai hukou tudi tianfu tongji* [Historical statistics on population, land, and taxes of China], 401, cited in Kong Jingwei (1990), 166. 1910: Chen Chang-heng, cited in Waller Wynne (1958), 17.

Land: 1820: *Zhongguo lidai hukou tudi tianfu tongji* [Historical statistics on population, land, and taxes of China], 401, cited in Kong Jingwei (1990), 166. 1909: *Man Meng quanshu* [Complete book of Manchuria and Mongolia], zhuan 3, page 3, cited in Kong Jingwei (1990), 313. The latter figure is supported by Xu Shuming (1990), 119, who cites the figure of 10,801,420 shang (108 million *mu*) of cultivated land in the Northeast in 1908.

The available figures for population and land under cultivation in the Northeast bridge the longer period, 1820–1910 (Table 1), and thus do not provide the detail needed to document the changes that occurred during the first decade of the 20th century. But the substantial increases in both categories, especially in the central and eastern Manchurian region of Jilin, where population grew tenfold and land under cultivation nearly 25 times, support the contention for a late Qing surge in migration and the reclamation of land.

The impact of the "New Policies" may actually have been greater in the Mongol areas than in Manchuria, for the reason that less had changed in these areas during the preceding half century. The policy "to move people to strengthen the borders," which had prompted the settlement of Chinese farmers in the north and east, had little effect in the west: first, because this region lay outside the path of the Russian advance and was therefore of less strategic value; and second, because the Manchu rulers had been reluctant to challenge the Mongol princes for control of land within their domains. After 1902, these reservations were no longer sufficient to stay Beijing's hand. The need for additional income compelled the Qing to seize and dispose of land in what had been autonomous Mongol territories.

The first land bureaus in the Mongol areas were set up along the Sungari and Nenjiang (Nonni) Rivers and the Chinese Eastern Railway (CER), which cut across this territory from central Russia to Vladivostok. The creation of Chinese settlements along these lines of communication strengthened the Qing in areas vulnerable to the Russian advance, while the rivers and railways provided the transportation needed to bring migrants in, ship produce out, and make these areas profitable. A special effort was made to target banners whose chiefs had fallen into arrears. When the creditors were Chinese, it was enough to allow the Mongols to sell the land and pay off their debts. In some cases, however, Mongol banners had borrowed from Russian banks and secured the loans with mortgages on land, mines, livestock, or forests. To forestall the expansion of foreign interference, Beijing was forced to intervene, seize the mortgaged property, and, after negotiations with the Russians, allow the banners to sell the assets to Chinese buyers and use the income to repay the foreign lenders.[15]

Government intervention also extended further west, into areas that were *not* in the path of the Russian advance, demonstrating that the purpose of the "New Policy" on land was as much to raise revenue as to provide for the region's defense. The military commanders of Fengtian and Heilongjiang expropriated, surveyed, and sold millions of *mu* of land in the Mongol banners of Zhelimu League, along the western border of Manchuria.[16] The creation of government tax offices in this region demonstrates the breadth and depth of the change.[17] Finally, the Mongol banners west of Beijing were deeply impacted by the late-Qing crisis. The western provinces, which had contributed mightily to the destruction wrought by the Boxer Rebellion (1900), were obliged to pay their share of the indemnity imposed on China by the foreign powers. After 1902, when Beijing began to expropriate, sell, and tax land in the Mongol banners, the "New Policies" were applied with particular vengeance along both sides of the western Wall.[18]

[15] Kong Jingwei (1990), 272–73.

[16] For figures on the area of land reclaimed and cultivated in Zhelimu League, from 1800–1902, and 1902–11, see: Tian Zhihe (1982), 190–91; Tian Zhihe (1984A), 89–93; Kuang Haolin (1985), 47–48, Wang Bingming (1990), 71, and Kong Jingwei (1990), 274–76. For examples in Taonan and Zhaozhou, which lie west of Harbin, see: *Kotoku gannendo*, site 10, and *Kotoku sannendo*, site 2.

[17] Wang Bingming (1990), 67–70; and G. C. Binsteed (1913), 43–45; Owen Lattimore (1934), 204–5.

[18] Liang Bing (1991), 53–56, 61, 114–15; He Yaozhang (1978), 149; Kuang Haolin (1985), 48; Wang Bingming (1990), 63–65. See also Flemming Christiansen (1992), 29.

C. Conclusion

Part One ends on an ironic note: for it is just when the Manchu rulers acted most decisively that they did the most to advance the Chinese takeover of the Manchu homeland. During most of the Qing period, the rulers in Beijing appeared ambivalent, their policies toward Manchuria were indecisive, and the spread of Chinese into this region depended primarily on the efforts of the Chinese themselves. Near the end, however, the Qing acted with resolve, in unprecedented ways, and with results that greatly expanded the area of Chinese settlement. The Manchus inserted the government into practices, including the buying and selling of land, which previously lay outside the purview of the state. In the process, they greatly expanded the area of private landownership in Manchuria and the spread of the market economy as practiced in China proper. The very outcome that the dynasty had previously tried to avoid was now largely a fact.

Analysis

IN THE COURSE OF THE QING DYNASTY, the Manchu rulers tried and failed to establish a system of land tenure in Manchuria and Inner Mongolia that favored the dynasty and its allies, while Chinese settlers succeeded in transplanting into this region their own system of free markets in land and labor based on the model practiced in China proper. As a result of these events, the patterns of land use and land tenure above the Great Wall came to resemble practices previously established in China proper. The credit for this outcome belongs principally to those Chinese who reclaimed and farmed the land of this region during the Qing period. Although as yet shadowy figures in this account, Chinese migrants are the main actors in Part One, and will dominate the story in Parts Two and Three. Before moving on, however, we should pause to consider the role of the Qing Dynasty, and ask: Why attempts by the Qing to establish novel land tenure practices in Manchuria failed? How Qing policies in this region compare with those toward the other borderlands? And how the Chinese case compares with Russia, the other great landed empire that was expanding across Eurasia at this time?

A. The Border Policies of the Qing

An examination of how the Qing ruled the peoples and territories of Manchuria and other borderlands leads to the more fundamental question of the Dynasty's identity and purpose. For previous generations of China scholars, the prevailing view of the Qing and the explanation for its demise, best captured by Mary Wright (1957), was that by the 19th century, if not before, the dynasty had succumbed to the process of "Sinification": that is, the Manchu elite adopted Chinese ways, the Chinese literati captured most public offices and set cultural norms, and the Chinese gentry took over the functions of local government. In this view, the failures of the Qing were not the fault of the Manchus, but of the Confucian order itself. Recently, this interpretation has been challenged by a new school of Manchu studies, led by Evelyn Rawski (1998), Pamela Crossley (1990, 1997), Edward Rhoads (2000) and Mark Elliott (2001), who argue, using Manchu as well as Chinese sources, that the Qing Dynasty, rather than failing, succeeded to a remarkable degree, and the reason for their success was that Qing rulers, far from being "Sinified," maintained a strong Manchu identity, which kept them apart from their subjects and gave their enterprise cohesion and purpose. Complementing this Manchu-centered thesis is a related interpretation, proposed by James Millward (1998) in his study of another border region, Xinjiang, who argues that the Qing succeeded in building the largest empire in Chinese history by presenting itself as the head of a multiethnic, multiregional system in which all groups enjoyed a common, if not exactly equal, status. Millward agrees with the aforementioned Manchu scholars that the Qing was not "Sinified," but neither, he adds, was it distinctly Manchu. Rather its identity lay in imperial governance itself.

These accounts offer refreshing alternatives to the old orthodoxy, which viewed the Qing through Chinese eyes and conflated the Qing empire with its successor state of China. Appreciation for this scholarship should not, however, cause us to miss an equally important point, which is that for the Qing, as for several preceding dynasties, the Chinese heartland, or China proper, occupied the central and most important part of the empire. The borderlands, including Manchuria, were peripheral in location and status; their function was to insulate and protect the core; and the Qing Dynasty succeeded in large part because it recognized and embraced these priorities.

This book focuses on one border region, but does so in a way that reaffirms a China-centered account of the Qing and it successor state, China. The principal theme is that Manchuria was incorporated into the empire by the migration and settlement of Chinese and the transplantation or reproduction in this region of practices previously established in China proper—in contrast, for example, to theories that emphasize the creative power of the frontier (Frederick Jackson Turner), the interplay of forces in a "middle ground" (Richard White), the leadership of the Manchus (Evelyn Rawski et al.) or the joining together of separate coequal regions and peoples (James Millward). A secondary theme, explored here, is that the Chinese takeover of Manchuria was made possible by the priority the Qing placed on the defense of China proper and policies toward the borderlands that followed from this choice. The Manchus recognized that China proper was the core of their empire and the main source of its wealth and power, while Manchuria was part of a periphery that must serve the function of protecting and preserving this core. Despite their special interest in the Manchu homeland and neighboring Inner Mongolia, the Qing treated these territories as a buffer zone. And left in this subordinate status, the areas above the Great Wall fell victim to an overwhelming number of determined and capable Chinese.

Absent from the Qing agenda in Manchuria, Inner Mongolia, or any other border region was an ideological or developmental drive to conquer, convert, and control these territories. This is not to say that the Manchus lacked a capacity or enthusiasm for military action; on the contrary, the empire was conquered and constructed by the generous application of imperial force. But the Qing took the initiative and made commitments beyond China proper only in response to external threats and for the derivative purpose of defending the core. In the absence of threats from *without*, they were more concerned about threats from *within*— including, or especially, from within the borderlands themselves—than about the expansion, development, or transformation of these regions on behalf of some larger design. Qing border policies were reactive, defensive, and once the empire's borders were secure, produced a weak, stable, or in less seemly terms, stagnant periphery.

The choice of the Manchus to focus on China proper and treat Manchuria as a dependency or buffer zone was evident from the very beginning of the dynasty. As the bulk of Manchu banner troops crossed the Great Wall and continued south in pursuit of remnant Ming forces, the Russians advanced down the Heilongjiang and up the Sungari into central Manchuria. With their numbers depleted, there was little the Manchus could do to defend Manchuria against the Russians, while the strategy of concentrating forces in the south was risky, because if it failed, the Manchus might find it difficult to return home. Yet this is precisely the strategy they chose: for nearly four decades, the Qing concentrated its forces in China proper; only after the defeat of the Three Feudatories in 1681 were banner units redeployed in the north, where they succeeded in defeating the Russians and forcing them to retreat beyond the Heilongjiang.

When the Qing did show sufficient interest to commit resources to Manchuria, they acted in response to threats from the Russians, first in the 17th and again in the 19th centuries, rather than out of any positive impulse to transform or develop this region. Qing policies and programs in the Northeast that had explicit economic goals, such as the creation of "manors" and "agricultural military colonies," were designed to produce food or provide for the livelihood of military forces, the elite service class, or other allies of the Qing, rather than to expand the area of occupation, increase the production of goods, or enhance the wealth and power of this region on behalf of some imperial enterprise. And when, at the end of the 19th century, the dynasty did adopt an aggressive program to sell and tax farmland in the northern territories, the impulse came from a combined strategic and financial crisis in China proper rather than a concept of expansion and growth.

Finally, except in those instances when they focused on repulsing external threats or raising money to address financial needs, Qing policies toward Manchuria and Inner Mongolia were changing, conflicting, and followed no consistent logic, save perhaps to preclude the rise from within these territories of a force powerful enough to challenge the dynasty itself. This ambivalence was evident in the constantly changing policies to "close" or "open" passage through the Great Wall to migrants from the south and in the restraints placed on Manchus in Manchuria (and elsewhere), who were precluded from entering commercial and technical trades as a way of preserving Manchu identity, while preventing them from taking part in the process of economic and social development. In any case, events on the ground were determined more by migrants seeking work and landowners seeking labor than by officials in Beijing or the inadequate forces deployed to implement their orders.

A comparison of Qing policies toward the empire's most important borderlands suggests that in these respects Manchuria was more typical than unique. In most, if not all cases, the Qing acted forcefully, even aggressively when the security of China proper was at stake or the coffers of the central government were empty, while in the absence of such problems, the Manchus favored policies that divided and weakened the borderlands, rather than developing their resources, making the emergence of a power from within these regions unlikely. The major initiatives that led to the expansion of the Qing northward into Mongolia or westward into Xinjiang and Tibet all came in response to threats from the Dzungar Mongols of Central Asia. And in each instance, following the defeat of the Dzungars, the victorious Qing favored a balance among competing forces. This precluded higher levels of production or more coherent organization in these regions, but that was less important to the rulers in Beijing than having a cushion to insulate and defend China proper. A survey of the periphery of the Qing empire reveals local variations on otherwise consistent themes.

Mongolia Preoccupied with the conquest and control of China proper, the early Qing made no effort to extend its power north of the Gobi Desert into Outer Mongolia or Khalka. The conquest of Outer Mongolia came in response to the threat from Galdan, leader of the Dzungar or Oirat Mongols of Central Asia, who battled their way across Asia to the borders of the empire. Facing attack, the Emperor Kangxi led Qing armies against Galdan in 1690 and 1696, forcing his retreat and ultimate demise. Peter Perdue (1996) agues that whereas Kangxi's first expedition was purely defensive, the second was fueled by a "personal vengeance" that exceeded any reasonable assessment of strategic needs. In neither case, however, was the Qing guided by an imperialist purpose or rationale. Having secured domination over Outer Mongolia, Kangxi and his successors pursued a balancing act among Qing officials, Manchu banner forces, Mongol nobles, Llamist religious leaders, and Chinese merchants. The result in Mongolia, as in Manchuria, was an ambiguous policy by which the Qing claimed to protect the existing Mongol order and prevent Chinese immigration, while in fact allowing Chinese merchants to take control of the economy and the Mongol social structure to decay. This produced a weak and divided Mongolia, and a secure Qing monarch, while preventing the development of the region for the benefit either of the Mongols or of the empire as a whole.[1]

Xinjiang The Qing conquest of Xinjiang occurred later, in 1759, again in response to the emergence of Dzungar power in Central Asia. Following the conquest, Beijing tried to protect its interests in Xinjiang by maintaining a balance among the imperial military government, Chinese Green Standard forces and civil administrative offices, Chinese merchants and farming communities, and autonomous Turkic (*beg*) and Mongol (*jasagh*) leaders, who were made responsible for administering their own communities. This enterprise was supported in part by taxes on trade and other devices to raise money locally, but in the end it depended upon "silver transfers" from the surplus provinces of China

---

[1] C. R. Bawden (1989), 39–100.

proper. For more than a century (1759–1864), these practices afforded the empire protection against Central Asian armies and prevented the rise of rival powers within Xinjiang. Later, during the early-19th century, Chinese critics of the "statecraft" school charged that the Qing had failed to develop Xinjiang to enhance the wealth and power of the nation. But for the Qing that was quite beside the point. Their objective was to defend against attack from without, prevent the rise of threats from within, and pay for the whole thing as best they could, so that the core of the empire was safe and its wealth secure.[2]

Tibet Intervention by the Qing into Tibet followed the same pattern and produced similar results. Until the early 18th century, the Kingdom of Tibet and the Empire of the Qing had few contacts, conflicts, or shared interests. It was the entry into Tibet of the Dzungar Mongols that prompted the Emperor Kangxi to send a military expedition to capture Lhasa (1720) and drive the Dzungars out of Tibet. This intervention prompted no resistance from the Tibetans and resulted in the creation of a Qing protectorate that left the Tibetans in effective control. Thus, a pattern was set that was repeated during the next century: The politics of Tibet would take a course that invited the return of the Dzungars or some other outside force; Beijing would send troops to Lhasa to forestall an intervention, reorganize the government, and remain for a time to oversee the transition; the interest of the Qing overlords would wane and they would withdraw; finally, events in Tibet would trigger an intervention and another cycle of advance and retreat.[3]

Taiwan Completing this *tour d'horizon* is the record of Qing policy toward Taiwan. Again, the impulse to advance came in response to threats from this direction: The use of Taiwan as a base of power by the Ming general Zheng Chonggong prompted the conquest of the island in 1683; thereafter, Qing forces intervened periodically to settle conflicts among Chinese settlers and island aborigines; finally, a program to build up the economy and strengthen the forces on Taiwan occurred at the end of the Qing, a similar response to the same problems that prompted changes in Qing policy toward Manchuria. In the absence of compelling security needs, Beijing vacillated, according to John Shepherd (1993), between attempts to quarantine the island in some periods and colonize it in others—a see-saw pattern that recalls the proclamations to "open" and "close" passage through the Great Wall.[4]

[2] James Millward (1998), especially 32–36, 241–45.
[3] H. E. Richardson (1962), 41–72.
[4] John Shepherd (1993), 14–21 and passim.

B. China and Russia

A comparison of Qing and Russian, or Romanov, strategies for expanding control over peripheral areas demonstrates striking similarities in approach and equally striking differences in outcomes. In both cases, during the 17th and 18th centuries, established empires based on bureaucratic governance and an agrarian economy offered grants of land to hereditary elites in thinly settled but potentially arable border regions, along with military protection and support for a system of enforced labor, in exchange for service to the state. In the Chinese case, this model proved ineffective and gave way to a system of markets along the lines practiced in China proper. In the Russian case, the system of manors not only survived, but deserves much of the credit for enabling the tsars to extend their control from the forests of Muscovy onto the steppe, forming the basis for the powerful and expansive Russian state that emerged in the 19th century.

In both Qing and Romanov cases, the imperial rulers had good reasons to favor the creation or extension of "manors" and to expect them to succeed. Both monarchies had established alliances with favored hereditary elites, whom it wanted to reward for service in the past and count on for service in the future. Both were surrounded by territories, which had not yet been incorporated into their empires, were occupied by nomads and other elements that posed threats to their regimes, and offered arable land that could be settled, cultivated, and taxed for the benefit of the expanding agrarian economy and bureaucratic state. Both had surplus populations, whose relocation to the frontier would help expand the scope and power of the state and at the same time remove a potential source of instability within the core. Both had large standing armies that could enforce and help implement this program of expansion. And both chose to pursue this goal through a program of land grants, enforced labor, and a service elite.

The expansion of Moscow, between the 16th and 18th centuries, southward to the Black Sea and eastward to the Urals, began with the military conquest over the Crimean (Krim) Tartars and other steppe nomads. After each advance, Moscow built forts to secure a new line of defense, granted land within this defensive perimeter to nobles and landlords in exchange for military or administrative service, and strengthened the control of landed elites over rural labor. There was a weakness in this system, for peasants transferred from European Russia to serve on frontier estates could flee to become tenants of independent landlords or reclaim land on their own. Perversely, this tendency of workers to flee from estates on or near the frontier raised the pressure for tighter control over labor, leading eventually to the codification of the institution of serfdom in 1649. Independent mounted bands, or Cossacks, were formed by settlers on the southern steppe as a means of self-defense, while Moscow tried to co-opt these forces to defend this territory and impose control over rural labor.[5]

There are at least three reasons why the Russians had greater success than the Manchus in establishing a system of manors in frontier or newly occupied areas. First, the Russian tsars, unlike the Manchus, were exporting a system that had deep roots in the politics and society of the parent regime. Beginning in the 14th century, Muscovy had grown by military conquest, the establishment of landed estates, and a social structure based on powerful landed elites, subject rural labor, and a small, weak commercial middle class, all held together by a centralized, even despotic state. The various parties within this system knew their roles and were expected to follow them. By contrast, the Manchus and the social and economic structures that had emerged during their rise to power were of recent and, to the Chinese, foreign vintage. Most Manchus, Mongols, and others who received land grants under the Qing had little experience with agriculture or the management of a large workforce, as was common among the gentry of Russia. Chinese peasants, who provided the bulk of the rural labor, had a much better knowledge of farming than the men they worked for and brought with them their own ideas about how production should be organized and managed, the relationship between landlord and tenant, and ultimately the ownership of land. Whereas the Russian tsars had only to move an existing social and economic system from one locale to another, the Qing had to create new patterns or change old ones.

Second, the threats to settlers on the Russian steppe were much greater than in Manchuria or Inner Mongolia. Even as late as the 18th century, mounted horsemen, heirs to the Mongol invaders who had plagued Russia for centuries, remained a clear and present danger to anyone who ventured beyond the protection of Russian forts and forces. This created pressures on all parties to stick together, reinforcing

---

[5] William McNeill (1983), 24–27, describes the tension between forced labor and freedom on frontiers prior to 1750. William McNeill (1964), 192–93, Donald Treadgold (1957), 14–16, and Joseph Wieczynski (1976), 60–61 and 78–79, make particular reference to this phenomenon on the borders of Russia west of the Urals.

the power of the tsar over the landlords and of the landlords over the serfs. The situation in Manchuria and Inner Mongolia was quite different. During their rise to power, the Manchus had either defeated or co-opted the Mongol and other native tribes in the north, and after the defeat of the Russians and the Oirats at the end of the 17th century, there remained no organized resistance to the Qing above the Great Wall. The presence of bandits and wild beasts made safety a problem for individuals who wandered too far afield, but for the bulk of the population in or near settled areas, the dangers on China's northern frontier were not nearly as great as those on the Russian steppe.

Finally, there was a fundamental difference in the degree of commercialization of the two empires, which favored the development of manors in tsarist Russia and hindered their operation in Qing China. A commercial economy provided the tax base for government bureaucracies and professional armies, which made it possible for agrarian empires of the 17th and 18th centuries—in China, Russia, or elsewhere—to conquer and control the neighboring steppe. Absent the commer- cialization of agriculture, the tsars of Muscovy could not build the military and bureaucratic machinery required to seize the territory north of the Black Sea from the Tartars or to defend it against the Habsburg or Ottoman empires.[6] Compared to China, however, the Russian economy was very modestly commercialized, the Russian peasantry had little experience with commercial agriculture, and the Russian merchant class was small and weak. Lacking stiff competition from market forces, the landed elite of Russia exercised disproportionate power both at home and on the neighboring steppe, whereas the more commercialized economy of China created the opposite conditions: Migrant farmers from China proper brought to Manchuria the knowledge and skills needed to practice commercial agriculture and the determination to apply these practices for their own benefit. Chinese merchants gained financial leverage over the Manchu and Mongol heads of banners, bannerlands, and estates. And both peasants and merchants used their commercial skills to gain control and eventually ownership of land throughout the territories above the Great Wall. At both ends of Eurasia, the institution of the manor was in competition with the market; in Russia, the former prevailed, and in China, the latter.

[6]See William McNeill (1964), 125–79.

PART TWO

People

Introduction to Part Two

SINCE THE PURPOSE OF THIS BOOK is to describe the Chinese occupation and takeover of Manchuria, it may seem odd to begin with a discussion of land use and land tenure, the subject of Part One, rather than
the migration and settlement of people, which are dealt with in Part Two.
In part, this reflects the choice to stick with chronology, start from the
beginning, and to the fact that for the first two centuries of the Qing the
sources say more about the land than the people of this region. And in
part, it is because the number of migrants to Manchuria and the area
covered by their settlements increased quite slowly during the earlier
period, but with increasing speed and scope from the late 19th century
on. When the sources begin to fill in the picture, around 1900, the story
of migration and settlement becomes both more interesting and more
visible.

It is unlikely that scholars will ever be able to trace with precision
the demographic history of Manchuria during the imperial period. The
first reliable census was conducted by the government of Manchukuo in
1940. Before then, in 1910, the Chinese Ministry of the Interior carried
out a provincial census, which included Fengtian, Jilin, and Heilongjiang. Although falling short of modern standards, this census serves as
a useful reference point, whereas the numbers gathered by Qing officials
before then offer only a rough approximation of actual conditions. In a
careful study of the subject, Waller Wynne (1958) projects data from the
1940 census backward to map the growth of population in Manchuria
over the preceding half century. Wynne's findings, supplemented
by the earlier Qing figures, are as close as we are likely to come to a

demographic profile of this region during the Qing and Republican periods. They show, consistent with other evidence, that the growth of
population in Manchuria was gradual from the mid-17th to the mid-
19th century, then quite steep from the late-19th century on. The distribution of population within Manchuria also changed over time, with
the south, Fengtian or Liaoning, filling up first, followed by Jilin, then
Heilongjiang (Figure 1).

Finally, it should be noted that most of this growth occurred as a result of migration from China proper. Again, the statistical evidence
on the composition of the population of Manchuria is uneven: sketchy
for the period before 1890, somewhat better for the years 1891–1922,
and considerably more reliable after that date. Thomas Gottschang and
Diana Lary have reconstructed a statistical series for the period 1891–
1942 (Figure 2), based on reports of the Maritime Customs Service
(1891–1922) and the South Manchuria Railway (1923–43). These data
show that during this period, 25.4 million people migrated from north
China to Manchuria, 16.7 million (66%) returned, leaving a net transfer
of 8.7 million (34%). The number and net increase of migrants rose
steadily, with fluctuations from year to year, following events that impacted on conditions both above and below the Great Wall. Peak migration occurred during the first tide of railway construction in Manchuria
(1900–03), the chaos that followed the 1911 Revolution, the outbreak of
famine and warlordism in Shandong and Hebei (1927–29), and the industrialization of Manchukuo (1939–42). Intervening troughs of out-
migration and peak returns of migrants to China proper followed the
major conflicts in Manchuria: the Sino-Japanese War (1894–95), the
Russo-Japanese War (1904–05), the Manchurian Incident (1931), and
the outbreak of the War of Resistance (1937).[1] At its high point, between
1927–29, more than one million people passed this way each year,
which was more than entered Canada or the United States in any single
year during the great boom of migration to the New World.[2] Waller
Wynne estimates that the average annual increase in population during
the period 1910 to 1940 was between 2.2 and 2.5%, about half of which
was due to immigration and half to natural growth.[3] The 1940 census
also records the distribution of population by nationality, showing that
more than 85% were Chinese, followed at a considerable distance by
Manchus (6%), Koreans (3%), Mongols (3%), and Japanese (2%).[4]

[1] Thomas Gottschang and Diana Lary (2000), Figure 1.1, 38.
[2] C. Walter Young (1928A), 241.
[3] Waller Wynne (1958), 20.
[4] Waller Wynne (1958), 63.

Population
(millions)

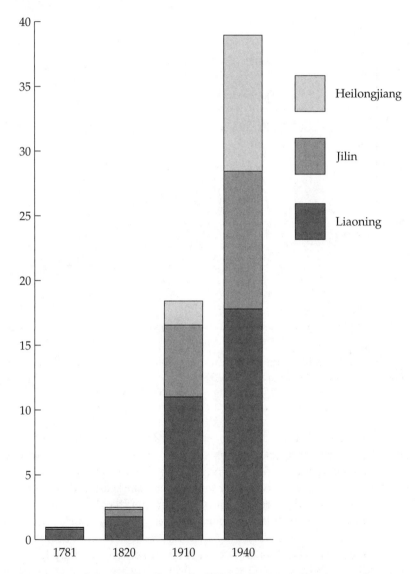

FIGURE 1. Population of Manchuria, by Military Region or Province, 1781–1940
SOURCES: 1781: SJTZ (1784), 36:1–13. 1820: *Zhongguo lidai hukou tudi tianfu tongji*
[Historical statistics on the population, land and taxes of China], 401, cited in
Kong Jingwei (1990), 166. 1910: Waller Wynne (1958), 17. 1940: Waller Wynne
(1958), 24.

Migrants
(thousands)

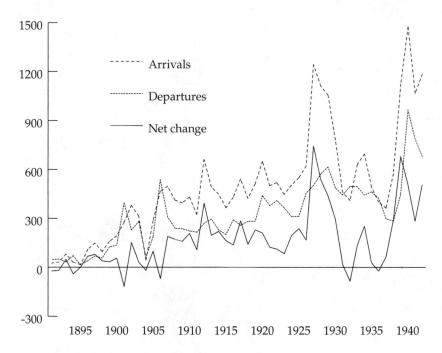

FIGURE 2. Migrants from North China to Manchuria, Arrivals, Departures, and Net Change, 1891–1942
SOURCE: Thomas Gottschang and Diana Lary (2000), Table A.9, 180.

Study of the Chinese who moved to, settled in, and ultimately made up the overwhelming majority of the population of Manchuria confirms the theme introduced in Part One: that the society and culture of this region has been defined more by the transplantation or replication of patterns and practices from China proper than by the innovation or invention of new frontier ways. The twig of Manchuria's Chinese population was bent before the migrants crossed the Great Wall. They were "sojourners," rather than emigrants or settlers, for they left their homes in north China with the intention of remaining only as long as was needed to earn money, before returning home to resume life where it was most worth living, alongside the ancestors. Chapter 4 traces the origins of these migrants in the villages of Shandong and Hebei, and shows that their decision to migrate was governed by the needs of the family and that their mission was to go, to earn, and to return.

Once on the road, would-be sojourners were taken up by "networks" that moved teams of young men from rural north China to the fields and eventually cities of Manchuria. Without abandoning their sense of belonging to a home in China proper, indeed while holding tightly to this identity, many of the migrants gradually became settlers, forming villages, creating networks of communication and trade and extending their way of life northward. Chapter 5 describes the transition these migrants made from temporary sojourners to permanent residents and shows how networks channeled, controlled, and insulated them against their new surroundings, precluding, or at least hindering, the formation of a distinct culture or regional identity of the sort associated with "frontier" society or a "middle ground."

Finally, by the 1920s and 1930s, the character of Manchurian society began to change, less because of the interactions between Chinese and native peoples or landscapes than because of the same process of urbanization and industrialization that was shaping other parts of China that were exposed to foreign influence and international trade. Chapter 6 shows how economic and political factors limited the spread of rural settlement and channeled Chinese migrants into the cities, mines, factories, railroads, and ports of industrial Manchuria. In contrast to the Russian Far East, where one is struck by the strength of regional cultures and the tension between metropole and frontier, the Chinese occupation of Manchuria appears as the seamless extension of an existing society and culture across the fading boundary of the Great Wall.

CHAPTER 4

Sojourners

"SOJOURNERS" IS THE TERM that has been used to describe Chinese emigrants, who left China with the intention, not of relocating or settling in a foreign country, but of using their temporary stay abroad to earn money that they would remit or bring back to make a better life for themselves and their families in their native place.[1] Sometimes, this characterization has been used to distinguish Chinese sojourners from European "settlers" in America. Viewed in this way, Chinese went to America (and elsewhere) only to make gains that could be realized back home, whereas Europeans made a one-way trip and a principled commitment to their adopted land. Recent scholarship has demonstrated that this dichotomy is false: Emigrants from many countries, including such major suppliers to the United States as Italy, returned home at rates that actually exceeded the Chinese; and the return rate of Chinese was due to discrimination and other factors they faced in America as well as to the motives that took them there in the first place.[2] Meanwhile, new work in the field of Chinese history has shown that sojourning was practiced by migrants within China as well as those who went abroad.[3]

With these caveats—that sojourning is not unique to Chinese emigrants, nor among Chinese migrants is it unique to those who have gone overseas—it remains that this term best describes the attitudes and experience of Chinese who went to and eventually settled in Manchuria

[1] Academic discussion of this concept dates from the article by Paul C. P. Siu (1952). For a recent review of the literature on this subject, see Philip Q. Yang (1999).

[2] See, especially: Mark Wyman (1993). A recent study of this subject from the perspective of the Chinese is Sucheng Chan (1990).

[3] William T. Rowe (1984), 220–21.

during the Qing and Republican periods and thus serves as the starting point for the account that follows. The evidence shows that most migrants who crossed the Great Wall left their homes in China proper with the intention of returning, that most did in fact return, and that most of those who stayed behind adapted in ways that tied them continually to the people and places of their native land. These facts had a decisive impact on the society and culture that emerged in Manchuria during the 20th century.

The decision to sojourn reflects a trade-off between competing demands. Material conditions—especially the balance between population and land, which was decidedly more favorable above than below the Great Wall—attracted peasants to the north. At the same time, subjective factors—such as an affinity for family, village, and place—held them back. In the end, the decision was most often made by the family or household, which wielded power over its members and chose to send its young men out to earn and return with money that would improve the family's conditions back home.

A. Material Conditions

Given the material conditions—the natural resources, distribution of population and arable land, methods of transportation, and dangers one might meet along the way—one might ask why more Chinese did not choose Manchuria? Although decisions to move are always fraught with risk, in this case a rational analysis of the balance sheet seemed to favor going over staying behind. The fact that so few did move, that they moved such short distances and for such short periods of time, and that the migration and settlement of large numbers of people was postponed for so long all indicate that other factors must have played a significant role in their individual and collective choices.

1. Natural products

The highlands of Manchuria offered a wide range of valuable products to foresters, hunters, fishermen, prospectors, and anyone willing to risk the adventure of crossing prohibited barriers, gathering proscribed items, and returning with them for sale. By the 18th century, when most forests in China proper had been stripped bare, the northern territories remained cloaked in what appeared to be endless woodlands. At the upper elevations, the mountains of Manchuria were covered by a taiga (moist, subarctic) forest, dominated by larch in the west and the more valuable cedar and spruce in the east, and at lower levels by oak, walnut, birch, and maple, often of gigantic size.[4] "We were nine days in passing through one of [these forests]," remarked an 18th-century traveler, "and obliged to have several trees cut down, by the Mantcheou soldiers, to make room for our observations of the sun's meridian."[5] The eastern forests, especially those along the Korean border, which are accessible by the Sungari and Yalu rivers, remain a valuable resource even today.

In addition to forests, the mountains had other attractions. Fur-bearing animals, especially the sable, and deer, valued for their antlers, which were used to make Chinese medicines, were in great supply. The Sungari and Heilongjiang rivers teemed with sturgeon and pearl-bearing oysters that fetched high prices in Beijing. By the end of the 19th century, nearly all of the gold mined in China came from deposits in Manchuria. The largest mines were at Moho, on the Heilongjiang, which was being worked by 10,000 miners and protected by a thousand soldiers, while other sites could be found along the Nenjiang and Sungari rivers. Coal, iron, copper, lead, tin, and other mineral deposits were also mined or waiting to be mined in this region. Finally, the forests along the Russian and Korean borders contained wild ginseng, a medicinal plant of exceptional rarity and value, which fetched 7 to 8 times its weight in silver in Beijing. The Qing emperors collected sables as tribute from Manchurian tribesmen and declared imperial monopolies on ginseng, pearls, gold, and other valuables.[6] But the Manchurian highlands, which contained these riches, were vast, sparsely populated, and beyond the control of Beijing, offering opportunities to hunters, prospectors, and men-of-fortune, to private investors willing to risk their capital, if not their lives, and government officials who saw the potential to enrich the coffers of state and, as was often the case, themselves.

2. Land and Population

Throughout the Qing and Republican periods, the most striking features of Manchuria were the enormous breadth of its farmland, both

---

[4] Arthur Sowerby (1919), 79. For more on Manchurian forests, see: CER (1924), 173–90; and Zhao Songqiao (1986), 101–4.

[5] Jean-Baptiste Du Halde (1741), 96.

[6] For details on the natural products of Manchuria, see: Jean Baptiste Du Halde (1741), 94, 97–98, 112–14, 147; Père d'Orleans (1971), 112; Alexander Hosie (1904), 121, 145; B. L. Weale (1904), 151–56; and Henry James (1888), 272.

actual and potential, and the sparseness of its population. The vast central Manchurian basin is banked by rolling hills to the south and east and gives way to a wide plain stretching to the west. The soils, formed by a combination of alluvial and aeolian (loess) deposits, vary among brown in the forests, black in the piedmont, and chernozems or mollisols on the steppe, all quite suitable for cultivation. The growing season in Manchuria is shorter than in China proper, but the summers are warm (mean July temperatures, 20–25° C) and long (100–200 frost free days) enough to support one crop per year throughout the length and breadth of the region. The average annual precipitation in the central basin ranges from 700 mm in the southeast to 400 mm in the northwest, most of which falls during the growing season (June–September), when it produces the greatest plant response. Ground water is adequate, and drainage is good, except in the west, where the dry climate acting on low-lying areas causes the accumulation of salts that render the soil unsuitable for farming.[7]

Wide slices of potential farmland lie within easy reach of China proper. During the early Ming (1368–1644), hundreds of thousands of peasants crossed the Great Wall into Jehol and the Yanshan Mountains into southern Manchuria.[8] By the early-18th century, visitors to the Liaodong found "very good" farmland, abounding in wheat, millet, roots, and cotton, and with great herds of oxen and flocks of sheep rarely seen elsewhere in China.[9] A century later, travelers who ventured further north into Jilin and Heilongjiang discovered still more land, unoccupied and "of extraordinary fertility."[10] "Agriculturally," reported one journalist who had traveled widely in China and other parts of Asia, Manchuria "is rich beyond the dreams of avarice, and that is the last word about it."[11] But migrants did not have to go all the way to Manchuria to find land. A broad expanse of prime farmland lay just above the Great Wall in Jehol, a region of forests and meadows formed by the peaks and valleys of the Yanshan Mountains. Passing this way at the turn of the last century, travelers found "a rich agricultural valley with sweeps of from 1 to 2 miles wide, and with perhaps some of the finest arable land that could be desired."[12] To the north and east, these

[7] *Manchoukuo Year Book, 1934*, 16–19, 243–44; Zhao Songqiao (1986), 97–107, 112–13.
[8] Henry Serruys (1959), 15–24.
[9] Jean-Baptiste Du Halde (1741), 92.
[10] Francis Younghusband (1898), 27. A similar view was expressed by Henry James (1888), 11.
[11] B. L. Weale (1904), 183.
[12] John Hedley (1910), 111. See also ibid., 117.

mountains taper off into broad valleys and rolling hills that were among the first to be settled and farmed.

The attraction of Manchuria lay not only in its riches, but in the imbalance of population and resources above and below the Great Wall. During the course of the Qing, conditions for farmers in the heavily populated areas of north China, including Shandong and Hebei, worsened. Virtually all of the arable land in these provinces was occupied and under cultivation by the beginning of the Qing era, while the growth in population during the 18th and 19th centuries reduced the amount of farmland per person by 40%. By the 1930s, the area of cultivated land per capita was around 3 *mu* in Shandong and 4 *mu* in Hebei, which was less than in nearby Fengtian (5 *mu*), and much less than in the northern territories of Jilin (8 *mu*) and Heilongjiang (11 *mu*).[13] More detailed data, based on village or household surveys, reveal an even wider gap in farmland per capita above and below the Great Wall. Studies of particular locales in Shandong and Hebei during the 1920s and 1930s found that the average size (cultivated or crop area) of the family farm could be 9 *mu*, 14 *mu*, or 21 *mu*.[14] John Lossing Buck, in his massive study *Land Utilization in China*, discovered even greater differences in the average size of family farms in the various counties of Shandong and Hebei, which was as low as 6 *mu* in some counties and as high as 85 *mu* in others.[15] Although none of these sources provides comprehensive provincial estimates, it seems likely, using the data provided by Perkins and Buck, that during the 1930s, the average crop or cultivated area per family farm was around 24 *mu* in Shandong and 31 *mu* in Hebei.[16]

Surveys of rural households in Manchuria conducted during the 1930s reveal striking contrasts with conditions in north China. Two surveys, referred to in this text by their brief titles, *Kotoku gannendo* and *Kotoku sannendo*, were carried out by the (Japanese) Manchukuo government in 1935 and 1936 and covered 1,776 households in 37 counties of

[13] Shandong and Hebei: Dwight Perkins (1969), 207, 212, 234–36. Liaoning, Jilin, and Heilongjiang: SMR, *Third Report* (1932), 13, 140; and *Manchoukuo Year Book, 1934*, 27.

[14] See: Wang Yaoyu (1938), 181; Philip Huang (1985), 314–20; and Sidney Gamble (1954), 209–12.

[15] John Lossing Buck (1937B), 286.

[16] These estimates are based on two separate findings or calculations: First, Dwight Perkins (1969), 212, 236, estimates that in the 1930s, the area of cultivated land per capita was 3 *mu* in Shandong and 4 *mu* in Hebei. Second, John Lossing Buck (1937B), 300, 416, 420, reports that the average size of the farm household in the "Winter Wheat-Kaoliang Area," which included Shandong, Hebei, and Henan, was 6.7 persons, and that 85% of all households in this area were on farms. Therefore, doing the calculations, 3 *mu* (Shandong) or 4 *mu* (Hebei) per person, times 6.7 persons, divided by 0.85 yields an average cultivated area of 23.6 *mu* per farm in Shandong and 30.7 *mu* per farm in Hebei.

Jehol, Fengtian, Jilin, and Heilongjiang.[17] The results of these surveys were reported separately for each village in 16 standard tables, showing the composition, history, budget, landownership, land use, and other details for each household, and a brief history of the village from the time of its settlement. For the purpose of our analysis, the survey villages have been organized into five regions as shown in Map 7. Region 1 includes sites in Jehol and the Liao River basin that received migrants beginning in the 17th and early 18th centuries. Region 2 is the central plain of Jilin, which became the focus of settlement during the 19th century. Region 3, surrounding Harbin, began to receive migrants after 1860. Region 4 extends to the northern and eastern frontiers that were occupied only in the late 19th and early 20th centuries. The northern-most site, Aihui on the Heilongjiang River, was settled by soldiers and enforced workers in the 17th century, a history that makes it unique and justifies placing it by itself in Region 5.

The figures from these survey sites show the steady increase in farm-land, actual or potential, that was available to migrants who made their way north. By the 1930s, the average area of cultivated land per farm household in Shandong (24 *mu*) and Hebei (27 *mu*) was somewhat less than in southern Manchuria—Kotoku Region 1 (37 *mu*) and Region 2 (34 *mu*)—but much less than in northern Manchuria—Region 3 (82 *mu*) and Region 4 (122 *mu*).[18] Even more telling was the amount of arable, but as yet unreclaimed, land in each region. By the 18th century, there was virtually no arable virgin land remaining in Shandong or Hebei—or at least none that could be exploited with existing technologies.[19] Later, as the population increased, conditions in these two provinces grew worse. By contrast, in the 1930s, more than half of all potential farmland in Man-churia still awaited the plow, while the percentage of arable land that re-mained uncultivated increased along a gradient from south to north—27% in Fengtian, 52% in Jilin, and 68% in Heilongjiang.[20] Of course, the description of land as "arable but uncultivated" is open to challenge, since its arability must be demonstrated by successful farming, which

[17] See bibliography for full citation of the Kotoku surveys, which are also described in Ramon Myers (1976), 593n. Each of the Kotoku survey teams focused on one site in each of 37 separate counties. Since some sites included two or more neighboring villages, the total number of villages, 42, is slightly larger than the number of sites. In describing these surveys, we will treat each site as a single village and use the terms, site and village, interchangeably.

[18] These averages are calculated using data in *Kotoku gannendo*, Table 6, and *Kotoku sannendo*, Table 7.

[19] Dwight Perkins (1969), 236.

[20] These percentages are calculated using data in *Manchoukuo Yearbook, 1934*, 237.

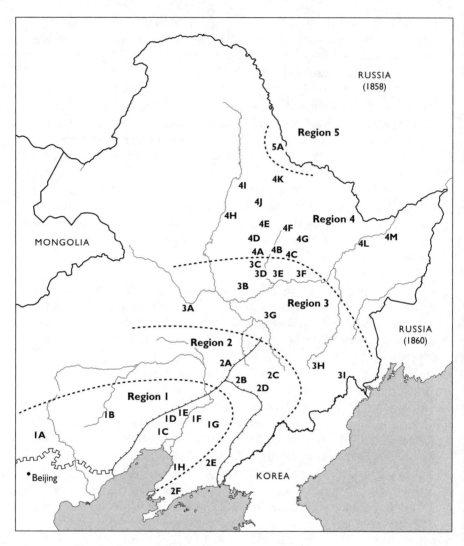

RUSSIA
(1858)

Region 5

5A

4K

4I

4J

4H

4E   4F

4D   4G

MONGOLIA

4A 4B 4C

3C

3D 3E 3F

3B

3A

Region 3

3G

Region 2

2A

2B   2C

2D

Region 1

1B

1D 1E

1F 1G

1C

1A

1H   2E

•Beijing

2F

KOREA

Region 4

4L   4M

RUSSIA
(1860)

3H

3I

MAP 7. Kotoku Survey Sites

Map 7 Legend

Region and Site	Location	Source and Site Number (S = *Kotoku Sannendo*; G = *Kotoku Gannendo*)	Region and Site	Location	Source and Site Number (S = *Kotoku Sannendo*; G = *Kotoku Gannendo*)
1A	Fengning	S-20	3F	Bayan	G-6
1B	Ningcheng	S-21	3G	Yushu	S-7
1C	Panshan	S-19	3H	Dunhua	S-5
1D	Heishan	S-18	3I	Yanji	S-8
1E	Xinmin	S-14	4A	Qinggang	G-7
1F	Liaozhong	S-12	4B	Wangkui	G-2
1G	Liaoyang	S-11	4C	Suihua	G-3
1H	Gaiping	S-13	4D	Mingshui	G-14
2A	Lishu	S-15	4E	Baiquan	G-13
2B	Xifeng	S-16	4F	Hailun	G-1
2C	Panshi	S-6	4G	Qingcheng	G-4
2D	Hailong	S-17	4H	Fuyu	G-11
2E	Fengcheng	S-10	4I	Nahe	G-12
2F	Zhuanghe	S-9	4J	Keshan	G-15
3A	Taonan	S-2	4K	Longzhen	G-16
3B	Zhaozhou	G-10	4L	Huachuan	S-3
3C	Anda	G-9	4M	Fujin	S-4
3D	Lanxi	G-8	5A	Aihui	S-1
3E	Hulan	G-5			

had not yet occurred. One way to test the accuracy of estimates made during the 1930s is to compare the percentage of land under cultivation in these provinces then (1934) and later (1990), when the reclamation of all or almost all arable land in this region was complete. After adjusting for changes in the boundaries of these provinces, this comparison shows that the earlier estimates were essentially correct.[21]

At the same time that the balance between population and farmland in north China was worsening, natural disasters could turn hardship to desperation. During the great famine of 1743–44, the Qing government, then operating at peak efficiency, was able to import grain into Hebei and Shandong from the Yangzi Valley and areas outside the Great Wall.[22] In the even more devastating drought-famine of 1876–79, however, when the capacities of the regime to store and move grain were much reduced, the death toll spiraled, reportedly exceeding 10

[21] 1934: *Manchoukuo Yearbook, 1934,* 237. 1990: U.S. Department of Agriculture (1992), Table 6; and *Encyclopedia Britannica*.

[22] Pierre-Etienne Will (1990), 153–58, 170–71.

million people in five northern provinces.[23] "All that my eyes could see were those thin and emaciated human figures," reported the imperial commissioner for famine relief in Shaanxi province, "and all that my ears could hear were the howls of males and screams of females. . . . Sometimes my cart had to detour in order to avoid rolling over human skeletons which piled up on the highways."[24] At the height of the famine in 1876, nearly a million refugees fled to Manchuria by land and sea.[25]

There are limits on the degree to which material conditions—the distribution of population, land, and other resources—can be used to explain migration. The documented decline in cultivated land per capita in Shandong and Hebei occurred almost entirely between 1766 and 1893, after which there was relatively little change, at least until 1933.[26] But the migration northward increased only modestly during the earlier period and then quite sharply in the second. This suggests that the worsening of the man-land ratio was not sufficient, and certainly not decisive, in explaining the move north. Natural disasters also had mixed effects on migration. A minority of wealthy people with the means to survive a famine might be able to profit from the troubles of their neighbors, and thus prefer to stay and defend their growing assets. Conversely, the most impoverished members of the community might be too weakened by starvation or disease, too poor to pay for the trip, or too demoralized to make decisions of any type. Surveys conducted during the 1930s and interviews with former migrants show that it was rarely the poorest peasants who moved or the poorest districts that provided the largest number of migrants.[27] The decision to migrate often depended more on the particular situation of an individual or family than on the general conditions of a village or region as a whole. The encouragement of a cousin who had gone to Manchuria and returned could make more difference than the appearance of a swarm of locusts.

[23] Paul Bohr (1972), xv, 13–15; Lillian Li (1982), 687.

[24] From the *Shaanxi tongzhi gao*, Ho Ping-ti (1959), 231.

[25] CIGC, *Reports on Trade* (1876), 8, cited in Thomas Gottschang and Diana Lary (2000), 47.

[26] Dwight Perkins (1969), 207, 212, 234–36.

[27] A survey conducted by the National Agricultural Research Bureau in 1935, cited in Thomas Gottschang and Diana Lary (2000), 7–8, found that 49.5% of emigrant families owned 0–5 *mu* of land, while another 37.4% owned 6–10 *mu*. A separate survey of 150 refugee households, carried out in 1928, found that 88% owned between 5–15 *mu*. According to Gottschang and Lary, some of the richest counties in Shandong produced the most migrants, while the poorest counties produced few.

3. Transportation

Migration depends on a means of moving, and during most of the Qing, travel to and through Manchuria was difficult. Migrants from north China had to cross formidable barriers on land or sea and make their way along primitive roads, through thick forests and brush. In summer, when monsoon rains turned the region into one vast swamp, progress was virtually impossible, whereas during the winter, when most seasonal workers moved back and forth, the roads were frozen hard and the migrants could walk or, if able to pay, ride one of the many carts used in trade with the hinterland. On the whole, travel for pioneers was hard, and the scope of their journeys limited, until 1903, when the opening of the railroads began to carry large numbers of migrants rapidly and to more distant frontiers.

Travel overland began with the Yanshan Mountains, north of Beijing. The Emperor's Road from Beijing to the Summer Palace in Jehol was one of the best kept thoroughfares in China, yet the British ambassador, Lord Macartney, who passed this way at the end of the 18th century, found it "so steep and rough" that he had to be transferred to a palanquin, while his carriage was hauled piecemeal over the rocky crags.[28] Travelers could avoid the Yanshan Mountains by going east, along the coast through Shanhaiguan. But this route had its own travails. On the banks of the lower Liao, alluvial deposits on a sinking valley formed a mudflat or marsh, appropriately dubbed the "Southern Great Wilderness."[29] One traveler, who had made the trip before, could only look forward to this part of his journey "with a degree of horror."[30]

Upon entering Manchuria, the 19th-century traveler discovered a network of roads, that included major trunk lines from Beijing via Shanhaiguan and from the port of Newchwang to Fengtian (Map 1), the capital of southern Manchuria and distribution center for trade from that point on. The oldest and safest route northward was from Fengtian to Jilin City,[31] east of the Willow Palisade and the Sungari River, and thus

[28] Sir George Staunton (1797), 176. See also, Sven Hedin (1933), 12; and John Hedley (1910), 29–30.
[29] Zhao Songqiao (1986), 116.
[30] A. Michie (1863), 158.
[31] Three problems regarding names of Chinese cities that arise in this study are demonstrated here: First, are changes in names of particular cities, such as Fengtian, which was originally called Shengjing, and later became Fengtian, Mukden, and finally Shenyang. In such cases, I use whatever name was current at the time or used in the source cited. Second, is the use of the same name for a city and the region surrounding it, as Fengtian or

beyond the reach of the Mongols. At Jilin, the road branched in four directions: northwest, along the Sungari to Petuna; north to Alachuke, an old Manchuria city, where the road again split, north to Hulan, or east to Sanxing; east to Ninguta, thence to Hunchun; and finally southeast to the Korean border. With the development of a major trading center at Kuanchengzi on the Yitong River (near the present site of Changchun), a second road was open from Fengtian due north to that city, and then on to Petuna. Petuna could also be reached by a westerly route, from Xinmin on the lower Liao, up the river to Faku and Zhengjiatun (Shuangliao), then overland to Petuna. From Petuna there was only one road north, through Tsitsihar and Mergen to Aihui on the Heilongjiang River. The westernmost route bypassed the central plain entirely, crossing the Great Wall at Xifengkou and the Tao'er River west of Taonan(fu), and then on to Tsitsihar. Finally, there were roads from Newchwang to the southeast through Gaizhou to Jinxian at the tip of the Liaodong Peninsula or eastward via Fenghuangcheng to the Korean border.[32]

But what roads! Prior to 1924, when the first modern intercity highway was opened to traffic along the 55 kilometers from Port Arthur (Lushun) to Dairen (Dalian),[33] a "road" in Manchuria was simply a cart track, established by necessity, reinforced by use, and eventually abandoned when the trail became impassable and the next carter to pass that way edged his mule a few steps to one side, cutting a new track alongside the old. What made the process of continuous road-building and destruction both necessary and wretched was (and still is) the unfortunate combination of soil and climate. Manchuria's alluvial and loess soils are high in clay, low in sand and organic content, and thus drain poorly and form a compact mass when wet. The problem of flooding is exacerbated by the concentration of rainfall in summer and the flat topography of the plain. Thus, tracks laid down in the spring sink into pools of mud in July and August, making travel by any conveyance virtually impossible. The first cold snap freezes these ruts, creating a bumpy obstacle course for early winter traffic. Finally, by late winter, the frozen ground becomes smooth, hard, slick, and dangerous. Since the Manchurian plain lacks natural stone, there was no material to

---

Jilin, which are names of both provinces and their capital cities. When there is possible confusion, I will attach the word "city," as Jilin City, although this does not correspond to the Chinese. A third problem arises in the choice of romanization. In cases where a traditional spelling is widely recognized and used, such as Mukden, I have adopted it. Otherwise, I have transliterated the Chinese characters, using Pinyin.

[32] Alexander Williamson (1870), 30–31; CER (1924), 373–75.

[33] Baron Sakatani (1932) 91.

reinforce vulnerable lowlands, much less construct a proper road over any appreciable distance. For centuries, Manchurian travelogues have paid homage to the ordeal of overland travel.[34] Even today, travel through this region during the rainy season is an adventure.

Travelers stuck to the roads, despite their defects, because the rivers were in many ways worse. At first glance, one is struck by the enormous reach and volume of Manchuria's rivers. The Heilongjiang-Sungari-Nenjiang system ranks second in China, behind the mighty Yangzi, in drainage area and annual discharge, providing a course for timber and other products coming out of the mountains, water for irrigation and transportation for agricultural goods across the plans, and a highway for people and produce to the sea.[35] But closer examination reveals the shortcomings of this system. The Heilongjiang, Nenjiang and Sungari Rivers and their tributaries originate in highlands that lack direct contact with China proper, flow north and east still further from the centers of population and commerce, and exit into the Sea of Okhutsk, one of the coldest and least hospitable outlets of any of the world's major rivers.

A second problem is the uneven depth and pace of these rivers. The Sungari flows swiftly from the uplands of southeastern Manchuria to Jilin City, and again eastward across the border between Jilin and Heilongjiang provinces, But in its midsection, on the broad plain from Jilin to the point where it joins the Nenjiang, the Sungari flattens and slows to a muddy crawl, at best a mile wide and 3–4 feet deep, in places a mass of capillaries ten miles wide, and at worst a "vast swamp." Both the Nenjiang and the Liao are wide, shallow, slow-moving, silt-laden rivers that cross flat alluvial plains, providing limited scope for travel and commerce. Finally, during much of the year, all of these rivers are frozen: from November to March in the south, and from October to early May in the far north.[36] From the point of view of human utility, Manchuria has one of the largest and least functional river systems in the world.

[34] The earliest such account by the Jesuit Priest, Ferdinand Verbiest, who accompanied the Kangxi Emperor to Jilin in the summer of 1682, appears in Père d'Orleans (1971), 106–7,113–14. For 19th- and early-20th-century accounts, see: A. Michie (1863), 158–66; Alexander Williamson (1870), 31–32, Henry James (1888), 386; Francis Younghusband (1898), 42–43; Alexander Hosie (1904), 237; Arthur Sowerby (1919), 79; Arthur Sowerby (1922), 18; CER (1924), 373–77; and Baron Sakatani (1932), 87–91. The tragicomedy of a great "quagmire" appears in the novel *Tales of Hulan River* by Xiao Hong. See Hsiao Hung (1979), 118–23.

[35] Zhao Songqiao (1986), 99.

[36] For accounts of Manchurian rivers by 19th century travelers, see: Alexander Williamson (1870), 52; Francis Younghusband (1898), 34; Henry James (1888), 296; and Alexander Hosie (1904), 236–37.

The route and method of travel changed with the opening of the Manchurian railroads in 1903, and the growing reliance on steam over sail from the late 19th century on. During the 1920s, three out of four migrants arrived by steamship or junk, most through the port of Dairen, others by way of Yingkou and Andong, while the remainder came overland, walking or by rail to Mukden.[37] Although there are no comparable statistics for the Qing period, travel by sea would have been primarily through Yingkou into the Liao River basin, while a much larger proportion of migrants must have gone on foot. Travel overland was always difficult, because the roads were long and hard, the established population was hostile to poor, hungry refugees who competed for land and jobs, and the migrants had to find food and provisions along the way. But in the early years, this was the most direct route between north China and the Liao, which was the first stop for most migrants.

Railroads attracted migrants in several ways. First, construction of the railroads required large numbers of unskilled workers and gave rise to a secondary economy of producers and suppliers of food, construction materials, and fuel. Several of the upswings in migration (Figure 2) were associated with the building of new railroads. The construction of railroads consumed an enormous volume of timber for sleepers, bridges, tunnels, and other facilities, and to drive the wood-burning steam engines of the Chinese Eastern Railway. After the southern branch of the CER was taken over by the Japanese, the South Manchuria Railway, as it came to be known, changed over to coal, prompting the development of coal-mining, another industry and employer in the south.

Second, the railroads transported migrants more quickly, comfortably and easily to more distant places. Railroads ran rapidly and reliably in all seasons and passed through or near fertile and unreclaimed wasteland. Authorities in charge of the railroads came to appreciate the value of Chinese migrants: to the Chinese, they were a strategic asset in the battle to secure Manchuria against foreign rivals; to the Japanese and Russians, they were a market for imports and suppliers of exports, which paid the freight and made imperialism economically viable. To encourage immigration and settlement, during the 1920s, the

[37] Franklin Ho (1931), 4–5, reports that during the period 1923–29, migrants entered Manchuria through the following ports: Dairen, 52%; Yingkow, 16%; Andong, 6%; Mukden, 26%.

Manchurian railroads reduced their lowest fares and in some cases offered free transportation to women, children, and old people.[38]

Third, railroads encouraged migration to distant places by providing a measure of security and the means to ship supplies in and exports out. A landless peasant might be willing to reclaim land in a remote area, provided that he could avoid or pay off the bandits. An especially desperate or enterprising peasant might raise opium, a cash crop that could be used to buy protection from bandits or soldiers (the two being largely interchangeable), and the surplus smuggled to markets in China proper. But the establishment of a permanent frontier community required the physical security and access to markets in bulk goods, which depended on the railroad.

Finally, railroads were the harbinger of a modern urban and industrial economy that provided jobs for migrants who were making the transition, not only from China proper to Manchuria, but from countryside to city and from the farm to mines, factories, and other urban trades. The infusion of Japanese capital and Tokyo's program to build a modern industrial base in the puppet state of Manchukuo commenced in 1936. Even before then, however, the growth in international trade fueled the development of the modern sector in Manchuria at a rate exceeding that in any other part of China.

4. Dangers and hazards

The frontier, in Manchuria as elsewhere, was fraught with peril. By far the most notorious adversary was the tiger. The 18th-century French missionary, Jean Baptiste Du Halde, reported that for soldiers assigned to Eastern Tartary, the "chief danger is from wild beasts, and especially tigers, against which they must be continually on the guard: If any one is missing, after the signal for the return of the troop, they conclude him devoured by the beasts, or lost thro' his own carelessness. . . ."[39] Henry James, traveling in the same region in the 1880s, reported no encounters with tigers, but he did come up against other animals which he found "no less ferocious":

I have not words to express to you the multitude of mosquitoes, gnats, wasps, and gadflies which attacked us at every step. Each of us, armed with a horse's tail fixed on an iron prong, endeavoured to strike them, and this weak defence

[38] C. Walter Young (1928A), 247–50.
[39] Jean Baptiste Du Halde (1741), 98.

only served to render the enemy more vicious in his attacks. As for me, I was completely beaten, without strength either to advance or protect myself from the stinging of these insects; or if, at times, I raised my hand to my face, I crushed ten of twelve with one blow.[40]

In most cases, however, the greatest danger came from other human beings. "In the Ussurian taiga," warned the 19th century Russian explorer V. K. Arseniev, "one must expect at times to meet with a wild beast, but the most dangerous meeting of all is with a man. . . . When a man sees another man in the forest the first thing he does is to hide behind a tree, and the second to have his rifle at the ready."[41] Jilin, in the view of another experienced traveler, the British consul at Newchwang, Alexander Hosie, "is, *par excellence*, the province of outlaws and ex-soldiers, who, well mounted and armed, collect into bands, and, issuing from their mountain fastnesses. . . , swoop down on villages, caravans of goods and travellers and plunder and rob without mercy. Even the great trade highways of the provinces are invested with them. . . ."[42]

While the threats were real, however, it is unlikely that pioneers in Manchuria and Inner Mongolia faced dangers as great as those on the Russian steppe or the American Great Plains. The unification of Manchuria and co-optation or defeat of the Mongols removed organized resistance to the Qing north of the Great Wall. There were no mounted bands in this region comparable to the Crimean Tartars or American Indians. So long as they did not wander too far afield, migrants in Manchuria were, if not entirely safe, at least safer than pioneers in other times and places.

This was the northern frontier that awaited the Chinese during the Qing and Republican periods. On the whole, the material conditions—the distribution of population, cultivable land and other resources, and the modes of transportation linking the two—made the north seem attractive and the method of getting there difficult, but not prohibitively so. There were obstacles and risks, of course, but not notably more numerous or serious than those confronting other pioneers. Indeed, one might well ask: Given these conditions, why did peasants on the crowded and disaster-prone north China plain not make the move earlier, in larger numbers, and to more distant locations? Part of the answer lies in the subjective considerations that influenced the view Chinese peasants had of the world beyond the village and of themselves.

[40] Henry James (1888), 425.
[41] V. K. Arseniev (1941), 69–70.
[42] Alexander Hosie (1904), 169.

B. Subjective Factors

Several factors described in the literature, both contemporary and ret-rospective, on this subject may have made peasants in Shandong and Hebei reluctant to leave home, even for the more abundant land and greater opportunities that awaited them in the north. The economic and social structures of north China made villagers insular in outlook and at the same time able to sustain their small-farm economy even un-der the most difficult circumstances. Allegiance to one's ancestors and religious beliefs that favored local objects over universal principles pro-vided a pull toward home without any countervailing push toward the remote or unknown. The common culture, at least in the eyes of foreign observers, placed little value on curiosity, adventure, or risk, and priv-ileged the familiar over the strange. All of the habits of mind that were common among villagers in north China seem to have favored the impulse to stay rather than go.

The small family farms and agricultural villages of north China were stable, insular, and resistant to change. Compared to south China, the north had a low level of commercialization, few handicraft industries, low rates of tenancy, limited social differentiation, and few opportuni-ties for individuals or families to rise in wealth, status, and power. Housing was concentrated on high ground to avoid floods, irrigation that depended on individual wells provided no stimulus for the forma-tion of water-control societies, lineage and clan structures were weak, and village leaders were commoners who differed only slightly from their neighbors. These characteristics contributed to the insularity of the village, the absence of channels for social or geographic mobility, and the lack of contact with a larger world. In all these respects, the vil-lages of north China differed from those in the south, where the oppo-site conditions contributed to a higher level of social and geographic mobility, in what G. William Skinner has called the "standard market-ing community." Compared with Chinese in other parts of the empire, the villager of north China had less experience beyond the walls of his village and less motivation to seek it out.[43]

In surprising ways, material conditions in north China may also have discouraged migration. Although land was scarce, it was equitably dis-tributed; barring natural disaster, most farm families had enough land to work and enough food to eat for most of their members most of

[43]Philip Huang (1985), 219–48, makes the case for the insularity of the north China vil-lages. This case is supported by the material presented in: Sidney Gamble (1954), 209–12, and Ramon Myers (1970), passim.

the time. Peasants in Hebei and Shandong lived on a narrow margin and had little hope of improving their situation, individually or as a whole. But the small family farm was remarkably resilient, surviving even, or especially, when its landholdings shrank and family size increased to the point of "involution," or an excess of labor for the given area of land.[44] The system was not evolving in a direction that promised a higher standard of living for future generations. But it was remarkably effective in sustaining the family farm, squeezing peasants onto the margins of existence, and keeping them there.

The most important religious impulse in rural north China— "religious" in the sense that it addressed fundamental questions about the nature and purpose of life, death, and destiny—was the focus on ancestors and the continuity of the family line. "The northern Chinese peasants have, through the generations, developed a deep-rooted passion for the place of their ancestors," noted the anthropologist Martin Yang, who grew up in a village on the southern coast of Shandong. "They cannot resist the idea of coming back home. . . ."[45] Chinese have little feeling for China as a nation, Yang observed, but would fight to the last ditch to "protect our ancestors' graveyards."[46]

Running parallel to concerns about the ancestors and the family line were other manifestations of a spiritual kind that served to reinforce the insularity of village life. First, was the worship of local deities or folk gods, beginning at the lowest level of the divine hierarchy with the family "kitchen god," working up through the "earth god" [*tudi shen*] who oversaw the neighborhood or village, to the *Guandi*, who represented a larger sphere. The family, clan, neighborhood, or village ministered to its god(s) through temples that were financed and managed by wealthy and influential members of the community, and included all who belonged to the particular locale. The festivals, ceremonies, fairs, and operas sponsored by the temple drew the community together around the symbol of its religious identity. On her birthday, the local goddess might be taken out to visit a neighboring temple, after which she was returned to her niche at the end of the lane. Peasants who left the village had to leave the goddess, the temple, and the temple community behind.[47]

[44] The concept of "involution," which was developed by Clifford Geertz in his study of Indonesia, has been applied to rural China by Philip Huang (1985 and 1990).

[45] Martin Yang (1945), 200.

[46] Ibid., 164. See also ibid., 46, 88.

[47] For descriptions of folk religion in rural North China, see: Arthur Smith (1899), 98–105; Martin Yang (1945), 197; and Joseph Esherick (1987), 63–67.

There were, in addition to folk gods, religious activities and institutions that extended beyond the villages of north China and exposed villagers to a larger world. Societies dedicated to conducting pilgrimages to the sacred mountain of Tai Shan in Shandong or other revered sites gave many peasants an opportunity to venture beyond the neighboring market town. During the 19th and 20th centuries, millennial sects such as the White Lotus, Red Spears, or Boxers united villages and villagers across northern and eastern China on behalf of some larger cause. As studies by Elizabeth Perry (1980) and Joseph Esherick (1987) have shown, however, these movements focused on the acquisition or defense of power and resources within a particular locale, region, or the empire as a whole. None called on followers to go beyond the boundaries of China, convert the barbarians, conquer new territory, or build a refuge in the wilderness.[48] In contrast to those Western religions that have sent and continue to send missionaries and other adherents abroad, in China, the devotion to ancestors, folk gods, and millennial causes served to strengthen the centripetal force of family, village, and locale and to discourage crusades or missions into the unknown.

These factors did little to encourage an interest in people and things that lay beyond the horizon—a fact noted by many foreign visitors. The testimony of Europeans and Americans on the attitudes of Chinese should be taken with a grain or two of salt. Many foreigners went (and still go) to China with motives—adventure, curiosity, or the desire to convert the natives to their beliefs—that cause them to be disappointed when the Chinese fail to respond as they hope. Still, it is striking how many foreigners who traveled or worked in north China during the 19th and early-20th centuries found the people they met devoid of interest in the world outside their own neighborhood and personal experience. Walter Mallory observed that the Chinese had a particular "love of home and unwillingness to leave it for new fields." Every year, workers left Shandong for Manchuria to work temporarily on farmland that they could have purchased outright at a very low price. "It cannot be said that the people do not realize the benefits," Mallory noted, "for they see them with their own eyes and share in them for a short time every summer; but they are unwilling to change their homes and their mode of life."[49] "Anything beyond a man's own town or the road he works on has no interest for him," said the experienced Asian traveler Francis

[48] Elizabeth Perry (1980) has described the alternative strategies of predators (Nian) and protectors (Red Spears).
[49] Walter Mallory (1928), 19–20.

Younghusband, who along with his companion, Henry James, provided the earliest and most detailed accounts of Manchuria in the late-19th century. "How different all this is from what one sees in the bazaars of Central Asia, where the merchants—some from India, some from Turkestan, some from Afghanistan—meet and talk over the countries they have travelled over and the state of the roads, and where a traveller can always obtain a fair general idea of any caravan route now in use!"[50] "The Chinese farmer prefers his traditional environment, and it is only by force of compelling circumstances that he will go abroad," Walter Young, the leading foreign observer of Chinese migration to Manchuria during the 1920s, notes. "Not being an adventurer of the Western buccaneer type of the 15th, 16th, and 17th centuries, the Chinese forsakes his home principally for economic motives, and the farmer from the necessity of seeking a livelihood under circumstances less rigorous than are to be found at home."[51] "Wanderlust, which is characteristic of the Westerner," Young concluded, "is not a characteristic of the Chinese."[52]

In 1980, Philip Huang visited villages on the Shandong-Hebei border, whose history he had studied through Japanese surveys conducted in the 1930s. Based on his previous research and his reading of the work of William Skinner, who describes rural China as a world of interdependent "marketing communities," Huang expected to find in this region of north China a similarly open, mobile, cosmopolitan society. But in this he was disappointed. The old men Huang interviewed had grown up in this area during the 1920s and gone to school with children from their own and the neighboring villages. As adults, they visited markets and tea shops, where they ran into their former classmates and other acquaintances from the surrounding area. Yet these men *never* (sic) stopped to chat with anyone not of their own village, even people living in the next village, which was located a mere 30 yards (sic) away. The fact that one should talk only to fellow villagers, Huang discovered, was "something taken for granted, so obvious that it needed no articulation."[53]

C. The Compromise

Peasants of north China who faced hardship and wanted to improve their lives were caught between opposing forces: on one side was the

[50] Francis Younghusband (1904), 61.
[51] C. Walter Young (1928A), 244.
[52] C. Walter Young (1927A), 617.
[53] Philip Huang (1985), 221–22.

imbalance in material conditions that made migration to Manchuria seem attractive; on the other was the compulsion to stay home, in the village, with the family, near the graves of the ancestors. If the choice had been left to the individual, it would have been difficult, even terrible, but one can imagine young men, women, or couples deciding either to stick it out, take care of the old folks and make their peace at home, or take the plunge, move out, and hope to build a better life for themselves and their children in a new land. But the choice was not left to the individual, and the most common outcome was neither to stay nor to go. Rather, it was made where the control of resources and power over individuals resided, in the family, and in most cases the family chose to send its spare men out to forage, to make a brief tour in the land of plenty, and return with as much treasure as time and trouble allowed.

In 1984, Diana Lary interviewed 58 Shandong natives who had migrated to Manchuria at some point during their lives, after which they had returned to Shandong or some other part of China proper. For the vast majority of these men, the driving force behind the decision to migrate was "the deep and unquestioned commitment . . . to aid their families by any possible means."[54] According to Lary, the typical migrant was a young man, tapped by his family to work for a time in Manchuria, in order to reduce the number of mouths that had to be fed and earn extra money, which would be sent home in remittances or brought back by the migrant on his return and used to buy land, pay for the young man's marriage, bury his father, or contribute in some other way to the family fortune. Most migrants and their families thought of migration as a tour of duty—a domestic alternative to military service—rather than a permanent departure from home. The young man was ready to migrate when he reached his mid- to late-teens. He was likely to be recruited and receive a recruitment bonus, or "comfort-the-family fee" [*anjiafei*], the first of what they hoped would be many such payments. Typically, the recruiter was a man from the same or some nearby village, who had gone to Manchuria, found a job, and been sent back by his employer to recruit more workers—in the same fashion that a soldier on temporary leave from his unit might look for recruits in his hometown. In fact, many young men accepted the invitation to go to Manchuria, because they knew that the next recruiter to visit the village might be a soldier who would make them an offer that they, or their families, could not refuse! To serve as a migrant was a passage to

54 Thomas Gottschang and Diana Lary (2000), 9.

adulthood, a way for the boy to join the men who were responsible for the family's fate and thus pay his dues.

The pattern of land tenure in rural north China reinforced the power of the family and its motive for sending sons to engage in temporary labor elsewhere. During the 1930s, over 80 percent of rural households in this region owned some or all of the land they worked, giving them control over the production, consumption, and thus the lives of their charges.[55] Partible inheritance, the rule by which the family estate was divided equally among male heirs of the next generation, reinforced the practice of temporary migration in two ways: first, as the property was divided into smaller pieces, each family unit had to find additional means of support; and second, after leaving home, the migrant knew that he would have to return to claim his inheritance.[56] Daughters were equally dependent on their success in marrying into another household and producing sons who could provide for them in old age. In this regard, Mark Wyman's study of return migration from America to Europe is instructive, for it shows that the goal of most "remigrants" was to purchase land back home and that success depended on the ability of the migrant worker to amass the maximum amount of money in the minimum amount of time and on whether or not land was available for purchase in the native village. Remigrants returned to areas were land was held in small parcels, but not to those dominated by large estates. The European practice of primogeniture worked against remigration, since most migrants had no inherited land to come back to, and estates were not always broken up for sale.[57] Conversely, the fragmentation of land among large numbers of smallholders and the practice of partible inheritance made north China, like similar areas of Europe, an ideal supplier of sojourners and haven for those who returned.

The departure and return of migrants followed the seasons, a timing dictated not only by choice, but by the climatic conditions and agricultural technology of the northern territories. Enormous effort was required to plant, cultivate, and harvest a single crop during Manchuria's short, hot summers, while there was little to do on farms during the long, cold winters. Owing to the shortage of fertilizer (a function of the sparse population), intensive weeding was required to remove the competition for nutrients, leaving little slack between sowing and

---

[55] John Lossing Buck (1937A), 34.
[56] Ibid., 71–72, 105, 134.
[57] Mark Wyman (1993), 129–32.

reaping.[58] Finally, primitive technology offered few laborsaving devices. Although the coming and going of the farmworkers followed the seasons, and most preferred to make their stay as brief as possible, the travel time was so long and the need to earn sufficient sums so great that most remained in the north for several years. Monthly figures for arrivals and departures at the port of Dairen during the years 1923–29, show a large number of arrivals in March and April, after the New Year Festival and before spring planting, and a corresponding bulge in departures from October to December, after the harvest and in time to get back home for New Year. Both outward and return trips occurred, as noted above, when the roads were frozen and passable. According to a separate study carried out during the same period, however, only ten percent of returning migrants had been in Manchuria for one year or less, the principal reason being that it was difficult to complete the round-trip and still earn enough to make the venture profitable in such a short period of time. Most migrants went north in the spring and returned south in the fall, but the intervening period was more likely to be between 2–4 years than either more or less.[59]

The evidence on migration across the Great Wall during the Qing period, while anecdotal, suggests a seasonal or temporary pattern similar to that documented during the 20th century. Edicts from the 18th and 19th centuries on the "opening" and "closing" of the border between Manchuria and China proper indicate that seasonal labor was favored by Chinese workers, Manchurian employers, and Qing authorities, who discouraged settlement of a permanent Chinese population north of the Wall.[60] In the 1860s, according to a native of Penglai, a port on the north coast of Shandong, "From almost every family a son went to Manchuria to seek his fortune . . . These wanderers came home at New Year's time to give their gain to their families. If unsuccessful, the great new country swallowed them up and they were heard of no more."[61] Martin Yang offered a similar account of his village on the southern coast of Shandong: "Almost all the single men who went to Manchuria, or elsewhere, have come back sooner or later after they have made some money. They come back to marry, to buy land, and to settle down."[62]

[58] *Kotoku gannendo*, site 10, reports on agricultural practices in one village in Heilongjiang, where yields increased by 100% or more, after weeding had been increased from one to three times during the growing season.

[59] Franklin Ho (1931), 3, 9.

[60] On seasonal migration during the Qing, see: Cheng Chongde (1990), 175–76; Cheng Chongde (1991), 27–28; Diao Shuren (1993), 212; Liang Bing (1991), 50.

[61] Ida Pruitt (1945), 7.

[62] Martin C. Yang (1945), 200.

Finally, the nature of this mission is confirmed by the testimony of those who made the trip—almost all of whom said that they did not want to go. When asked the reasons that they or their forebears left home, the vast majority of migrants and settlers in Manchuria responded that they were pushed by hardship or disaster rather than pulled by the promise of a better life abroad. In 1931, the Nankai University Economic Research Institute interviewed the heads of 1,149 migrant households in Manchuria. Their reasons for moving (Table 7), either personal or remembered as family history, were overwhelmingly material and negative: more than two-thirds cited "difficult living conditions" or other economic hardships, such as too little land, too many people and not enough to eat, accumulated debts, the lack of family property, or business failure; and most of the rest said they moved to escape banditry and warfare, natural disasters, or both. Only a handful expressed any positive view of the possibilities in Manchuria, such as the chance to "get rich" or the attraction of "going abroad."[63]

The Nankai survey included many migrants who arrived with the flood of refugees in the late 1920s, so it might be argued that the respondents harbored especially negative views and motives. But evidence from another survey, conducted by the Japanese Manchukuo government in 1935, suggests that these opinions were shared by migrants of both earlier and later times.[64] Most of the respondents in the Japanese survey were descendants of migrants who had arrived in Manchuria in the 19th century or before and knew the reasons for their forebears' initial move from China proper only as family history that had been passed down from generation to generation. Yet their responses were remarkably consistent with one another and with those of more recent migrants and refugees. They or their predecessors had moved to Manchuria primarily to escape "hardship," especially the shortage of land, natural disasters such as flood, drought or famine, and banditry, while only a minority cited positive reasons, such as the prospects for obtaining land, work, money, or a more peaceful life. According to C. Walter Young, an American who monitored Chinese migration to Manchuria during the late 1920s, Chinese left home only when forced by "the compelling necessity for a living. Food and clothing, not gold and finery, bring the Chinese immigrant laborer to Manchuria."[65]

[63]Survey by the Nankai University, Economic Research Institute, 1931, cited in Wang Yaoyu (1938), 180.

[64]*Kotoku gannendo* (1936). Note: the companion survey, *Kotoku sannendo* (1936), did not ask why the family had originally moved to Manchuria.

[65]C. Walter Young (1927A), 617.

TABLE 2

Reasons given for the family's initial move from China proper
to Manchuria and subsequent move to the Kotoku survey village

	MOVE TO MANCHURIA		MOVE TO SURVEY VILLAGE
Reason	Nankai, 1931 (%)	Kotoku, 1935 (%)	Kotoku, 1935 (%)
Negative			
Hardship	68.3	55.2	18.3
Natural disaster	12.3	27.0	8.3
Banditry, war	13.1	1.6	7.7
Other	2.2		
Total	95.9	83.8	34.3
Positive			
Land	0.0	8.1	27.6
Money, jobs	0.7	4.5	10.6
Family, friends	1.2	1.1	22.1
Other	0.2	2.6	5.4
Total	2.1	16.3	65.7
Other	2.1		
TOTAL	100.0	100.0	100.0

SOURCES: Survey by the Nankai University Economic Research Institute, 1931, in Wang Yaoyu (1938), 180; *Kotoku gannendo*, Table 2, and *Kotoku sannendo*, Table 2.

Of course, for a migrant who is moving to improve his condition, a pessimistic assessment of the place he is leaving implies optimism about his destination, and vice versa. Still, the notion that the original motive for leaving China proper was negative continued to dominate the telling of family history, even by later generations whose own experience in Manchuria had been positive enough to persuade them to stay. Thus, the same respondents who said their ancestors had been driven from China by hardship or disaster, explained that the family, after arriving in Manchuria, had chosen to move to the particular village where they finally settled, for more positive reasons (Table 2).

D. Conclusion

Two factors worked in opposite directions on the peasants of north China, one driving them out, the other keeping them at home. The sum of these conflicting pressures was a compromise by which many went north, but only for a limited time and a limited purpose. Material conditions, especially the imbalance in the distribution of population and arable land, made it attractive to move from Shandong or Hebei to areas north of the Great Wall. The traditions of peasant society, ties to the family and the locale, made it equally compelling to stay at home. The compromise between these competing forces was struck at the vortex of power and meaning, where all the important decisions were made: the family. Migrants were young men, sent by their families for a tour of duty that was supposed to last for season or at most a few years, during which they were to send home remittances, and after which they would return with the balance of their earnings to buy land, marry, settle down, and continue the family line. Most completed the mission as planned. Those who stayed or got stuck became the new Manchurians.

This experience left its mark on Chinese settlements in Manchuria and Inner Mongolia. The reluctance to leave home, the temporary nature of the assignment, the continued ties to family and village, and the determination to return limited the commitment of the pioneers and militated against the formation of a new identity and culture based on their engagement with new environments, neighbors, and circumstances. Not going to stay, wanting to stay, or expecting to stay, Chinese migrants invested little in what they took to be temporary quarters. As time passed and life in the new surroundings became more permanent, the attachments to home and native place helped to make settler society more cohesive within and less open to contact with the world outside.

CHAPTER 5

Networks

THIS CHAPTER CONTINUES THE STORY of the migrants, after they left their villages in north China and made their way through Manchuria to the outer edges of settlement on the expanding frontier. These were the young men sent by their families to find work in a neighboring territory and to return, the sooner and richer the better, so that they could get on with the task of improving life at home. Once on the road, however, they became increasingly subject to "networks" that channeled and shaped their movements. The effect of these networks was to reinforce the initial impulse that bound the migrants together and ensured their separation from the world outside. Even as they made the transition from sojourners to temporary and then permanent settlers, they remained more dedicated to their identity as members of an established society and culture than changed by their new surroundings.

Recent studies of migration have emphasized the dynamic and contingent role of networks over static and deterministic categories, such as sojourner. Labeling Chinese (or any other) migrants as sojourners implies that they embody essential features, which define their character and culture from the point of departure, through an intermediate but for them inconsequential experience, to the return home. This view of history ascribes enormous power and permanence to cultural identity and leaves little room for growth or change. To view migration, instead, as the patterns or networks that channel the movements of the migrants leaves open the possibility of choice and change at each step along the way.[1]

---

[1] See Adam McKeown (1999) on the operation of networks among Chinese, and Charles Tilly (1990) on European migration to the New World.

What is most striking about the networks that carried Chinese peasants across the Great Wall, however, is the degree to which they favored the replication of social and economic forms previously established in China proper, rather than the creation of something new. Migrants from the same province, county, or village shared a common identification and attachment. Most were recruited by people from their own locale, traveled with relatives and fellow villagers, and joined communities on the far side of the Wall where they were already known. The first stop was most likely an established settlement in southern Manchuria, a town, city, or village protected by walls and surrounded by farmland. Only after a period of adjustment did the migrant-become-settler move on to join the gradual spread northward. At each step, the force of family, community, and tradition held the migrants together, kept them tethered to their origins, and militated against the creation of distinctly new societies and cultures.

A. Pattern of Identity

1. *Origins*

Most migrants to Manchuria came from Shandong Province, and their heirs remembered and continued to identify with their native place, generations and sometimes centuries after they had lost all ties to home. Over 70% of the respondents in the Kotoku surveys, most of whom were from families that had left China more than 50 or even 100 years earlier, identified their "place of origin" [*chushendi*] as Shandong, while about half of the remainder were from neighboring Hebei (Zhili).[2] Travelers in Manchuria and Inner Mongolia during the early 20th century found whole villages of self-identified "Shandong people," who were five or six generations removed from their home province.[3] In interviews the author conducted in Manchurian and Inner Mongolian villages in 1998, most of the people who could trace their origins to China proper and sometimes entire villages called themselves Shandongese, even though no one spoke Shandong dialect, and few had ever been to Shandong, knew a relative there, or could name his or her ancestral village.[4]

---

[2] *Kotoku gannendo* and *Kotoku sannendo*, Table 2.

[3] John Hedley (1910), 155–56. Also Alexander Williamson (1870), 165–66.

[4] Of 27 Han respondents interviewed in July 1998, in villages located between Siping, Liaoning, and Dolon Nor, Inner Mongolia, 16 described the origins of their families as

This common identity played an important role in binding the migrants together, from the time they left home, throughout their journey, until after they settled down. Migrants from Shandong passing through the port of Dairen during the 1920s enjoyed the support of the "Shandong Guild," which raised money for the relief of indigent Shandongese, and provided food, lodging, and transportation to help fellow provincials complete their journey and start life in Manchuria.[5] According to Walter Young, common origins continued to shape the communities of Shandong immigrants above the Great Wall.

> The solidarity of the Chinese agricultural community of Shantung, the communal basis of organization centered in the family system, and the persistence of long-accepted standards of value and or social institutions are likewise characteristic of the pioneer society in North Manchuria. The pronunciation and idiom of the Shantung farmer's *patois* (a slight variation from the Peking dialect), his four-walled living compound, his simple farming implements, and, above all, his predisposition to live in Manchuria much as he and his ancestors in Shantung have lived, these are transplanted to North Manchurian soil. The process of this colonization has aptly been described as that of "transplantation of the entire Chinese social complex into new soil."[6]

2. Recruitment and Travel

The same forces that persuaded the peasants of north China to remain in their native villages bound those who left together at each step along the way. Some migrants signed on with professional recruiters, who worked for a Manchurian railroad, mine or factory or free-lanced as independent contractors. But strangers were suspect: If they withheld wages, gouged workers at the company store, or took their earnings in gambling, the migrant laborer had no recourse. Thus, it was far better to work for an uncle, cousin, fellow villager, or someone introduced through local connections, who had been to Manchuria, returned home to recruit among his neighbors, and could be counted on to stay with his work team during their outward voyage, tour of duty, and return.[7] "Most [migrants] have friends and relatives from their home towns who are already here, on whom they depend,"

"local" or from Jilin or Liaoning, and 9 from Shandong. In several cases, the entire village reportedly descended from migrants from the same part of Shandong.

[5] C. Walter Young (1928A), 250.

[6] C. Walter Young (1932), 349–50. See also: CER (1924), 68.

[7] C. Walter Young (1927A), 629–30, and Gottschang and Lary (2000), 60–63.

Migration. Most Chinese who migrated from Shandong or Hebei traveled by the cheapest and most direct method—on foot, *left* (5). When the number of refugees from China proper to Manchuria swelled to more than one million in 1927, many arrived by junk or steamship at the port of Dairen, *top right* (6). On their arrival in a village at the outer edge of settlement, most migrants found that land was unavailable for purchase or too expensive and became tenants, like this family in Qinggang County, Heilongjiang, *bottom right* (7).

SOURCES: No. 5: *Manchoukuo Year Book* (1934), 674. No. 6: SMR, 1st Report (1929), 14–15. No. 7: *Noson jittai chosa hokokusho* (1937), I, 3.

explained Tsao Lien-en, a Chinese scholar working in Manchuria during the late 1920s.

Usually a farmer returning home would spread news of promise in Manchuria and would try to bring out his friends and relatives to the Canaan flowed (sic) with milk and honey. *Hsien* organizations, or native district organizations, chambers of commerce and benevolent bodies would render them assistance on their way. In several cases, nearly the entire population of a *hsien* or district migrated to Manchuria.[8]

A survey conducted in 1930 of over 11,000 migrants passing through the port of Dairen found that most were single men, traveling in small groups, and accompanied by fellow villagers who were taking them to a prearranged location and job.[9]

[8] Tsao Lien-en (1930), 837.
[9] Zhao Zhongfu (1971), 338.

3. *Community Values*

"The communal element in Chinese society is of first importance," observed Walter Young. "In union the Chinese finds strength; alone he is weak."[10] Most migrants left home in the company of friends and relatives and headed for villages in Manchuria where other friends and relatives awaited them or gravitated to established settlements where they could become part of an existing community. There were, of course, a few true pioneers—"leg-runners" [*pao tui'er di*], drifters, wanderers, or masterless men—who struck out for the wilderness. But even they chose to live and work in groups.[11] Francis Younghusband came across bands of men in the forests of eastern Liaoning, clearing the land, "hacking and hewing . . . , digging up the ground and preparing it for a crop," and in the evening cooking their porridge in common dwellings, living together beyond the reach of established society, and when threatened by the encroachment of authority, moving on to a more remote location.[12]

Group solidarity was a function not only of culture, but also institutional arrangements, or what Walter Young calls the "spirit of association." "One finds whole communities in North Manchuria," Young reported, that "are, in the main, but transplanted organisms that grew to a maturity in the homeland of the immigrants." He noted the existence of community groups, such as the *baojia* or local security corps, chambers of commerce, professional guilds, and cooperative loan associations, all of which were based on models from, if not direct heirs to, similar organizations in Shandong. Along the road, indigent migrants could stay in the hostels, eat in the soup kitchens, and ride in the boats and carts of, or get small loans from provincial guilds and other organizations. "But of the associations that in the pioneer areas have great importance," Young concluded, "one is all-pervading, the family itself. . . . And over every community hovers the memory of the ancestral village, to which many will return eventually—some, however, only in wooden boxes by the ancient cart road south through the pass at Shanhaikuan."[13]

Perhaps the most striking feature of the villages covered by the *Kotoku* surveys is the dominant role played by one or sometimes two

[10] C. Walter Young (1928A), 244.
[11] Owen Lattimore (1932), 66–67.
[12] Francis Younghusband (1898), 16.
[13] C. Walter Young (1932), 351–52. For additional details on the Shandong Guild, see C. Walter Young, (1928A), 250.

families. Most informants in these surveys dated the founding of their village from the arrival of the first member of the leading family. Before that date, the collective memory of the community was vague, whereas afterward the oral history of the leading family and the village were essentially the same. In most cases, the first settler or settlers obtained large tracts of land and brought in relatives and friends to serve as tenants, workers, or in some cases to obtain land of their own. As the population grew, by immigration and natural increase, the composition, organization and physical construction of the village revolved around the richest and most powerful households of the dominant family or clan. Most of the survey villages were named after the leading family, with such titles as Cai Family Compound, Pei Family Bean Mill, or Sun Family Well.[14] When two or more families joined the same village, names might reflect the distribution of power among them. One village on the lower Sungari, which was composed of the Yue Family Neighborhood with 17 households and the Zhu Family Neighborhood with only 5, was predictably named for the Yues.[15] When one family eclipsed another, the name of the village changed accordingly. The physical layout and organization of Shandong villages of the late-19th and early-20th centuries, described by Arthur Smith and Martin Yang, reflected the same priorities, with lanes or neighborhoods named for resident families or clans.[16]

Associations or guilds also played important roles in maintaining and protecting the community, especially in areas where government institutions were weak or nonexistent. At the end of the 19th century, Henry James came across one such guild at Tanghekou, on the upper Sungari River in eastern Fengtian, which boasted one thousand members and governed this region from a magnificent guild-house in the hills above the river. Guilds of this kind often ruled with an iron hand over areas not subject to government control. "The guilds are most efficient institutions, and the only place within Manchuria where life and property may be said to be really secure is within their limits," James observed. "The mandarins never dream of going into the mountains."[17]

[14] These typical examples are from *Kotoku gannendo*, sites 3 and 12, and *Kotoku sannendo*, site 15.

[15] *Kotoku sannendo*, site 4.

[16] On village nomenclature, see Arthur Smith (1899), 16–19, and on layout of neighborhoods along family lines, see Martin Yang (1945), 6–7. Other aspects of the close relationship between village and family are described throughout these books.

[17] Henry James (1888), 251–54.

4. Religion

Religious practices among Chinese settlers in Manchuria reflect the same communal values that bound peasants of north China to their homes and villages, persuaded most who left home to return, and reinforced the cohesion of Chinese peasant communities at every step along the way. One expression linking group identity to the eternal spirit was the compulsion to return the remains of family members to the native village for burial. Observers at Shanhaiguan, the eastern terminus of the Great Wall and chief overland passage between China proper and Manchuria, noted the long line of coffins, airtight boxes made of heavy wooden planks, finely finished with paint and lacquer, strapped five abreast across great carts, and backed up waiting to return their occupants to villages in Shandong, which they had left some years, perhaps decades, before.[18] A caged rooster sat atop each coffin, although the men who accompanied the coffins on the trip south differed over the rooster's role. Some thought that without it only the body would be transported and not the spirit. Others said it served as a beacon to signal the coffin's whereabouts and prevent the spirit from wandering off or getting lost. There seemed to be general agreement that the rooster helped in some way to keep body and spirit together and assure that both would get safely back across the Great Wall. "However," said one skeptic, "cock or no cock, it's no use—no spirit can pass the Wall. When the great Emperor Kienlung [Qianlong] died, they wanted to send him to Moukden to be buried with his ancestors, but even his spirit could not get through, and they had to bury him at Peking."[19]

Another religious expression was the worship of local gods and deities, who were transported or reinvented to provide a focus for communal identity in Manchuria, just as they had done Shandong. "Nothing strikes a person travelling in Manchuria for the first time more than the number of little shrines to the *genii loci* which stand at the corners of the roads," noted Henry James, following his visit to this region in 1886.[20] At about the same time, the English missionary John McIntyre made a walking tour through eastern Fengtian, which was just then beginning to fill up with settlers from China proper, and found shrines

[18] Henry James (1888), 139–41, 384–85; Francis Younghusband (1904), 50; C. Walter Young (1928A), 244.
[19] Henry James (1888), 384.
[20] Henry James (1888), 186.

and temples "perched everywhere," in gardens, fields, and village corners, "even in the solitudes and on distant mountain-peaks, wherever
the fuel-cutter and the cattle-herd have had an errand."[21] McIntyre's
most notable discovery were the many shrines and tablets, devoted to
the "Venerable Headman." "Headman," McIntyre explains, was the
term used for a head boatman on the Yalu River, a farm steward, or foreman over other servants, a figure of authority, someone with special
knowledge of the territory, and thus a suitable title for the mythical
founder of the local settlement:

[F]ollowing the spirits of ancestral worship, the new settlers thus sought out a
first ancestor, a man who was in the land before them and knew its ways, whose
"spirit" would naturally have an abiding interest in the territory and have
power to protect its denizens from malignant demons whether of mountain,
forest, or flood. . . . He knows the place. His spirit hovers over it. Therefore,
every new comer sets up his twelve inches of wood for a tablet, gets a scribe to
write the inscription, offers incense in its season. . . .[22]

5. Bandits

The same communal character that marked legitimate frontier society
was also evident on the far side of the law, among Chinese bandits. Banditry was a cardinal feature of the Manchurian frontier, as it has been
on other frontiers, where men are free, wealth is mobile, and the police
are few in number. Here, as elsewhere in China, many outlaws were organized into large bands, which had a complex organization, shared resources among their members, and carried out their activities through
a web of relationships, partly legal, partly illegal, that wove banditry
into the fabric of the larger society.

One account of Manchurian bandits is provided by Harvey Howard,
an American doctor who was captured and held for ransom by a band
of "Red Beards" [*honghuzi*] in Heilongjiang Province during the summer of 1925. Howard's bandits were typical of the gangs that operated
along the edge of settlement and authority in the Northeast. Bandit
groups recruited new members from among the flotsam and jetsam of
frontier society: men on temporary contracts with railroads, mines, or
timber gangs who lost their jobs, fell into debt, or simply drifted off.
Many bandits were former soldiers who had broken away from their

[21] Rev. John McIntyre (1886), 44.
[22] Ibid., 63–64.

units or members of a unit that moved as a whole from inside to outside the law. Movement also occurred in the opposite direction, as officials recruited bandits or bandit gangs into their armies. In fact, some of the most successful military forces moved back and forth from legal to illegal status in response to changes in local conditions. Most bandits made their living by stealing valuable and easily traded goods, such as opium and human hostages. Howard's bandits consumed vast amounts of opium and raided or sold protection to opium growers, who were the first to reclaim and cultivate land in remote locations. He himself was a captive whom the bandits hoped to exchange for ransom.[23]

The gang that held Howard was well organized, with a recognized leader and a staff of specialists who handled banking and bookkeeping, records and letter-writing (essential for communicating with officials in correct literary style), a cook and clean-up crew, lookouts, guards, messengers, and supply officers. Members of the gang shared all their possessions. Cash that had been stolen or received as ransom was deposited in a common treasury and the proceeds divided at the end of the year. Some bandits sent their earnings home to families in Shandong; others went to town for an annual fling and returned to the band when their money ran out. Power was also shared. The bandit leader never acted arbitrarily, but reached important decisions after consulting with the band's "elder statesmen." In especially dangerous situations, the leader might refer decisions to the group, in which case, "Each bandit, as his name was called, in a low voice, voted 'yes' or 'no.'"[24]

Owen Lattimore considered the bandits of Manchuria to be similar in most respects to legitimate frontier society. "The Manchurian bandit tends very strongly to adhere to a group," Lattimore explained. "In fact the bandit not only seeks the comfort of plurality; he likes to belong to an organic body, with a recognizable place in the community . . . , through various affiliations, there is always a degree of communication between the outlaw community and the law-abiding community." The coherence of bandit organization and its connections to legitimate society made it possible to deal with the bandits through negotiation or by enlisting them into the military or the police.[25] These factors insulated both societies—licit and illicit—against the transforming influences of their new surroundings.

[23] Harvey Howard (1926), 98–100, 165. For a similar account of the role of opium and bandits, see Owen Lattimore (1932), 187–97.
[24] Harvey Howard (1926), 98, 161–62, 167–68, 186.
[25] Owen Lattimore (1932), 225–26.

B. Pattern of Migration

The pattern by which Chinese moved into and through Manchuria, where they settled, and for how long demonstrates their reluctance to break ties with their native place or adapt to the world outside. The *Kotoku* surveys provide details on when and where each of the survey households arrived in Manchuria, how many times they moved, and where they finally settled. Read as history, these data reveal a pattern of migration that proceeds over time, from the mid-17th to the early-20th century, and over space from south to north, while the migrants retained the commitment to family and village at each step along the way.

Households in Jehol and southern Manchuria (Region 1) had been in the region longest, on average 180 years, and had moved the fewest number of times. Nearly half of the survey households were still in the village where their forebears had arrived in the 18th century or earlier. Comparing this experience with villagers in Regions 2, 3, and 4, we see that the histories of these communities changed along a gradient from south to north. Households in the north had arrived in Manchuria at progressively later dates, were more likely to have first landed in a location further to the north, and moved more often before finally settling in the village where surveyors found them in the 1930s.

This indicates that at each stage, Chinese crossing the Great Wall moved only as far as they had to. Most settled in the south, where natural conditions, previous acquaintances, and established communities made life seem familiar, comfortable, and promising. The earliest arrivals were often successful in renting or reclaiming land, founding new villages or joining communities that were sparsely populated and welcomed new recruits. As these areas filled up, later migrants arrived, adding to the burden of overpopulation and triggering a secondary migration into the next ring of land, which was more sparsely populated and able to absorb newcomers. For two centuries, the process unfolded in this way, with each generation of migrants trying to squeeze their way into an already established area, and either recognizing the difficulty of this task and moving on or finding a place and in the act pushing more marginal members of the community out of the village and onto the road north.

Contemporary observers who followed the progress of the migrants noted the serial character of this advance. "The newly arriving immigrant in Manchuria seldom pushes northward to the frontier of his adopted country," explained Franklin Ho, on the contrary, he takes his abode close to the port in the South at which he landed. In that way, by providing and creating labor he assists in the economic expansion of the regions in South Manchuria; but rarely does he undertake work of a pioneer nature. This he leaves to the older settler, or, at any rate, until the time when he himself may no longer be considered a new comer. Thus . . . , the writer finds a large number of immigrant families who first settled in Liaoning Province and, later, migrated to the North in Kirin and Heilungkiang in order to escape the pressure of those arriving afterwards.[26]

The evidence on serial migration suggests that it proceeded by the same mechanism that brought migrants from China proper to Manchuria in the first place: that is, young men were initially sent out on temporary assignment by families who expected them to remit their earnings and return to the village, while eventually some of the intended sojourners chose to remain, got lost, or became trapped far from home. A recent study of Daoyi, a banner settlement 20 miles north of Mukden, illustrates this process in a village located midway between China proper and the receding frontier. The household registers for Daoyi during the period 1774–98 show that a number of young men who left the village in their youth returned later in life, often accompanied by wives and children whom they had acquired during their absence. Most of the returnees first moved in with their fathers, elder brothers, or uncles and after a few years set up separate residences of their own. Just as families in Shandong had sent young men to places like Daoyi, in hopes that they would return with the wherewithal to resume life in the native village, so too families in Daoyi sent their young men out and with similar expectations. And just as some Shandong men returned, while others remained in the north, so too some of Daoyi's young men returned, while others broke loose to establish new settlements on a still more distant frontier.[27]

Evidence from the *Kotoku* surveys also shows that over time many migrants adopted a more positive view of moving as a way of improving their lives. Most migrants, as noted in the preceding chapter (Table 2), described the original move by themselves or their forebears from China proper to Manchuria in negative terms—an effort to escape economic hardship, natural disaster, or war. By contrast, the same informants, once established as permanent settlers, had more positive assessments of the family's final move to the village where surveyors found them in the 1930s. Whereas over 80 percent of the *Kotoku* respondents described their family's initial move from China

[26] Franklin Ho (1931), 20–21.
[27] James Lee and Robert Eng (1984), 40–44.

proper as compelled by "hardship," nearly two-thirds said that they had moved to the survey village because they believed or hoped that their lives would improve. In most cases the motive was economic—they expected to obtain more or better land, a better job, or higher income. A significant portion (22%) said it was a way to join family or friends, and some (5%) said they expected a more peaceful way of life.

Several of the village histories also show that when, during the late-19th or early-20th century, an area was opened to settlement and the land offered for sale, enterprising farmers who had previously settled in southern or central Manchuria, worked as a laborers or tenants and saved or invested their money, came north to buy tracts of undeveloped land. In many cases, these migrants were able to sell cultivated land in the south at a much higher price than they paid for wasteland in the north. Then, they and their families, relatives, and friends reclaimed the land and laid the foundations of an entirely new village. The village of Zhang Family Kettle in Qingcheng County was founded by Zhang Sheng, who arrived in this region in 1862 and bought 20 *fangdi* (900 *shang*, or 9,000 *mu*) of land for only 600 coppers [*wen*] per *shang*. Zhang's ancestors had previously settled in Fengcheng County in southern Manchuria, raised tobacco on rented land, and ran a general goods store and inn. The elder Zhang immediately began to reclaim his land and four years later was able to move his entire family north.[28] Similarly, the village of Yue Family Neighborhood in Fujin County on the lower Sungari was the creation of a farm family from Benqi County, south of Mukden. Beginning with the purchase of land in 1908, various members of the Yue family moved back and forth between Benqi and Fujin, a distance of 600 miles, to reclaim land and build a homestead. Finally, in 1915, the entire family moved north, followed by friends and relatives who became tenants of the founding household.[29] The same pattern of serial migration accounted for the settlement and creation of villages in the Mongol areas of the eastern steppe.[30] During his travels through this region in the 1920s, Owen Lattimore met many "secondary migrants," who in the course of a lifetime made several moves, developing and selling land for a high price in a densely settled territory, moving on to buy at a lower price, and repeating this process in some location yet further out on the steppe.[31]

[28] *Kotoku gannendo*, site 4.
[29] *Kotoku sannendo*, site 4.
[30] See, for example, *Kotoku gannendo*, sites 11 and 13.
[31] Owen Lattimore (1932), 221–23.

The experience of migrant households in reaching the fringes of settlement in northern and eastern Manchuria is confirmed by the age and sex profile of their members. Since the original migrants from China proper were overwhelmingly single men, primarily teenagers and young adults, one would expect communities of new arrivals to include a disproportionate number of males between the ages of 15–30, whereas older communities, or communities made up of the descendants of migrants, should have a normal balance among men and women and the various age groups. In fact, the households covered in the *Kotoku* surveys were monotonously normal: The gender balance was 51% male, 49% female, and the age structure included large numbers of young and old that one would expect to find in a stable rural community. Only 13% of the total sample were males between the ages of 15 and 30.[32] None of the 37 communities in the survey varied significantly from these averages, suggesting that all had reached a high stage of maturity.

The opposite example—pioneers who had moved directly from China proper to some remote location to wrest land and livelihood from the wilderness—is conspicuous by its absence. Figures on the arrival and departure of migrants in northern Manchuria during the period 1921–26 show that only about 7.5% of the new arrivals chose to stay in the north while the remainder returned to southern Manchuria or to China proper.[33] "The career of the adventurer," Owen Lattimore observed, was not to "strike out for the wilderness," but to head for an established community, find work under an employer, make money and return to home.[34]

C. Pattern of Settlement

The strength of the Chinese migrant community—both the cohesion within and the resistance to influences from without—was affirmed by the pattern of settlement: the clustering of houses to form compact villages, protected by walls made first of mud and later brick or stone, and surrounded by fields that expanded from the central core across an unbroken stretch of farmland to the edge of wilderness.[35] Unlike Mongol herders and farmers who dwelt in isolated tents or houses that numbered

[32] *Kotoku Sannendo* (1936) and *Kotoku Gannendo* (1936), Table 3.
[33] Zhao Zhongfu (1972), 354.
[34] Owen Lattimore (1932), 68.
[35] J. A. Wylie (1893), 449.

in twos or threes and made use of pastures and fields just outside their doors,[36] Chinese lived and worked in densely populated towns and villages, surrounded by farmland that expanded gradually like a tree trunk, adding a new ring of growth each year. According to Walter Young, this tendency to settle in groups, congregate in villages, and expand the area of cultivation slowly away from centers of population and commerce was one of the things that "militates against rapid absorption of outlying areas,"[37] and helps to preserve the character of the original community.

Accounts of foreign travelers who crisscrossed Manchuria during the 19th century describe walled villages and towns, and "sudden" or "abrupt" changes from forest or steppe to farmland—all evidence of the pattern of settlement that insulated Chinese communities against the world around them.[38] In 1845, the French missionary, M. de la Brunière, heading out of the densely cultivated area surrounding Alachuke, reached the edge of cultivation, 25–30 miles east of the city, where "the country, hitherto sufficiently peopled, suddenly changes to an immense desert, which ends at the Eastern Sea." It was obvious to de la Bruniere that the change was produced by human artifice rather than natural geography, for the dense forests and tall thick grass, "were convincing proofs of fertility of the soil, as yet untouched by the hand of man. . . ."[39]

Forty years later, the English travelers, Henry James and Francis Younghusband, found the same pattern of abrupt change between cultivated and uncultivated land along the arc of frontier that fringed the central Manchurian plain. The trip down the Sungari River from the Changbaishan Mountains toward Jilin took them for several days through thick forests. "But at length," Younghusband noted, "and very suddenly, we found ourselves clear of the forest, and in a populous district of extraordinary fertility. . . . Here, as before, we were impressed by the vigour and prosperity of these Chinese colonists breaking through the forest. . . ."[40] Settlement on the eastern frontier followed a similar pattern. For about 40 miles south of Sanxing, at the juncture of the Mudan and Sungari rivers, "cultivation is pretty general," remarked James, "but south of it the valley narrows, and population

[36] Alexander Williamson (1870), 206.
[37] C. Walter Young (1932), 350.
[38] See, for example, Henry James (1888), 315–22, 339–40; Francis Younghusband (1898), 28, 34, 37, 43; and Francis Younghusband (1904), 62.
[39] M. de la Brunière, 1845, cited in Henry James (1888), 424–25.
[40] Francis Younghusband (1898), 27–28.

almost ceases."[41] Then again, after several days travel, "the valley widened and for the last fifty miles into Ninguta we had a fair road, with numerous flourishing villages and a wide extent of cultivation. . . ." The Englishmen found the city of Ninguta booming, its population between 15,000–20,000 in 1886, up from 3,000 just 15 years before. "The country round is open and well cultivated," James remarked, "and there are numerous fertile valleys in the neighbourhood."[42] Finally, when they crossed the steppe from Tsitsihar to Hulan, north of the Sungari, the travelers again ran headlong into Chinese cropland. "Suddenly one day we drove right into cultivation," Younghusband reported.

We had crossed the boundary-line between the Mongol and Chinese territory. It is a purely artificial line laid across the downs, but up to that line the Chinese cultivate the land; beyond it the Mongols hold sway, and no attempt at reducing the land to cultivation is made. Consequently, the boundary-line between Chinese territory proper and that which the Chinese still allow to the Mongols is formed by rows of millet and wheat.[43]

Chinese settlements above the Great Wall in Jehol or further west to the great bend in the Yellow River produced the same pattern by expanding outward from densely populated and intensively cultivated villages. Reports by foreign visitors, including the French priest Père Gerbillon,[44] in the 17th century, the Russian envoy George Timkowski, in the early 19th century,[45] and the Central Asian explorer Roy Chapman Andrews, in 1925, make the same point. "It was interesting to see how Chinese cultivation was being pushed northward toward the edge of the desert," Andrews noted.

Every two or three years the Chinese open a new tract for settlement and, as soon as this is occupied by farmers, the border line of cultivation is advanced still farther. In the last seven years [1918–25], it has gone northward forty miles. The Mongols who occupy the frontier region are simply forced to retreat as the Chinese progress.[46]

Finally, the surest sign that Chinese migrants had come to rest, that the transition from sojourner to settler was complete, was when the village established a graveyard. The coffins that were used to ship the

[41] Henry James (1888), 337.
[42] Henry James (1888), 339–40. See also Francis Younghusband (1898), 42–43.
[43] Francis Younghusband (1904), 24. See also Henry James (1888), 314–15.
[44] Jean-Baptiste Du Halde (1741), 327–31, 359.
[45] George Timkowski (1827), 276.
[46] Roy Chapman Andrews (1932), 241. See also Dudley Buxton (1923), 399–400.

bodies of deceased migrants back to their homes in China proper were made of thick wooden planks and closed tight, so that they could be left above ground until it was convenient to move them. In a new village, uncertain of its own future, the coffins were simply lined up to await shipment south. But a permanent village must provide a home for the dead, so that older settlements had family burial grounds, many of which, according to Henry James, were "neatly walled in, with carved tombstones resting on the back of tortoises, and often a handsome p'ailou [archway] at the entrance. . . ."[47]

D. Conclusion

Most Chinese who found themselves, owing to the vicissitudes of life, outside the Great Wall were neither happy nor proud to be there. The movement of migrants and refugees was rarely driven by a quest for fortune or adventure or by a religious, political, or ideological calling. Instead, young men were sent out by their families to earn and return, while the punishment for failure was exile. "The sentiment of the Chinese people still regards these colonists as dwellers in a strange land beyond the pale of civilization," remarked the scholar Dudley Buxton after visiting migrant communities in Inner Mongolia during the 1920s, "and for the most part this feeling is shared by the colonists as far as can be judged; if possible, their bodies are carried within the Wall for burial."[48] Owen Lattimore met settlers, who, even after living in Manchuria for decades, clung to the oxymoronic status of "long-term temporary immigrants," because to accept the fact of permanent settlement was "a mark of exile, failure and defeat."[49]

It is easy to understand why migrants who failed to make a go of things in Manchuria should long for home. More interesting are the successes—those settlers who through a combination of hard work, wise investments, and good luck managed to acquire land, find a wife, raise a family, and earn respect in a community of their own making. One might expect such men to appreciate the virtues of their new way of life, to become pillars of frontier society and spokesmen for frontier values. But according to Lattimore, Chinese settlers who had "graduated" to the ranks of the Manchurian elite invariably abandoned their identity as pioneers, "faced about toward China," and devoted their wealth,

[47] Henry James (1888), 140–41.
[48] L. H. Dudley Buxton (1923), 402.
[49] Owen Lattimore (1932), 200.

talent, and energies to the traditional pursuits of classical learning and government service. Absent was the sense of being part of or wanting to create something new.[50]

Why was this the case? Lattimore offers a cultural or psychological explanation, emphasizing the dichotomy between the Chinese and what he took to be the essential character of the American West. In the West, Lattimore notes, the term "pioneer" elicits an image of the "lonely settler," an individual who travels to the far edge of civilization to carve out a life of his own. In China, however, these "psychological characteristics of individualism" are unknown. Instead, "The frontiersman forms for himself a group-connection by attaching himself to Mongols, Manchus or other non-Chinese tribes; the second-line frontiersman moves forward as part of a group; the squatter is always found as an extension of the group never wholly removed."[51]

Lattimore attributes this behavior and the underlying attitudes to a "general instinct" in Chinese society, "not to get away from the old order, nor to found any new order, but merely to extend the old order, and to reproduce it as fast as possible."[52] In America, he argues, hearty individualism and the quest for something new produced the "instinctive and urgent *drive* of a spontaneously expanding nation," whereas in China, the preference for group solidarity and preservation of the social order favored "a tentative and uncertain *spread*."[53] "Psychologically," Lattimore concludes, "[Chinese] colonists are less pioneers, carrying with them a young and confident tradition, than refugees, looking over their shoulders at a homeland unwillingly abandoned."[54] Based on her interviews with Shandong migrants, Diana Lary reaches a similar conclusion: A corollary of migration as a service to the family "is that the individual expression of free will—the bold courage of the pioneer so celebrated in the history and lore of migration to North America—is absent here."[55]

Some of the evidence presented in this chapter supports this explanation. Family values, communal spirit, and religious beliefs are all parts of the culture or identity that contributed to the reluctance of Chinese pioneers to integrate or change themselves to fit with their new surroundings. But there is a danger in relying exclusively on cultural or

[50] Ibid., 69–70.
[51] Ibid., 224.
[52] Ibid., 224.
[53] Ibid., 66. Italics original.
[54] Ibid., 100.
[55] Thomas Gottschang and Diana Lary (2000), 10.

psychological explanations, because they imply that Chinese were unchanging or unchangeable, that some essential "Chineseness" determined their fate. In this regard, the use of "network" theory is helpful: not because it shows how Chinese changed in the process of migration to Manchuria, for the record seems quite the opposite, but because it shows how some networks reinforced established habits and weighed more heavily on the side of persistence than change.

The networks by which Chinese moved into and through Manchuria all served to strengthen their original identity and militate against the influence of their surroundings. Migrants were generally recruited by and traveled with relatives, fellow villagers, or friends, while the institutions that aided their move were operated by fellow provincials. In most instances, settlements were established and settlers recruited through family ties, while the villages established in Manchuria were extensions of the families that created them. Villages were laid out in lanes or neighborhoods defined by blood relations, and the fields surrounding the villages were sharply delineated from the wilderness beyond. Most migrants moved, not in a single leap from China proper to a distant frontier, but by serial migration through established communities, beginning in southern Manchuria and advancing to Jilin and Heilongjiang. Bandits posed a threat from without that pressed migrants into densely populated and compact towns and villages, while the institutional arrangements of the outlaw band made it a refuge for migrants who had lost their place in the legitimate order and connected the bandits to the larger fabric of Manchurian society.

In addition to factors that channeled and shaped the migrants on their way north, physical realities or constraints also limited their adaptation to the new surroundings. The smallholder economy of north China favored a rapid turnover in landownership that made it possible for returned migrants to buy land, while the practice of partible inheritance made it necessary for those with claims to return home. From south to north, the climatic gradient shortened the growing season, making conditions progressively less favorable for crops grown in China proper. Agricultural technologies used in north China were crude and ill-adapted to conditions in the forests or on the heavily matted steppe. Migrants from Hebei and Shandong were used to an intensive, commercialized agriculture that depended upon a dense population and connection to urban markets, and ill-prepared for the self-sufficiency demanded by settlement on a remote frontier.

Were the factors that have thus far been adduced to explain the constancy of Chinese behavior in Manchuria sufficient to continue this process, or were Chinese migrants susceptible to change under different circumstances? One way to answer this question is to observe the migrants under different conditions, when their choices narrowed and their predilections, if they had any, were constrained. Such a test came during the late 1920s, when famine and war devastated north China, driving refugees northward in unprecedented numbers and with little freedom of choice. Under extreme conditions, the preferences of migrants and patterns of migration were swept aside in a tide of desperation. This process and its outcome are the subject of the following chapter.

CHAPTER 6

Refugees

THE PATTERN OF MIGRATION and settlement described thus far was challenged by the events of the late 1920s. During these years, famine and warlordism in Shandong and Hebei drove an unprecedented number of refugees north. Caught up in this flood of humanity were not only the young men who had been dispatched to Manchuria as temporary wage-workers, but women, children, old people, and whole families who took to the road with no hope of returning and nothing to return to. Southern Manchuria was already densely occupied, leaving little space for new arrivals, while a well-developed network of railroads offered transportation to sparsely settled areas in the north, east, and west. These conditions promised to thrust the hapless refugees directly onto the frontier and prompt an engagement with the wilderness that had been lacking in the previous history of this movement. Rather than the gradual, cohesive, filtered spread through occupied territory, a disorganized mass of humanity was thrown helter-skelter into the unknown.

These conditions make the explanations presented above appear inapplicable or outmoded. Refugees tossed into the maelstrom could have no plans to sojourn, nor indeed any plans at all. And the networks that moved migrants of earlier generations along carefully designed routes to and from workstations in the north were swept away in the tide. Yet the results of these adventures were surprisingly similar to those previously observed, as the refugees of the late 1920s, despite the changed conditions, ended up in the densely populated areas of southern Manchuria rather than on the labor-short, land-rich frontiers. The explanation for this outcome seems to lie with a factor thus far ignored in this account—namely, the politics and power over landownership in the outlying areas—as well as the characteristics of the migrants or migration per se, which have been the causes cited above.

A. The Flood to the North, 1927–29

The terrible suffering and massive flood of refugees from north China to Manchuria during the late 1920s captured the attention of the entire world. Beginning in 1927, a cruel combination of drought, banditry, warlordism, and famine drove more than a million people per year across the Great Wall. In parts of Shandong able-bodied men had left the villages, the very old and young had died, and those who remained were living on chaff and cottonseed. The land was worthless, because there was no one strong enough to work it or confident that they would live to see the harvest. The only thing left to sell were the people themselves. "Boys are selling for something like $10," a relief worker in western Shandong reported, "girls for from $10 to $30, while young women bring as much as $100 or more."[1]

Flight from the areas affected by famine was no longer limited to young men and temporary workers, nor did those able to escape have any hope of returning. Surveys of refugees arriving in Manchuria in the late 1920s show that the percentage of women, children, young, and old people increased, along with the number who said they intended to remain in the north. In fact, many refugees had no means to return or, having sold all they owned, anything to return to. "From April to October 1927, I observed them week by week in Dairen," wrote Walter Young, "streaming down the gangplanks of the steamships which brought them from the Shantung ports. . . ." Their meager luggage—"a well worn plough share, a bit of wood intended perhaps for a scythe handle"—showed that they brought all that they owned. They were refugees, not migrants, Young observed, for "such as these do not travel for the season alone."[2]

Driven by hardship and famine, more refugees arrived in Manchuria, more moved to remote areas where they could find land to support their large numbers, and more stayed on. The figures reported by Thomas Gottschang and Diana Lary (Figure 2) show the sharp increase in the numbers of refugees who arrived and remained in Manchuria during the crisis of 1927–29. According to Franklin Ho, three out of four

[1] Franklin Ho (1931), 16.
[2] C. Walter Young (1928A), 244.

migrants who entered Manchuria during this period headed for the northern, eastern, and western frontiers, which had the most cultivable but as yet uncultivated land. By contrast, much smaller numbers were drawn to areas along the Beijing-Mukden Railway in central Manchuria, which were already densely settled and cultivated.[3] A separate study of the 630,000 migrants who arrived in Manchuria during the first six months of 1927 reached the same conclusion: more than 80% went to marginal areas in the north, east, and west, whereas fewer than 20% remained in the central core.[4] The opening of additional tax offices during the period 1911–31 (Map 8) attests to the spread of cultivation into outlying areas.

B. Return to the Old Order

Despite these reports indicating dramatic changes in the size, nature, and direction of migration, however, in the end the older pattern changed little or was quickly restored. Other than a brief uptick in the numbers, there is little to distinguish the pattern of migration in this period from the one that preceded it. The gradual spread of population, at first temporary, reluctant to move or change, and only eventually seeping into the surrounding wilderness, remained the defining features of this enterprise.

Beginning in 1930, the numbers of migrants to Manchuria and of those who chose to remain in this region fell back to the level of the early 1920s. Events conspired to discourage migration during the 1930s: The end of the drought in northern China and the victory of the Guomindang reduced the ravages of the warlords, made life in north China more bearable, and gave peasants less reason to flee; the clash between Chinese and Soviet forces on the Chinese Eastern Railway in 1929 ended the Guomindang forward policy and made Russian authorities less amenable to Chinese immigration; the Great Depression reduced the market for Manchurian soybeans and put a damper on the development of this region; and after the Japanese takeover of Manchuria in 1931, the new masters of the puppet state Manchukuo were more resistant to the influx of Chinese.[5] A massive study of rural migration in China during the mid 1930s, concluded that the movement of

[3] Franklin Ho (1931), 22–39, gives statistics and maps, showing the distribution of population, migrants, and land use in Manchuria during the period 1927–29.
[4] C. Walter Young (1928A), 297; (1928B), 533; and (1932), 342.
[5] Owen Lattimore (1932), 102, 200–203.

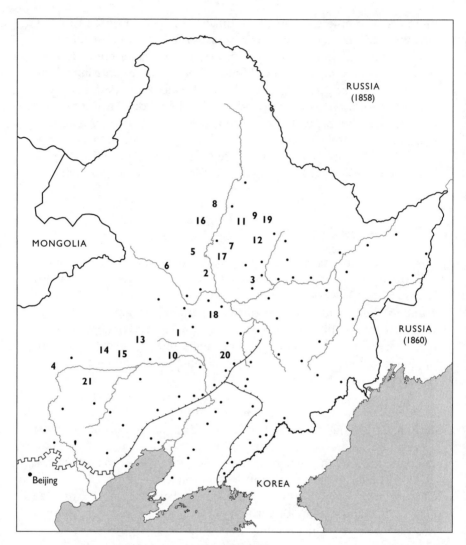

MAP 8. Government Offices, Northeast China, 1912–31

Map 8 Legend

Map No.	Est. Date	Place	Status
1	1912	Danyu	County
2	1913	Tailai	County
3	1913	Zhaodong	County
4	1914	Jingpeng	County
5	1914	Jingxing	County
6	1914	Solun	County
7	1914	Lindian	County
8	1915	Buxi	County
9	1915	Keshan	County
10	1918	Tongliao	County
11	1923	Yi'an	County
12	1923	Mingshui	County
13	1924	Lubei	County
14	1925	Lindong	County
15	1926	Tianshan	County
16	1926	Gannan	County
17	1926	Taikang	County
18	1927	Qian'an	County
19	1929	Kedong	County
20	1929	Shuangshan	County
21	1931	Quanning	County

SOURCE: Owen Lattimore (1934), 288–289.

peasants from Hebei and Shandong to Manchuria had been "practically suspended."[6]

Meanwhile, the composition of the migrants, the dominance of single men on temporary assignment from families in Shandong, changed only briefly and on the margins. The share of women and children increased, although less than some observers claimed, from 12% in 1926, to 18% between 1927–29. In 1927, when the flood of refugees was at its peak, a Japanese survey found that 70% returned home after three years or less.[7] A separate survey, conducted by the South Manchuria Railway in 1930 and covering 11,284 migrants arriving at the ports of Dalian and Yingkou, yielded similar results. The majority were single men, traveling in small groups of friends and relatives and accompanied by fellow villagers who had recruited them to work in Manchuria for a specified length of time, while almost all (90%) declared that they had come either to inspect conditions in Manchuria before deciding how long to stay or intended to return home in three years or less. Taking the entire sample, which included women, children, old people, and

[6]National Agricultural Research Bureau (1936), 171.
[7]Franklin Ho (1931), 9–10.

destitute families who had no means of returning home, more than 60% said they planned to stay in Manchuria for no more than three years.[8] The reluctance of Chinese to abandon their homes in China proper apparently survived even the most devastating crisis.

Finally, there is the question of where in Manchuria the migrants of the late 1920s actually went or, if they went, stayed. The reports cited above claim that 80 to 90 percent moved to the peripheral areas, where the population was sparse and land plentiful, leaving only a small minority in the central Manchurian plain. But later studies that tracked the movement of these migrants show that either they did not go where they said they would, or having gone there, decided not to stay, and instead ended up in a village, or more likely a city, on the central plain.

The 1930 survey by the South Manchuria Railway found that over 80% of the migrants passing through Dalian and Yingkou boarded trains headed for Changchun or Mukden, and almost half planned to settle in areas south of Mukden or around Harbin, rather than on the open and rugged frontiers. By contrast, only about 10% said they were headed for Heilongjiang.[9] Follow-up studies of these migrants showed that over time they gravitated to cities and to jobs on railroads, in mines, factories, or other urban trades. Nearly 80 percent of the respondents in the 1930 SMR survey described themselves as "manual laborers" and a third of these as "agricultural laborers." Since most came from farming backgrounds, it is reasonable to suppose that they would look for work in this field. Yet, only one in four of the "manual laborers" ended up in agriculture, while the majority went to cities and nonagricultural work. Those who came with their families were more likely to sacrifice short-term income in favor of long-term security and settle on farms. But nearly 80% of the unmarried males, who made up the majority of all migrants, went to Mukden, Changchun, Harbin or other large city, or to work in the mines, factories, railroads or as coolie trade.[10]

A recent study by Zhao Zhongfu also demonstrates that while the balance between land and population continued to favor northern Manchuria, most migrants nonetheless chose to settle in the south.

[8] "Statistical investigation of the migration and settlement of Chinese in Manchuria," by the Investigation Department of the South Manchuria Railway (Dalian, 1931), cited in Zhao Zhongfu (1971), 336–38. This survey covered 11,284 individuals in 2,571 groups. Groups that boarded the train at the port of disembarkation were headed for: Changchun (57.8%); Fengtian (25.4%), Siping (4.4%), Fushun (4.4%), other (8.0%). They reported that their eventual destination was in: Jilin (53.2%), Liaoning (35.0%), Heilongjiang (10.2%), other (1.6%).

[9] Ibid.

[10] Zhao Zhongfu (1971), 339.

Zhao estimates that between 1915 and 1930, the area of cultivated land per person in the agricultural sector of northern Manchuria actually increased [*sic*], whereas the south was becoming more crowded and the area of farmland per capita declined. Still, a Japanese report based on data for the year 1936, claims that there was a shortage of 670,000 agricultural workers in northern Manchuria and a surplus of 500,000 workers in the south.[11] In other words, migrants were crowding into areas with little land and few jobs, while shunning those where land was plentiful and labor in short supply. Clearly, the old patterns persisted despite the change in circumstances. Why was this so?

C. Hardship on the Frontier

One reason that migrants, even refugees with few choices in life, after traveling as far as the railroads or their legs would carry them, returned home or to densely populated southern Manchuria was that land on the frontier was expensive and tightly held by a minority of large owners who were disinclined to sell or in some cases even to rent the land to the new arrivals. The policies of the late-Qing to sell land and settle population in Manchuria and Inner Mongolia, which were ostensibly designed to raise money and strengthen the nation's defense, also had the effect of shifting wealth and power to a minority of well-connected landowners. By the early 20th century, the ownership of land in these regions was concentrated in very few hands, and the refugees of the 1920s found little for sale or even for rent at prices they could afford.

The histories of villages covered by the *Kotoku* surveys attest to the practice by which official land bureaus set up to dispose of public lands sold vast tracts to "speculators" or "monopolists" [*landou*] at bargain prices. In one case, a wealthy individual in Taonan reportedly bought land at 40% of the price available to ordinary farmers. It was not uncommon for local magnates to take control of hundreds or even thousands of *mu* of potential farmland.[12] The warlord Duan Qirui is said to have owned 20 million.[13] Many speculators had no interest in farming

[11] Zhao Zhongfu (1972), 349–50, 362.

[12] Taonan: *Kotoku sannendo*, site 2. For other examples, see: *Kotoku gannendo*, sites 1–8, 10–11, 13–14; and *Kotoku sannendo*, sites 2–5, 9, and 15–17. For a similar account of class conflict regarding land sales in a Manchu banner near Shengyang, see: *Manzu shehui lishi diaocha* (1985), 17–18.

[13] Zhao Zhongfu, (1971), 343; Zhao Zhongfu (1972), 356–58; Franklin Ho (1931), 40; Owen Lattimore (1932), 110–11; 213–14. The Taonan case is reported in *Kotoku sannendo*,

and simply subdivided the land and sold it to others, turning a quick
profit. Such sales favored very large buyers who themselves became (often absentee) landlords. The evidence from the *Kotoku* surveys shows
that whereas villages in southern Manchuria (Regions 1 and 2) were
generally formed by tenants who first rented land from banners or estates, those further north (Regions 3 and 4) were invariably established
by one or more households that bought very large tracts (in the hundreds or thousands of *mu*) either directly from a land bureau or through
an intermediary. In either case, land ownership in these villages was
concentrated in the hands of a few individuals, leaving later arrivals
with limited opportunities.[14]

On the steppe-lands of western Manchuria, Chinese migrants faced
powerful Mongol landowners and officials, who colluded in the same
way as the Chinese themselves.[15] In the south, where Chinese warlords
held sway, migrant farmers found they could gain greater leverage by
moving in behind the advancing armies. "The colonisation was bru-
tally carried out," Owen Lattimore reported, in 1930, of the situation
in western Liaoning, "the Mongols were evicted at the point of the
bayonet and Chinese colonists planted on their land. If any Mongols
resisted, they were dealt with as 'bandits.'" In such cases, Chinese settlers fared no better than the dispossessed Mongols, however. For, as
Lattimore observed, the generals rented the land out to refugees from
famine areas at exorbitant rates, keeping them poor, powerless, and
under control.[16]

Conditions on the Manchurian frontier were also surprisingly unfavorable to new arrivals. As noted, the availability of arable land, both
cultivated and uncultivated, increased along a gradient that ran from
Shandong and Hebei through Liaoning to Jilin and Heilongjiang. At the
same time, however, the ownership of this land was concentrated in
fewer and fewer hands. The percentage of farmers who owned all or
some of their land declined from a high of 88% in north China to 71%
in southern Manchuria and a low of 35% along the arc of villages
that made up the outermost region (Region 4) covered by the *Kotoku*
surveys.[17] Similarly, the concentration of landownership—measured

---

site 2. Virtually all of the northern Manchurian villages covered in this survey report that
the initial buyers obtained huge tracts of land, which they held or resold to others.

[14] Kong Jingwei (1990), 279–81.

[15] *Kotoku gannendo*, sites 11 and 13.

[16] From Owen Lattimore and Fujiko Isono, *The Diluv Khutagt* (Wiesbaden: Otto
Harrassowitz, 1982), cited in Robert Newman (1992), 17.

[17] John Lossing Buck (1937B), 57, cites an agricultural survey based on 30 sites in the
"Winter Wheat-Kaoliang Area," which includes Shandong and Hebei, that shows 68.9%

by the percentage of farmland owned by the two largest landowners in each of the Kotoku sites, a group that constituted only 4.2% of all households—increased from just over 30% in Regions 1 and 2 and more than 60% in Region 4.[18] Migrants who went to distant frontiers in search of land were likely find it, but also to discover that the land was owned by a shrinking minority, while the majority of villagers were landless tenants or workers who would compete with the new arrivals for land and jobs.

The problems facing the ordinary migrant farmer did not end with the inequality of ownership. Newcomers could still have benefited, if the large, and often absentee, landlords had been willing to sell land in small parcels or develop it for agriculture through rental arrangements. In many cases, however, the owners viewed their holdings as investments or objects of speculation, rather than as real or potential farmland. Land values fluctuated wildly, following rumors about which areas might be opened up by new railroads, and insiders with access to reliable information could make a killing. The price of land around Zhengjiatun on the middle Liao, increased four to eight times, between 1912, when it was first offered at auction, and 1919, when construction of the Siping-Zhengjiatun Railway was completed. A separate study of farmland in 29 counties of northern Manchuria during the early 1920s, revealed a high rate of turnover, which contributed more to the profits of speculators than to the development of agriculture.[19] For those who played the game, land was a commodity to be traded, not a resource to be developed.

Under these conditions, the purchase of land by newcomers was difficult. During most of the Qing, land prices, rents, and taxes were lower in Manchuria than in China proper. Prices began to rise in the

---

"owners," 19.0% "part-owners," and 12.1% "tenants." Buck's findings are supported by other land surveys carried out in China proper during the 1930s. See especially: National Agricultural Research Bureau (NARB) (1936); Nationalist Government Land Committee [*Tudi weiyuanhui*] (1937), and Li Wen-chih et al., *Zhongguo jindai nongye shi ziliao* [Historical material on agriculture in modern China], Vol III, 728, cited in Dwight Perkins (1969), 91, 242–43, and Joseph Esherick (1981), 393–96. Esherick (1981) provides an assessment of the distribution of land ownership in pre-1949 China that supports the findings reported here. For detailed analyses of particular locales in Shandong and Hebei, see: Sidney Gamble (1954), 212–13; Philip Huang (1985), 313–20; and Wang Yaoyu (1938), 181. *Kotoku gannendo*, Table 6, and *Kotoku sannendo*, Table 7, show the following percentages of households in each region that owned at least some land: Region 1 (71%), Region 2 (42%), Region 3 (39%), Region 4 (35%).

[18] *Kotoku gannendo*, Table 6, and *Kotoku sannendo*, Table 7, show the following percentages of land held by the two largest landowners in each village, by region: Region 1 (32%), Region 2 (32%), Region 3 (39%), Region 4 (62%).

[19] Zhao Zhongfu (1972), 359.

late-19th century, while the intervention of the government after 1900 was accompanied by an increase in taxes. Landlords demanded that rents be paid in silver, which rose in value relative to copper. When this happened, many migrant farmers who did the hard work of reclaiming the land, found that they could not afford to buy it.[20] By the 1920s, the price of land in many parts of northern Manchuria was in the range of 10–16 yuan per *shang*, in addition to which a homesteader needed between 500–600 yuan of start-up capital to buy tools, draft animals, food, and other materials.[21] It is unlikely, however, that many migrants had that much money. Surveys of Shandong migrant households during the 1930s found that most, after selling all they owned to finance the trip, left home with 100 yuan or less. Since this was not enough to pay their travel expenses to northern Manchuria, many migrants encountered financial problems along the way, and a significant number were reduced to begging for food.[22] During the 1920s, Manchurian railroads offered reductions on third-class fares, and in some cases allowed children and old people to ride for free. Still, most migrants were too poor to travel by train, no matter how low the price. "The great majority actually walked," Walter Young reported, "men, women and children, carrying infants and even grandmothers on their backs at times," 400 to 500 miles from Dairen to Changchun or Harbin.[23]

Unable to purchase land, the typical migrant had to choose between working for wages or entering into an arrangement that might enable him to obtain land over time. But it was difficult for most peasants to earn and save enough to buy land. According to one source, annual salaries for new arrivals in northern Manchuria were in the range of 130 yuan for an adult male and 80 yuan for a youth. At these rates, in 5 to 10 years, a man and two sons who saved one-third of their earnings could amass the capital required (700 yuan) to buy land and start a farm of their own. Alternatively, a family or group of men with sufficient labor might contract with a landlord to rent farmland or reclaim and develop a patch of arable wasteland. But this left no room for crop failure, illness, or other mishap. Generally, migrants who arrived before an area was developed found more land available, obtained better terms, and had a better chance of rising to the rank of independent land-owner.

[20] Kong Jingwei (1990), 264, 278–79. Kong, 264, cites evidence that the price of one *shang* of land in Lishu County increased tenfold between 1855 and 1894.

[21] Franklin Ho (1931), 41.

[22] Surveys by the Nankai University Economic Research Institute, cited in Wang Yaoyu (1938), 184–85.

[23] C. Walter Young (1928A), 247–50.

Those who arrived later had to travel further or accept less desirable land, paid higher prices, and had less chance of converting their status from tenant or worker to freeholder.[24]

Whatever the conditions of his employment—whether as tenant, wage laborer, or partner in a sweat-equity arrangement—the frontier farmer faced many obstacles. While some farms in remote locations may have been self-sufficient, the great attraction of Manchurian agriculture was the chance to produce wheat, beans, and other crops for the market. But small farmers were vulnerable to the power of local grain merchants, wholesalers, and exporters, who normally extracted around 20% of the value of the crop, as it made its way to market. In spring or summer, after the winter stores had been consumed, many farmers needed cash to tie them over to the next harvest. Lacking both capital and credit and unwilling to pay the high interest rates charged by pawn shops and moneylenders, these farmers turned to futures contracts or "green sales," under which they sold their crop while it was still in the ground and received a fixed price based on an estimated output, which was generally one-third below the rate available in the fall.[25]

The currency system (or systems) was also a nightmare for farmers. The value of the most widely used currency, *guantie*, paper notes denominated in strings of copper cash, fluctuated on a seasonal basis. Their value rose in autumn, when demand for cash to settle grain sales was high, so that farmers who sold their crops at harvest were paid with a smaller number of higher-value bills, and declined in spring and summer, when there was little demand for cash, but when farmers who needed food and other supplies to tie them over until the harvest, had to pay with large numbers of devalued bills. Meanwhile, inflation reduced the value of the *guantie*, leaving peasants who held this currency with less buying power. Nor was that all, for the enormous diversity of Russian, Japanese, Chinese, provincial, and regional currencies in use on the frontier imposed an additional cost on all who had to exchange one currency for another. Taxes, which were normally around 5% of the value of the land, were not as high as in China proper, but still onerous. Finally, if financial pressures were not enough, small farmers in scattered settlements were vulnerable to bandit gangs that operated throughout Manchuria, especially on the frontiers, and might rob, destroy, or demand protection payments from the local inhabitants.[26]

[24] Zhao Zhongfu (1972), 357–58; Franklin Ho (1931), 41–44; C. Walter Young (1928A), 297; (1928B), 533.
[25] Franklin Ho (1931), 46–47.
[26] Ibid., 45–50.

Officials, both in Beijing and in the provinces, who were aware of the challenges faced by the lower classes and the dangers of alienating them, ostensibly offered to help. In the late-19th century, the Qing distributed "livelihood lands" [*shengjidi*] or "charity lands" [*enchangdi*] to impoverished Mongol herders,[27] and required the Mongol banners to set aside rangeland, so that "ordinary Mongols who do not have any land will have pastures to raise their livestock." They also limited the power of land speculators, by restricting the area that could be reclaimed or owned by one individual.[28] Government-sponsored land development projects in Jilin and Heilongjiang provided settlers with building materials, tools, seed, and food, to reclaim and settle wasteland that had previously been sold to absentee owners. The settlers received 40% of the land they reclaimed in the form of sweat equity, and enjoyed a tax holiday of six years, after which the taxes on their land remained lower than in southern Manchuria or China proper.[29] Similarly, the provincial governments of Jilin and Heilongjiang promulgated "seize and reclaim" [*qiangken*] laws that recognized the rights of squatters on undeveloped wasteland, even though this land was owned by some other party.[30] In the end, however, these measures were too little, came too late, and lacked the commitment required to offset the avarice and power of local landlords and officials who defended their interests against all comers.

D. Conclusion

The crisis of the late 1920s triggered an unprecedented wave of refugees, including large numbers of women, children, old people, and whole families, who were forced to search for new homes in faraway places where land was plentiful and the prospects for survival greatest. Yet these pressures failed to change the established pattern of migration and settlement, which remained limited in scope and duration and focused on the most densely populated areas of southern and central Manchuria, rather than the northern, eastern, and western frontiers. The practices of successive Chinese governments in selling land on the frontiers of the empire and the reported collusion in this process among government officials, military commanders, and wealthy individuals

[27]Wang Yuhai (1990), 202–3; Liang Bing (1991), 49–50; and Tian Zhihe (1986), 57.
[28]*Yuzhe huicun*, regulations of 1902 and 1907, cited in Tian Zhihe (1986), 57.
[29]Owen Lattimore (1932), 213–18.
[30]Franklijn Ho (1931), 40.

left migrants and refugees with little chance of obtaining land. In the end, many returned home or sought refuge in the cities and already densely populated areas of central Manchuria. Walter Young, perhaps the most knowledgeable foreign observer in Manchuria during his period, noted that despite the tremendous number of refugees and their desperation, the "deep-grained Chinese tendency to settle only in groups" prevailed, while the conversion of wasteland to agriculture "naturally expands but slowly away from the population, market and communication centers."[31]

[31] C. Walter Young (1932), 350.

Analysis

THE ANALYSIS AT THE END of Part One compared Qing policies toward Manchuria with its policies toward the empire's other borderlands and the Qing strategy of establishing manors in areas north of the Great Wall with the Romanov strategy for occupying the steppe-land adjacent to Russia west of the Urals. This state-centered analysis followed the principal concern of Part One, which was the attempt and failure of the Qing Dynasty to establish a novel system of land tenure in Manchuria and Inner Mongolia, and the success of the Chinese in introducing their own system of markets in land and labor into these areas. The focus of Part Two has been less on the state and more on the Chinese migrants themselves. Here, in analyzing migrants and migration to Manchuria, we will make comparisons with the same or similar cases: first, Chinese migration to two of the empire's other borderlands, Taiwan and Xinjiang; and second, Russian migration into the region west of the Urals and beyond the Urals to Siberia.

A. Migration toward China's Borderlands

The small number of English-language studies of China's borderlands during the Qing and Republican periods share a state-centered approach, which focuses on policy debates and government programs, while dealing only tangentially with the motives and behaviors of Chinese who moved to and settled in these regions. Since government policies responded to and in turn affected conditions on the ground, however, the authors of these works perforce back into the questions of migration and migrants. Their findings reveal both similarities and differences between Manchuria and two other border areas, Taiwan and Xinjiang.

John Shepherd's (1993) findings on Chinese migration to Taiwan during the Qing period are remarkably consistent with the experience of Manchuria. In Taiwan, as in Manchuria, the Qing state acted as a gatekeeper: alternately working to "close" or "quarantine" border areas against Chinese migrants, who might create conflicts, require supervision and drive up administrative and military costs, or to "open" or "colonize" these areas in order to relieve pressure on densely populated China proper, beef up frontier defenses, and build a population and tax base to pay for it all. Yet, in both cases, Manchuria and Taiwan, the forces that moved people arose not from government programs or directives, but from the imbalance in population and natural resources between China proper and the borderlands and the quest of Chinese peasants for land. The vanguard of migrants to Taiwan, like Manchuria, were men who left home as sojourners, on temporary assignment from their families, and evolved over time into permanent settlers. Most were poor peasants who went as seasonal or short-term workers, although merchants, craftsmen, and land speculators were also included in the mix. Migrants to Taiwan were recruited, moved and settled as members of subethnic groups based on common place of origin, and followed networks of brotherhoods, worship groups, and regional associations. Intergroup violence fortified the ties that bound separate groups in Taiwan together and discouraged their integration with other peoples, native or Chinese, and with the surrounding environment.[1]

Studies of Xinjiang during the Qing period—by James Millward (1998), Dorothy Borei (1992), and Peter Perdue (1996)—present a different picture. In contrast to both Manchuria and Taiwan, where Chinese went voluntarily and at their own expense, Xinjiang was settled by active recruitment, generous incentives, and government direction. There were two reasons for this difference: First, after the conquest of Xinjiang in 1759, the Qing state had an overriding interest in stationing troops in this region and establishing colonies to produce the agricultural and other goods needed to support them. Except for a brief period in the 17th century, when Manchuria was threatened by the Russians, and again at the close of the Qing era, when imperialist forces appeared on

---

[1] John Shepherd (1993), 310–19.

China's coast, the Qing had no comparable concern in Manchuria, Taiwan, or any of its other borderlands. In this regard, the conditions in Xinjiang and the policies adopted to deal with these conditions at the height of the Qing were unique. Second, since those areas of Xinjiang that are suitable for farming lie in mountains and oases, separated by long distances and intervening deserts from China proper, left to their own devices, most Chinese would hardly have known of Xinjiang's existence, much less contemplated going there. Manchuria and Taiwan, by contrast, enjoyed abundant arable land and a suitable climate and were located right next door to the major centers of Chinese population. Most Chinese who settled in Xinjiang moved under government direction: as soldiers in banner and Green Standard armies, peasants attracted to military-agricultural colonies and relocation projects by offers of free land, travel allowances, and start-up expenses, or convicts sent to state farms. The exception were merchants, many of whom went to Xinjiang of their own volition, although the Qing also created incentives to lure them there.

Unfortunately, none of these studies says much about who the migrants were, where they came from, how and why they moved, or what their lives were like after settling in Taiwan or Xinjiang. Robert Lee's *Manchurian Frontier in Ch'ing History* (1970) is similarly silent on these questions. The focus of the literature to date has been on the Qing, how it constructed its empire, and what it did to allow or encourage the settlement of outlying regions. These are, of course, interesting questions, but they do not shed much light on the topics covered in Part Two of this study. In particular, they say little or nothing about Chinese society in these border areas, whether it continued along lines established in China proper or changed as implied by the previously mentioned studies that stress "frontier" experience or the "middle ground."

B. Migration in China and Russia

Chinese migration to Manchuria can also be compared with the experience of migrants and migration in Russia, during the same period, from the 17th to the 20th centuries. This comparison must be made in two parts, however, because the Russian experience was quite different in the regions to the west and the east of the Urals. West of the Urals, Russian landlords, officials, and soldiers wielded enormous power over the serfs and used this power to prevent them from fleeing the estates to which they were bound. Serfs on estates at the outer edge of Russian expansion could cross the boundary that separated imperial domination on one side from freedom and opportunity on the other and seek their fortune on the open steppe. But this move was fraught with danger, because freedom from imperial control meant the loss of imperial protection, and the steppe was rife with mounted horsemen and marauding bands who could make quick work of an unprotected farm or village. The Russian gentry was hesitant to move forward without the protection of the state, and Russian serfs had to choose between a certain, if unpleasant, future at home and an uncertain, albeit potentially worse, fate on the frontier.

Chinese migrants in Manchuria faced no comparable choice. The original estate workers and bannermen in Manchuria were less constrained than Russian serfs, and, if dissatisfied with their conditions, found it relatively easy to buy their freedom or escape. Later migrants came to the region voluntarily, struck deals with Manchu or Mongol landholders, and operated with relative freedom, renting, reclaiming, and in some cases gaining control over land of their own. Chinese migrants who chose to move beyond the circle of Qing military power confronted fewer dangers than their counterparts in western Russia. Russian serfs who fled to the steppe broke the bonds of serfdom and ventured into unknown territory where, acting in self-defense, they created Cossack bands and invented communities shaped by the need to survive. Chinese who moved to Manchuria experienced no similar change in circumstances—either liberation or self-defense—and were never called upon to invent an entirely new way of life.

Russian migration east of the Urals to Siberia was also different from the Chinese experience in Manchuria, but in almost exactly opposite ways: in the west, the power of the Russian state, military, and landlords was greater, the freedom of migration less, and the threat from without more serious than in Manchuria; whereas in the east, Russian authorities had little leverage, there were few threats to security, and settlers were free to create entirely new societies and cultures, all of which was quite different from the experience of Chinese who moved outside the Great Wall. Virtually all of the conditions that shaped Russian behavior west of the Urals contrasted with those in the east. Unlike the Crimean Tartars, who menaced the steppe, the natives of Siberia lived in small scattered groups, practiced hunting, fishing, or reindeer herding, produced no bands of mounted horsemen, and posed little threat to migrants, who in turn did not depend upon or feel subject to the Russian army. Siberia is too large and was too sparsely populated to require or support a permanent military and administrative presence of the sort Moscow wanted and needed west of the Urals. The riches of Siberia lay in furs and other natural resources that could be tapped and traded by a small, mobile, adventuresome workforce; stable agricultural settlements could draw on other forms of income, and individuals could move back and forth between these economies. The Russian gentry, who managed estates west of the Urals using a subject labor force, had no interest in Siberia, so that the manorial system and institution of serfdom never appeared in the east. Moscow oversaw the movement to Siberia of certain categories of people: convicts, prisoners, and exiles; peasants on state farms; and after Emancipation in 1861, former serfs who were moved from communes in the west to communes in the east. Still, the vast majority of migrants went to Siberia though unofficial (i.e. illegal) channels, and upon arrival organized their own villages, societies, economies, and cultures. In contrast to Russian settlement west of the Urals, which operated under the thumb of Moscow, favored the landed elite, and kept labor in check, settlement in the east involved greater freedom of movement and choice on the part of peasants and less control by the military, the nobles, and the state.

This pattern of migration and settlement produced in Siberia a society and culture with a distinct identity and separate regional character, of a sort unknown among Chinese communities in Manchuria. Russians migrants came to Siberia from throughout the "Black Earth" region, an area more than five times as large as Shandong and Hebei, with the result that settlers in the Russian Far East were more diverse and less likely to share a common identity than their counterparts in Manchuria. Russians moved as entire households, determined to leave the village for good, in contrast to Chinese who sent one or two young men on a temporary mission to find work and return with money to advance the fortunes of the family back home. Russians migrated to Siberia not only to change their place of residence, but to escape the system of communes and in hopes of owning land, whereas Chinese already enjoyed the system of private land tenure and were bent on reproducing it north of the Great Wall. Russian migrant households included men and women, young and old, quite unlike the bands of Chinese seasonal or temporary workers in Manchuria, which were composed almost entirely of young men. Russian settlers in Siberia lived next door to people from different families, villages, and regions and spoke different dialects. They preferred to settle in areas outside of government administration or control and banded together for protection and mutual help. The result was that Siberian villages and villagers, lacking a common past, had to invent their own future, which reflected the experience of diverse peoples in new surroundings. For most of these settlers, Donald Treadgold explains,

> it was the first time in their lives that it occurred to them, or became apparent, that in some fundamental manner they might order their own existence *de novo*. At home, their grandfather might have raised rye in Voronezh, but their grandfather was dead, they were in Siberia, and their neighbors were very possibly from Perm or Taurida. Questions could not be settled either with reference to ancestors or immemorial local custom.[2]

By weaving separate families into a new social fabric, Siberian Russia became a melting pot and a creature of its own creation—in contrast to the Chinese villages of Manchuria, which were largely reproductions, communities, and cultures transplanted wholesale from China proper, and relatively unchanged in the process.

Finally, these distinct patterns of migration and settlement in Siberia and Manchuria contributed to the similarly contrasting economies of these regions. All of the factors that produced Siberian farms and villages—the long-distance, one-way movement of entire families, who joined forces with total strangers to form new communities—assured that these settlements would be isolated, self-sufficient and disconnected from cities and markets. By contrast, the experience of Manchurian villages, which were built up by short-range, round-trips of sojourners who wove relatives and friends into tightly knit communities, produced integrated networks of commercial exchange. Long before the Qing conquest, rural China had become densely populated, Chinese peasants practiced intense cultivation tied to urban markets, and only when this reservoir was full did the surplus population overflow into adjacent areas. "The fundamental characteristic of Chinese colonization," according to one comparison of China and Russia made during the 1920s, is the "gradual and successive conquest of territory not only by way of agriculture but through the inevitable cooperation of the industrial city labor—in other words, only by creating conditions that justify intensive cultivation. . . ."[3] Russian expansion

---

[2] Donald Treadgold (1957), 141. For other details cited in this paragraph see ibid., 34, 88–92, 95–101, 132–41, 173, 206–13, 253–57.

[3] CER (1924), 67–68. A similar view is expressed by C. Walter Young (1932), 350.

into Siberia was driven by individual enterprise and long-distance calls, whereas Chinese expansion followed the gradual accumulation of pressure and spread of an integrated economic and social fabric from within. The former pattern favored the invention of new social structures and cultural forms, while the latter favored the transplantation or reproduction of proven ways.

PART THREE

Economy

Introduction to Part Three

PART THREE EXAMINES THE ECONOMY of Manchuria during the late-19th and early-20th centuries. Conditions in this region presented Chinese farmers and merchants with opportunities unavailable to their counterparts in China proper. In contrast to the densely populated north China plain, which suffered from a shortage of farmland and, ironically, a shortage of wage labor, Manchuria offered abundant land and an adequate supply of labor without the burden of overpopulation. The small family farm, although present in Manchuria, did not dominate this region to the same extent as in China proper, giving farmers in Manchuria much greater scope for large-scale production. Finally, after 1903, a modern infrastructure of trade and transportation opened Manchuria to vast markets for agricultural produce at home and abroad. These conditions invited Chinese farmers, merchants, manufacturers, and entrepreneurs to devise new and more productive technologies and organizations that would take advantage of what Manchuria had to offer and lead to economic growth and development unknown below the Great Wall. Yet, as the evidence presented in Part Three shows, such expectations were either unjustified, or the Chinese failed to meet them.

What is most striking about the economy of Manchuria during the late-Qing and Republican periods is the degree to which it remained within a traditional Chinese mold. The methods of production, trade, transportation, and finance inherited from China proper were reproduced or passed on with little or no change. Failing to come up with new and better solutions, Chinese in Manchuria were surpassed by the more dynamic Japanese, and to some extent Russian, alternatives. And after the railroads, docks, banks, and other facilities built by foreigners offered new opportunities to Chinese merchants and landowners in this region, those with the greatest assets, who were best equipped to take advantage of these opportunities, failed to do so.

The case for these findings is made in three stages and following three themes. Chapter 7 traces the production and trade of soybeans prior to 1903, when the railroads opened Manchuria to the world, and the whole way of doing business in this region changed. During this period, familiar systems of production, processing, and trade, centered on the port of Newchwang, met the modest needs of a traditional economy. When, after 1905, the Japanese built a modern infrastructure of trade and transportation running through Dairen, a process described in Chapter 8, Newchwang was eclipsed. From that point on, the economy of Manchuria was shaped to a large extent by forces outside its borders. Finally, Chapter 9 shows that the largest Chinese landowners, who had access to abundant land, labor, capital, and modern facilities built by the Japanese, failed to introduce new practices and techniques that might have made their farms more profitable and put Manchuria on the path to development. In sum, Chinese were not only reluctant to move to, settle in, and engage with their surroundings north of the Great Wall, they were also reluctant to adjust their behavior to take advantage of the opportunities Manchuria had to offer.

CHAPTER 7

Commerce and Trade (1644–1903)

PRIOR TO 1903, when the railroads began operation in Manchuria, the economy of this region was dominated by merchants and farmers from China proper, who had their own ways of doing things. The Qing rulers and their allies continued to operate bannerlands and estates and at the end of the dynasty sought to raise additional income by selling and taxing land. But the growing, purchasing, processing, shipping, and marketing of agricultural goods, which were the principal wealth of Manchuria, were the work of Chinese farmers and merchants. After 1903, the economy of Manchuria would be reshaped by foreign powers, Russia and Japan. Until then, it remained in Chinese hands.

This chapter focuses on two aspects of the Chinese performance prior to 1903. First, is the production, processing, and trade of soybeans, Manchuria's most important commercial crop. The purpose is to describe the various aspects of the soybean business and to ask how Chinese behavior changed (or did not change) to take advantage of the opportunities of working in a newly settled region and the demands of an expanding market. Second, is the degree of economic growth and development that occurred (or did not occur) in Manchuria prior to 1903, while this region remained under Chinese control. Again, the question is whether new conditions prompted new patterns of behavior that might propel the Chinese economy in new directions. The findings show that Chinese entrepreneurs did *not* change in response to changed circumstances, and the economy of Manchuria did *not* grow or develop with particular speed or in ways that distinguish this region from China proper. In commerce, as in society, the Chinese were successful settlers, but reluctant pioneers.

A. Trade in Manchuria and Inner Mongolia, 1644–1860

Before moving to the principal topic, soybeans, and the late-19th century, this chapter begins with a brief account of the economy and trade in Manchuria during the first two centuries of Qing rule. During this period, the commerce of Manchuria grew along three lines: first, private exchanges between Chinese merchants and Manchu and Mongol landlords, and later among Chinese themselves, primarily in southern Manchuria; second, the establishment of military installations and government-owned industries to support the defense of this region against the Russian threat in the north; and third, the trade of Manchurian raw materials for the manufactured goods of China proper. It was the export of soybeans, initially to China proper, later to Japan and beyond, that gave rise to the largest and potentially most dynamic sector of the Manchurian economy, which is the subject of the remainder of this chapter.

1. Domestic Trade: Manchus, Mongols, and Chinese

The rise of commerce in southern Manchuria and areas of Inner Mongolia adjacent to the Great Wall was prompted first by the demand of Manchus and Mongols for the products of China proper and over time by the migration, settlement, and cultivation of these areas by the Chinese themselves. The first Chinese in these areas included merchants and traders, whom the Qing admitted even under the "closure" policy. This may seem ironic, in view of the dynasty's concern that the influx of Chinese and development of the economy of this region would erase the boundary between north and south and transform Manchuria into an extension of China. But the Qing rulers recognized that in order to keep reliable Manchu and Mongol allies in the homelands, the dynasty would have to supply them with the luxury items coveted by the rich and everyday goods needed to maintain a comfortable lifestyle for all. Only Chinese merchants could provide this service. Yet the irony is well placed, for the effect of the merchants was to hasten the rise of a market economy, which in the long run undermined Manchu control.

There was great demand in Manchuria and Inner Mongolia for Chinese merchandise and merchants who could supply it. Under the practice of the late Ming, known as ruling with a "loose rein" [*jimi*], the northern tribes had grown accustomed to receiving luxury goods from the rulers in Beijing. Many Manchus had joined the invasion of China and stayed on after the conquest, because they preferred the comforts and riches of the agrarian empire to the simpler life of the forest or steppe. Those who remained at home and whom the dynasty counted on to manage the bannerlands and estates and provide for the security of these territories expected to receive grain, sugar, tea, handicrafts, and other goods from China proper. Bannermen were allowed to serve as soldiers, officials, or farmers, but were prohibited from engaging in trade or other occupations, which were reserved for the Chinese.[1] As long as Chinese merchants were limited in number and barred from the purchase of land, they could help satisfy the appetites of those who remained in Manchuria and Inner Mongolia and buttress rather than undermine the Manchu system of control—or so the Qing rulers imagined.

Many Manchus and Mongols who exercised control over land in the banners and estates developed an appetite for Chinese merchandise, found that Chinese merchants were willing to supply these goods on credit, consumed beyond their means, and as their debts mounted sought to satisfy their creditors first by renting land and ultimately by transferring control over the land itself. With the passage of time, the most successful merchants became land agents: taking large tracts on consignment from banners or estates, subdividing the land into smaller plots, and renting or selling these plots to individual tenants and farmers. The nobles and officials who controlled the land needed large sums of money to support their lavish lifestyles, while Chinese migrants had no cash to pay deposits or other start-up costs, enabling the merchants to step in and finance the transactions in both directions. In some cases, "speculators" or "monopolists" took control of hundreds or even thousands of square kilometers of farmland.[2] Depending on market conditions, they might dispose of the land at a profit or import workers to produce grain, which could be sold locally or exported to cities in China proper.[3]

In addition to sales to Manchus and Mongols, the spread of agriculture produced a more sustainable basis for trade among the Chinese themselves. Migrant farmers needed tools and household implements and, as their means permitted, traded grain, beans, cotton, and other crops for sugar, tobacco, tea, cotton cloth, and simple manufactures. Gradually, shops began to appear for the manufacture and sale of wood, metal, leather and ceramic wares, candles, soap, wine, vegetable oil, and other goods. From the mid-18th century on, privately owned

[1] Edward Rhoads (2000), 36; Shelley Rigger (1995), 200.
[2] Tian Zhihe (1984B), 88–90.
[3] Liang Bing (1991), 50–52.

factories were established in Fengtian and Jilin to press oil, brew wine, fire pottery, and spin silk. Capital for manufacturing and trade was provided by pawnshops [*dangpu*] and money houses [*qianpu*], established under both private and government auspices throughout the Northeast.[4]

The introduction of handicrafts and trade to service agriculture gave rise to periodic and later permanent markets. At the time of the conquest in 1644, a periodic market in the Manchu capital of Shengjing served the large administrative and military presence in this city and the surrounding communities. Other cities, such as Tieling, Liaoyang, Kaiyuan, Ninguta, and Sanxing, although visited from time to time by itinerant merchants, had no established markets. Gradually, buyers and sellers began to gather at more regular times and predictable places, in medium-size towns such as Tieling, where a periodic market appeared in late 1600s: Each day of the lunar calendar ending in the number 3, merchants displayed their wares on the North Road, each day ending in 6, on the West Road, and each day ending in 9, on the East Road. Livestock were traded at the city gate in front of the county magistrate's office, grain at the gate of the Great North Road above the Dongguan Bridge, melons on the Great South Road below the bridge, and meat and vegetables at the watchtower. Periodic markets, named for the days on which they met—in this case, the "3-6-9 market"—grew up in many towns and cities of Manchuria.[5]

During the 19th century, periodic markets were replaced by city streets lined with shops and stores. One list of commercial and manufacturing enterprises in Fengtian City includes 1,129 establishments in 34 different categories with nearly 9,000 employees. The number of stores and shops in Jilin City increased from around 300 in 1866 to more than 1,500 in 1902.[6] By the 1880s, Petuna had 200 stores of various types,[7] shoppers in Hulan could find stores selling "lacquered furniture, mirrors, china and pewter ware, furs, cloth, and, of course coffins," and Kuanchengzi (Changchun) boasted "the largest emporium in the north," a main street three miles long, "a splendid thoroughfare, a bewildering vista of sign-posts, and obelisks, and gilt inscriptions, and lamps."[8] "Every manner of merchandise can be found in K'uan-ch'eng-tzu,"

[4] Kong Jingwei (1990), 182–86.
[5] Ibid., 198–99. Today, one still finds "3-6-9 markets" in the less developed areas of Manchuria and Inner Mongolia.
[6] Ibid., 490–94.
[7] Ibid., 499.
[8] Henry James (1888), 315–16, 374–77.

reported one visitor to this city, whose population reached 250,000, in 1903.

From the north and east come all kinds of agricultural produce; from the west Mongolia sends its ponies, its skins, it hides, and its flocks; from the south Newchwang forwards bales of cottons, stacks of iron, and a thousand other things to be distributed over the country in payment for what has been bought for export. . . .[9]

Commerce also spread through Inner Mongolia. In the early Qing, Wudan, the capital of Wengniute Banner, which lies between the Xilamulun and Laoha Rivers, was a trading post and site of periodic markets that serviced Mongol nomads. After the arrival of the Chinese, the number of stores and shops increased from 14 or 15 in 1875, to 45 in 1894, and more than 100 in 1908, by which time Wudan had a permanent population of 3,000 and served as the base for itinerant merchants operating throughout the surrounding countryside.[10] Even larger and more important was Chifeng, the prefectural seat and commercial center for the Upper Liao region. By the beginning of the 20th century, Chifeng had 30 coal mines, 25 coking furnaces, 20 flour mills (the first steam-powered mill in Inner Mongolia was set up here in 1908), and more than 120 factories making textiles, leather goods, paper, foodstuffs, farm implements, and the like.[11]

2. Military Trade: The Garrisons of the North

Unlike southern Manchuria and the adjacent steppe, where commerce was driven primarily by private initiative, the economy of Jilin and Heilongjiang was shaped by the presence of military forces and government industries set up to support them. All of the cities established in Jilin and Heilongjiang during the 17th and 18th centuries began as military installations, surrounded by agricultural colonies, courier stations, and trading posts. These fort-cities included Jilin City, Ninguta, Petuna, Alachuke, Sanxing, and Hunchun in Jilin and Aihui, Mergen, Tsitsihar, and Hulan in Heilongjiang. Only after 1800 did there appear cities, such as Kuanchengzi (Changchun), that lacked an initial military or administrative presence and grew out of purely commercial activity.

[9] Putnam Weale (1904), 444–45. In 1896, Alexander Hosie (1904), 22, had estimated the population of Kuanchengzi at 120,000, but less than a decade later, Weale reported, it reached 250,000.

[10] *Wengniuteqi wenshi ziliao*, 9, 18, 69.

[11] *Chifeng shi*, 256–58.

The trade of the fort-cities began with the shipment of grain and other supplies to troops on the frontier. Merchants attached themselves to army posts, dealt with soldiers and supply officers, and built up a trade with the surrounding communities. Yet, most fort-cities were slow to move beyond the status of primitive garrisons. In 1741, the French missionary, Jean-Baptiste Du Halde, reported that there were only three cities in Jilin—Jilin City, Petuna, and Ninguta—all "wretchedly built, and surrounded with Walls of Earth."[12] Little had changed by the end of the 19th century. Tsitsihar, the seat of government in Heilongjiang, remained home to around 1,500 Manchu soldiers, a couple of inns, and shops bearing Russian goods, but generated little commerce of its own. Other garrison towns on the outer perimeter of the empire, such as Mergen, Sanxing, and Hunchun, had also failed to outgrow their garrisons.[13]

The only exception was Ninguta. The first Qing forces dispatched to northern Manchuria in 1652 established the garrison at Ninguta, which served as the military headquarters of this region until 1676, when the command moved to Jilin. Ninguta was also the gateway through which passed (legally and illegally) ginseng, sables, and other products from the eastern forests. During the 17th century, Chinese merchants flooded the city, transforming it into a bustling marketplace, filled with cartloads of cotton cloth and other goods from China proper and forest products destined for the return.[14] "The trade of Ningouta is considerable and draws a great number of Chinese from the most distant Provinces," observed Du Halde.[15] By the end of the 19th century, forty businesses in Ninguta had combined sales of nearly 600,000 strings of cash, which was five to seven times the level of trade in either Hulan or Tsitsihar.[16]

To support its forces in the Northeast, Beijing established mines, factories, and industrial works at various strategic locations. After 1676, when the Tartar General moved his headquarters from Ninguta to Jilin, the latter city, then known as the "shipyard" [*chuanchang*], became the center for the construction of junks, boats, and ferries for military use. Great rafts of timber were floated down the Sungari from the Changbaishan Mountains on the Korean border and dragged up the banks to

---

[12] Jean-Baptiste Du Halde (1741), 94.
[13] Henry James (1888): 304–9, 330–32, 346.
[14] Kong Jingwei (1990), 169, 198. Henry James (1888), 340.
[15] Jean-Baptiste Du Halde (1741), 94.
[16] Kong Jingwei (1990), 503. For additional details, see: Zhang Yaomin (1990), 167–210.

shipyards that lined both sides of the river.[17] The Qing tried, and failed, to enforce a ban on private shipbuilding, so that by the middle of the 18th century the Sungari was filled with boats of various types transporting passengers, agricultural products, and other commodities in all directions. Government mines and arsenals in Shengjing and Jilin produced gunpowder and lead shot for troops on the frontier. Officials oversaw the only coal mine in Manchuria, located at Benqi, while local government offices set up ironworks to refashion scrap iron imported from China proper. (In the 20th century, central Manchuria would emerge as a major producer of iron and steel, but before then blacksmiths in this area simply reworked imported iron.) Many of the official and imperial estates operated factories to spin yarn, weave and dye cloth, or manufacture salt, some of which were used to supply military forces in the north.[18]

3. External Trade: The Markets of China Proper

Finally, in addition to private markets that served Manchus, Mongols, and Chinese farmers in the south and governmental enterprises linked to military installations in the north, the commerce of Manchuria and Inner Mongolia responded to a growing demand in China proper for agricultural goods and other raw materials. At first, the trade was mostly in natural products, such as ginseng, pearls, and furs, which were subject to government monopolies and therefore favored by smugglers. Later, these products were eclipsed by agricultural goods: cotton, indigo, tobacco, grain, and especially soybeans. Whether legal (until 1906) or illegal (after that date), opium was a high-value, lightweight product that could be grown in marginal areas and fetched a high price in the cities below the Great Wall.

The question of trade, like migration, posed a dilemma for the Qing. The dynasty had to balance its commitment to maintain strong, reliable allies in Manchuria and Inner Mongolia and thus ensure their economic welfare, against the threat of political instability in China proper that could arise from either an excess of population or a shortage of food. With regard to migration, the question was whether or not Beijing should open the border to the movement of people northward. With regard to trade, especially food, the question was whether or not to open the border to shipments south.

[17] Henry James (1888), 293.
[18] Kong Jingwei (1990), 172–82.

When harvests in north China were good, the government could block exports of grain from above the Great Wall, and thus ensure a surplus that would hold down prices and benefit the dynasty's Manchu and Mongol allies. But when famine struck China proper, Beijing sent agents to Jehol and Fengtian to purchase and ship beans and grain to the affected areas. Such concerns and choices were not unique to Manchuria and Inner Mongolia; on the contrary, they were central to governing all parts of the empire. But they were especially sensitive in this region: first, because of the special role of the Manchu homeland, and second, because they involved coastal shipping. The threat that food might be smuggled abroad or captured by pirates, bandits, or rebels, meant that ships leaving port were prohibited from carrying more grain than required by their crews, and the embargo on sea trade [*haijin*] was always more rigorously enforced than that on exchanges between inland provinces.[19]

Owing to the multiple and changing pressures on Beijing, the stated policies and actual practices on trade across the Great Wall were as unstable, confusing, neglected, and unenforceable as those on migration. The same edicts, "opening" or "closing" the gate between Manchuria and China proper, applied (or failed to apply effectively) to goods as to people. After the embargo on coastal trade was lifted in 1684, junks and sand boats [*shachuan*] from northern and central China made regular calls on Newchwang and other Manchurian ports to exchange sugar, tea, and cotton cloth from the Lower Yangzi for beans, wheat, and raw cotton grown in southern Manchuria. Later, as the production of handicrafts shifted to north China, Manchuria became a supplier of cotton to and market for cloth from that region.[20] Trade between Manchuria and China proper was large enough to prompt the establishment of a customs office in Fengtian in 1707. However, Qing policies flip-flopped, so that it is difficult to say whether the normal status of the Manchurian ports was opened or closed. In some years, such as 1740, when the Qing imposed the "closure" policy in Manchuria, Beijing ordered the coastal provinces to prohibit merchant ships from calling on ports in the Northeast and instructed officials in Fengtian to prevent migrants from disembarking in this region.[21] In other years, such as 1743, when famine struck Zhili, Beijing opened the gates to imports from the north. Still later, in 1762, when the Tartar General reported shortages in Fengtian,

[19] Pierre-Etienne Will (1990), 211–16.
[20] Philip Huang (1985), 119.
[21] *Da Qing huidian*, zhuan 158, cited in Kong Jingwei (1990), 152.

the ban was reimposed. Over time, however, the trend favored greater trade: The ban on the export of soybeans was lifted in 1749, and all restrictions on exports of soybeans and wheat from Manchuria were removed in 1772. After this date, Beijing apparently made no further attempts to restrict trade between Manchuria and China proper, although the prohibition on the shipment of goods to foreign ports remained in force.[22]

B. The Bean Trade

The soybean, called by the Chinese the "yellow bean" [*huangdou*] or sometimes "big bean" [*dadou*], occupies a central place in the commerce of late-19th and early-20th century Manchuria. Throughout this period, beans and bean products, beancake and bean oil, occupied 70 to 80 percent of Manchuria's exports. At its peak, in 1930, Manchuria accounted for 60 percent of global production and a corresponding share of world trade in soybeans.[23] The bean industry proceeded through several steps, from growing, to processing, transporting, trading, and finally shipping. At each stage, the technology, organization, financing, and the particular character, what we will call "flexibility," of Chinese actors and institutions explain much about Chinese behavior in the bean trade and by extension in Manchuria as a whole. This section will examine each of these four factors and at the end assess the performance of the Manchurian bean business as a whole.

1. *Technology*

In his classic study, *The Great Plains*, Walter Prescott Webb describes a number of technological innovations—the six-shooter, cattle herding, barbed wire, windmills, and large farm machinery—that enabled American settlers to cross the divide from the moist, hilly, forested valleys of the eastern United States to the dry, flat, treeless plains of the West. Webb's argument is that these devices had little utility or market

---

[22] Pierre-Etienne Will (1990), 153–58, 170–71, 216–18, 222–24. For details on trade between Manchuria and China proper during the 17th and 18th centuries, see: Wu Chengming (1983), 102, and Xu Dixin and Wu Chengming (1985), 271–73.

[23] According to the SMR, *Third Report*, 143, in 1930, Manchuria produced 5.3 million metric tons (59.3 percent) and China proper 2.3 million mt (25.4 percent) of global production of 8.1 million mt of soybeans. Yields in Manchuria, 1.3 mt/ha, were higher than in any other country.

Transportation. Prior to 1900, trade and transportation in Manchuria followed the Liao River and varied with the season. In winter, when the ground was frozen hard and the peasants were freed from farmwork, carts, *top* (8), were used to haul produce to market. Thousands of carts, drawn by teams of horses and mules splayed out on hempen ropes, carried soybeans and other farm products over tracks formed by countless predecessors, *bottom* (9), to ports on the Liao. With the spring thaw, the overland tracks turned to mud, the peasant

carters and their draft animals returned to the fields, and the ice broke on the rivers, enabling a forest of junks to converge on Newchwang, *top* (10), bringing produce down from central Manchuria or picking it up for shipment to China proper and beyond. After 1905, the Liao-Newchwang system was eclipsed by the South Manchuria Railway, which carried larger volumes of produce faster and cheaper to the deepwater port at Dairen, and thence by modern steamships to the world market. The construction of railroads, *bottom* (11), not only changed the pattern of transportation but attracted larger numbers of Chinese workers to Manchuria.

SOURCES: Nos. 8 and 10: Putnam Weale (1904), 312, 520. No. 9: Adachi Kinnosuke (1925), 242. No. 11: SMR, *Fifth Report* (1936), 50.

value in the East, but were crucial in enabling Americans to settle and exploit the potential of the West, and that it was the new surroundings that prompted innovation in technology and organization. Although in theory Manchuria should have provided a similar stimulus for change, the record of the soybean industry suggests that the Chinese did not respond in the same fashion.

The cultivation of soybeans, which was introduced into the Liaodong by Chinese farmers as early as the Han Dynasty (ca. 200 B.C.) and was quite common in this region by the beginning of the Qing, followed practices that remained essentially unchanged into the early 20th century. According to a study published in 1911, the ground was broken in April, using a single-handled, steel-tipped plough, drawn by mixed teams of oxen, mules, and donkeys. The seed was sown and covered by hand, and fertilized, if at all, with a compost of manure and soil, which was also applied by hand. Since fertilizer was in short supply, it was especially important to remove weeds by turning and breaking the ground with a heavy hoe. The beans were harvested in September by pulling the plants up by the roots or cutting them with a sickle before they had fully ripened, lest the pods burst and the seeds scatter. After drying, the seeds were separated from the pods using a stone roller, which was dragged over the plants by a mule. Winnowing was done by throwing the mixture of beans and chaff against the wind.[24] Once dried and separated, the beans were ready for market or for pressing to produce oil and beancake.

Evidence from the Kotoku surveys shows that as late as the 1930s, farmers in Manchuria continued to rely on simple, even crude, tools and techniques. One exception was the heavy Russian plow, which was adopted by peasants in Jilin and Heilongjiang to break soil that was strewn with roots and rocks in the forested east and covered with a thick matting of stubborn sod in the west.[25] The extension of agriculture onto the Ukrainian steppe in the 17th century was made possible when the light horse-drawn Muscovite *sokha* was replaced by the heavy Polish iron plow, pulled by teams of oxen, and capable of turning the thick sod.[26] Russian migrants brought this device to Siberia and to sites along

[24] CIGC, *The Soya Bean* (1911), 4–5.

[25] CER (1924), 51–52, observes that in Northern Manchuria during the 1920s, Russian tractors and ploughs were used to break soil for colonization projects, because the Chinese plough was not up to the task. *Kotoku sannendo*, sites 1 and 16, describe use of heavy plows and other equipment drawn by teams of up to six horses. In Aihui County (site 1), this was due to Russian influence. For photographs of heavy plow see: *Noson jittai chosa hokokusho*, 48, 108.

[26] I. Stebelsky (1983).

the Heilongjiang. Chinese who moved northward found that the small plow pulled by a single ox, which worked well in China proper, could not bust sod on the Mongolian steppe or in Manchuria, and adopted a longer, larger iron plow, presumably inspired by Russian examples, which required two men and the power of five or six horses, mules, or oxen.[27]

For the most part, however, farmers in Manchuria were limited to the same hand tools and simple techniques that had been used for centuries below the Great Wall. In part, this was a sign of poverty: Chinese refugees, who made up the bulk of the workforce, had only the few implements they could carry with them or make on the spot—wooden, stone, or metal hand tools, which, although primitive, represented a considerable share of the rural capital. In part, it was a function of distance from the centers of population and commerce: The further one moved north, the more backward the equipment and methods. In the 1920s, the only mechanical device on most farms in Heilongjiang was a simple winnowing machine. And in part, it was due to the abundance of land and the shortage of labor in the northern territories: Under these conditions it made better sense to slash, burn, exhaust the land and move on, than to invest in expensive equipment or labor intensive techniques.[28] The evidence from the 1930s shows that Manchurian farmers rotated crops on a three- or four-year cycle, fertilized using animal manure or human waste in combination with the planting of beans, normally once within the cycle, and since fertilizer was always in short supply weeded intensively to reduce the competition for nutrients.[29] There are no reports of attempts at irrigation. Chinese farmers in Manchuria did the best they could with the knowledge and methods they brought with them from China proper. There is no indication they came up with anything new.[30]

[27] *Heilongjiang waiji* [External Notes of Heilongjiang] and *Heilongjiang zhigao* [Heilongjiang Gazette], cited in Sun Zhanwen (1981), 79. *Kotoku sannendo*, site 16, describes a plow of this type. For a photo, see *Noson jittai chosa hokokusho*, 3:48–49. A description of the light plow used in north China in the early 19th century, appears in George Timkowski (1827), II, 367–68.

[28] CER (1924), 51–52. *Manchoukuo Year Book (1934)*, 292–96.

[29] On the widespread use of crop rotation and fertilization, see *Kotoku gannendo*, sites 1, and 3–10; and *Kotoku sannendo*, sites 2, 5, 11, 14, 15, and 19. Although weeding is discussed less often in these village histories, *Kotoku gannendo*, site 10, contains a detailed description of the techniques and results of weeding three times during the growing season.

[30] According to Kong Jingwei (1990), 301–12 and Sun Zhanwen (1981), 96, reform-minded governments of the late-Qing and early-republican periods recognized the lack of progress and need for agricultural improvement in the Northeast.

The same was true for the processing of beans. Soybeans could be consumed directly or exported whole, but most beans were pressed to produce bean oil and the residue, beancake. Bean presses in Manchuria, as well as China proper, made use of simple techniques that date from the 14th century or before: a massive stone roller that was drawn around a circular stone base by two mules to crush the raw beans; a wood-burning stove and iron pots to steam and soften the crushed wafers; iron hoops and wooden cylinders to hold the bean mash in place; a press made of oak logs with wedges driven by hand to compress the tightly packed beans; and wicker baskets with paper linings to cart the beans and bean products from one location to the next.[31] A few skilled carpenters and blacksmiths, working with local materials and scrap iron imported from China or abroad, could build a mill and keep it running. Power was supplied by workmen and draft animals. Nothing in the design or operation of a 19th-century Manchurian mill would have surprised or been beyond the skill of craftsmen from the 17th century, or even before.[32] As the demand for beans and bean products grew, hundreds of small native mills were set up throughout Manchuria.[33] Mills of this type could extract about one-half (9 percent by weight) of the oil content of the soybeans, leaving the balance in the residue cake.

Modern devices were available, but Chinese were slow to adopt them. The first bean mill using state-of-the-art steam-powered equipment in Manchuria was built and operated by the British firm, Jardine, Matheson, in Newchwang between 1868–70. A study by Shannon Brown shows that this experiment was a technological and economic success: the company purchased raw beans and coal at competitive prices, the equipment worked as expected, and the margin of profits achieved by this foreign mill was higher than any of its native rivals. The problem, according to Brown, was that Chinese laborers balked at the intense and continuous work pattern required to offset the high cost of fixed capital of the modern mill. They refused to work at night, when the steam engines were charged and could not be shut down, and they refused to work in the slack season, when native mills with less fixed capital declared a holiday. "Essentially," concludes Brown, "the problem

[31] Sung Ying-Hsing (1966), 217–19; Francesca Bray (1985), 206.

[32] CIGC (1911), 13–14; Alexander Hosie (1904), 218–23.

[33] For example, in the 1870s and 1880s, bean mills in Tsitsihar, Ninguta, and Hulan were producing 3,000–5,000 piculs per year in each city, as compared with annual exports through Newchwang of over 750,000 piculs per year. Kong Jingwei (1990), 401–5, 504, 520–21.

was to get the Chinese workers to adapt to the needs of the foreign machinery."[34]

While cultural factors, such as work habits, may have inhibited the introduction of new technologies, these factors were later overcome by changes in the legal and political environment. The Treaty of Shimonoseki (1895), ending the Sino-Japanese War, gave foreigners the right to establish factories in the treaty ports. From that time on, a growing number of modern bean mills were introduced, first in Yingkou under British auspices, and later in other Manchurian cities under both Chinese and foreign control.[35] Most native mills had no more than three small presses, whereas the modern factories had from 20 to as many as 100 much larger steam presses. The larger scale and greater power of the modern presses produced yields of 10 to 12 percent, increasing both the quantity of oil and the quality of the beancake, whose value went up as the oil content went down. Later, in the 1920s, a chemical process for extracting oil introduced in Dairen produced yields of up to 14 percent.[36]

The next stage of the bean business, transportation, was dominated by even older devices, the cart and the junk. The choice of conveyance was seasonal: From November to March, Manchuria froze solid, closing the rivers to navigation and hardening the earth, so that it could support the "great carts" [*dache*], which were drawn by draft animals and driven by farmworkers temporarily freed from the burdens of agriculture. Conversely, in summer, the rivers melted and swelled under heavy rains, enabling shallow-draft junks to haul up the Liao or down the Sungari, while the roads were lost in mud and the carters and their animals returned to the fields. Before the creation of a network of railroads, steamships, and telegraph lines, carts and junks drove commercial development in the Northeast.

The construction and operation of the Manchurian great cart were derived from models familiar to merchants and farmers in China proper and made use of the same materials and skills found in the bean mills. In fact, a rig virtually identical to that described below is pictured in the *Tiangong kaiwu*,[37] the 17th-century textbook on industrial technology, and includes various elements that may go back two millennia or more.[38] The body of the four-wheel great cart, 15 feet long by 4 feet

[34] Shannon Brown (1981), 453–59.
[35] Alexander Hosie (1904), 223.
[36] CER (1924), 247–48, 252–54; CIGC, *Returns of Trade* (1901), 1; (1908), 19.
[37] Sung Ying-Hsing (1966), 181.
[38] Joseph Needham (1965), 79–82, 243–55.

wide, rested on heavy oak beams, while a lighter framework of elm held the 2 to 3 tons of freight. The element most challenging to build and most susceptible to damage was the wheel-and-axle assemblage. At the end of each axle was a wheel made of three wooden spokes: one massive beam that extended the full diameter of the wheel, and two smaller beams fitted at right angles and passing through the main spoke. The spokes were clasped with iron bands, and the side of the wheel studded with large iron rivets. An iron tire, fashioned in curved sections two inches wide and one inch thick, was nailed into a groove on the fellies of the wooden wheel. Each wheel-and-axle assemblage revolved as a piece and without lubrication—save for icy winds that mitigated the effects of friction between axle and beam. The number of draft animals varied with the size, weight, and range of the cart, from as few as two or three for small local deliveries, to as many as 8 or 10 for long-distance shipments of full loads. The driver, who sat atop the load, directed his team, splayed out on hempen ropes or traces, with a long whip of twisted cane, while a second driver walked beside the animals, helping to keep them on track. Both men kept gingalls, matchlocks, swords, and spears close at hand to fend off bandits.[39] A fully loaded cart could cover 25 to 40 kilometers per day, depending upon the conditions of the road. The most important route, from the bean-producing region surrounding Changchun and Jilin to Newchwang, measured 500–700 km and took 3 to 4 weeks.[40]

As the weather warmed and the roads softened, cartmen and livestock returned to the fields, while junks transported the remaining crops down the Liao to Newchwang. The junk, nautical equivalent of the great cart, was a wooden vessel with a shallow draft, that could be propelled on inland waters by sails, oars, poles, or towlines. The size of the junks varied from the relatively small, maneuverable type that could be hauled or dragged up river to secondary markets and transit points, to the large, heavy craft that sailed the open sea to Shanghai and beyond. Chinese oceangoing junks of much greater size and sophistication, of course, long preceded the hand-me-downs used in Manchuria.

Finally, the success of the bean trade depended on a technology for transporting the products, cake and oil. Soybeans come wrapped in a tough skin, well packaged for travel, while the weight of bean products are virtually identical to the beans from which they are made, so that there is no economic advantage in processing the beans at the point

[39] Alexander Hosie (1904), 237–38; Henry James (1888), 372.
[40] CIGC, *Returns of Trade* (1889), 3.

of origin rather than the destination. If Manchurian mills could press beans effectively, and Manchurian shippers move the products cheaply and safely, then Manchuria and the Manchurian hinterland could capture the value added by processing and move up the ladder of development. If not, then market forces would favor shipping the raw beans and pressing them nearer to the consumers, in which case Manchuria would lose the value added by the processing industry. During the 19th century, oil extracted by bean mills in the interior was transported to Newchwang in strong wooden boxes that could withstand the beating administered by frozen, rutted roads. On reaching the port, the oil was transferred to large jar- or carafe-shaped wicker baskets lined with waterproof paper, which were loaded onto steamers or seagoing junks.[41]

Junks enjoyed an advantage in shipping bean oil because of their simple, traditional technology. Foreign shippers attracted cargo because they charged low rates, called on both Chinese and foreign ports, and offered insurance not available on junks. But steamships were not built to store the irregularly shaped baskets, the crews on foreign ships were said to be careless in handling the baskets, which could weigh up to 500 pounds apiece, and since this delicate cargo was subject to spillage, foreign shippers charged higher rates for oil than for other products. By contrast, junks were specially constructed to accommodate the baskets, and their crews were trained to move the baskets with care, advantages that offset the lack of insurance on junks. Junks were restricted to Chinese ports, which was a handicap for shippers of beans and beancake destined for Japan and other foreign countries, but not bean oil, most of which was consumed in China. By the early 20th century, foreign ships moved more than ten times as much beans and beancake as Chinese craft, but junks continued to dominate trade in oil.[42]

All of the technologies related to the bean industry depended upon materials, including wood, wicker (willow), leather, hemp, and scrap iron, that were readily at hand, on draft animals, horses, oxen, donkeys, and mules, and on the modestly skilled labor of carpenters, blacksmiths, and other craftsmen. These materials and the techniques to work them were imported or derived from models that originated in China proper and were applied, more or less unchanged, in new surroundings. None was invented or improved in any noticeable way by

[41] Alexander Hosie (1904), 16, 245; CIGC, *Reports on Trade* (1877), 3.
[42] Alexander Hosie (1904), 245; CIGC, *Reports on Trade* (1878), 10.

virtue of contact with new circumstances north of the Great Wall. We find in this case no counterparts to Webb's barbed wire, windmills, or six-guns. Chinese in Manchuria got on, quite well, with the tools and ideas they brought from home.

2. *Organization*

In organization, as in technology, the Manchurian bean trade depended upon a large number of small, independently owned and operated enterprises, based on models imported from China proper. During the slack season, following the harvest, a cart, a horse, and a farmer were all that was needed to form a transport company, and enterprises of this type held their own, even after the introduction of the railroads and modern shipping lines in the 20th century. The Chinese Eastern Railway learned this lesson the hard way, losing out to horse-carts in a head-to-head competition for shipments between Harbin and Changchun in the years immediately following World War I.[43] During the peak season at the end of the 19th century, up to two thousand carts arrived in Newchwang each day, while one observer estimated that over 20,000 junks were engaged in river transport. As small carters and boatmen approached Newchwang, they came under the jurisdiction of one of the guilds that regulated and protected each slice of the business in this city.[44] The members of these guilds were separate small businesses that banded together only to keep the price of their service high. There were no large shipping companies upstream from Newchwang and no central control over the multitude of small entrepreneurs who took up the trade.

The business of buying and selling beans and other agricultural goods was conducted at three levels. At the base were the *liangzhan*, literally "grain warehouses," small companies that bought grain and beans directly from the farmers and sold to millers, distillers, or larger wholesalers further up the line. The typical *liangzhan* was a partnership, formed by as few as two and seldom more than six men, often including an official or military officer, who together contributed the capital, labor, and connections required to run the business. By the early 20th century, there were thousands of *liangzhan* in Manchuria. Although each one of them had limited capital, few employees, and a restricted range of operation, collectively they held most of the wealth and moved

[43] CER (1924), 79, 272–78.
[44] See Shannon Brown (1981), 453, for a description of Newchwang guilds.

most of the produce in this region.[45] At the opposite end were the export firms in Newchwang, which purchased large stocks of raw materials, processed and shipped them abroad or to the major cities on the China coast. Between these extremes were the "distribution markets," where cartloads of goods from the local traders were assembled into larger lots for transfer to Newchwang. Most *liangzhan* and wholesalers were Chinese, while the exporters were Europeans, Americans, and Japanese.

Another small business central to the bean trade was the country inn, temporary home to the farmer bringing his produce to market or the cartman on his journey south. The successful innkeeper, who doubled as agent for the storage and sale of produce and earned a reputation for prompt sales at good prices, could make a handsome living on commissions at the standard rate of 2 percent. As his business grew, the innkeeper sent his touts onto the road to find clients, who received free room and board in exchange for their consignments. Whether it anchored the local village or occupied a space along the road to Newchwang, during the fall and winter when the bean trade was at its height the inn was a bedlam of activity, its courtyard a tangle of carts, harnesses, and livestock, and its rooms filled with farmers and cartmen, who sat on the heated *kang*, dined on stewed mutton and hot wine, and smoked a pipe of opium, before resuming their adventure in the cold.[46]

Finally, the bean mill itself was a small business, generally a partnership formed by a handful of men, who pooled their savings to buy or build a factory of modest size at a location where beans could be gathered from farms and the products shipped to market. Until the introduction of steam-powered equipment, which was expensive, difficult to obtain and operate, and even more difficult to move beyond the treaty port where it was unloaded, the technology and economics of milling favored the small, low-budget local mill and limited partnership. Bean milling, like the bean trade as a whole, was a big business conducted by lots of small businessmen.

3. Financing

The structure of the grain trade and related industries, in which capital was dispersed among a large number of small businesses, was both

[45] CER (1924), 88–92; Kong Jingwei (1990), 349–54.

[46] For a colorful description of one roadside inn, which served as a stopover for carters en route to Newchwang, see Henry James (1888), 372–73.

Commerce. During the 19th and early 20th centuries, Manchuria's leading exports were soybeans and bean products. After 1905, peasants from northern Manchuria shipped their beans to the railroad yard at Changchun, *left* (12), the terminus of the Japanese South Manchuria Railway, bypassing both the Russian Chinese Eastern Railway and the Chinese port of Newchwang on the Liao River and enabling the Japanese to dominate the commerce of this region. The bean industry drew migrants together into villages and along trade routes, whereas another product, timber, which was cut in the mountains and floated down the Yalu or Sungari rivers, *top right* (13), scattered young men to the hills and turned some to banditry. The growth of commerce gave rise to towns and cities, such as Jilin, *bottom right* (14), capital of the province of the same name, which attracted migrants who preferred even menial jobs, such as pulling rickshaws, to the drudgery of farm work.
SOURCES: Nos. 12–13: SMR, First Report (1929), 116, 124. No. 14: Adachi Kinnosuke (1925), 286.

caused by and contributed to the third feature of 19th-century Manchurian commerce, which was the scarcity of capital and credit. The shortage of capital was due in the first instance to the transience of the Manchurian population, who as sojourners sent or took most of their money home. During the Russo-Japanese War (1904–05), enormous sums were spent to support the two armies, money flooded Manchuria from north and south, and all types of production and trade flourished. But these one-time expenditures quickly disappeared, because much

of the money went to pay dealers, carters, and coolies, who converted their earnings into sycee or silver coins and fled at the first opportunity back to Shandong or Zhili.[47]

Credit was also a problem. There were a few private banks in southern Manchuria, but none at all in the north. Banks attracted few

[47]CIGC, *Returns of Trade* (1907), 24.

depositors, because most people preferred to buy real estate, hoard silver, or invest directly in businesses, rather than put their savings in institutions that paid low interest and inspired little confidence. Instead, pawnshops, money changers, and other credit institutions were formed as partnerships among small groups of investors who operated on the basis of their pooled capital. In contrast to western banks, which take in deposits and make loans at low interest, for long periods, to total strangers with the proper collateral, Manchurian credit institutions loaned out their own capital, at high interest, on short terms (3 to 12 months), to people they knew and trusted or who had personal guarantors with similar credentials. As a result, credit was generally available only to a few men with good connections and then only for short periods, to finance trade or purchase discounted notes. There was virtually no credit for long-term investments, such as the purchase of land, buildings, machinery, or other fixed capital. The pawnshop, *not* the bank, was the model credit institution of 19th-century Manchuria. Its architecture bespoke the advantage of the lender and the dependence of those who came seeking loans:

When one enters a pawn shop, one's attention is struck by an extremely high (not less than 7 feet) wooden barrier made of boards and stretching from wall to wall, thereby separating the room for the public from the space reserved for the employees of the shop. The latter are behind the barrier on a specially arranged platform. Therefore, when talking the employees look down upon their clients, whereas the latter must raise their heads. In former times these barriers were made with the purpose of protection from possible attacks by robber, and they are being maintained up to the present day [1924] by the force of tradition.[48]

One novel form of credit, the system of "transfer money" [*guoluyin*] used in Newchwang, reinforced the dominance of small businessmen with personal connections. Transfer money was so called, because it existed as a deposit within one of the "sycee hongs" [*lufang*] that operated as a monopoly under the Great Guild of Newchwang and could be "transferred" from one "hong" [*hang*] to another without being converted to cash. By restricting the circulation of cash (except for small copper coinage for personal use) and requiring importers to repatriate their profits by transferring credits to buy and export agricultural goods, the Great Guild ensured that Newchwang would remain the principal conduit for trade with Manchuria. Small merchants in Newchwang and the interior derived particular advantage from the transfer system, which operated as follows: A Newchwang importer,

[48]CER (1924), 352; see also 349–54.

instead of borrowing money and paying the interest to finance the purchase of merchandise, opened an account at one of the sycee hongs and paid for his purchases with a check drawn on this account, which came due on the first day of the following quarter. No money changed hands at the time of the sale, and during the period between the purchase of merchandise and the settlement of his account, which might be as long as 90 days, the importer enjoyed interest-free credit, which he could pass on to merchants in the interior. The goods were shipped upstream to Kuanchengzi or some other distribution center, local merchants received and sold the goods, collected the money, and sent what they owed to Newchwang in time for the importer to cover his account at the *lufang*, before any interest was due. During the period when the transfer system was working smoothly, it made Newchwang the supplier of choice for merchants throughout Manchuria and helped small traders dominate the hinterland.[49]

There were no laws governing banking and finance in Manchuria during the Qing era, and in the absence of a secure legal framework, commerce in this region depended on personal relationships. "The influence of friendship becomes manifest at every stage of the highly complicated Manchuria grain trade," explained one study of this subject.

The broker does not hesitate to pay his farmer-friend full cash in advance for cereals to be delivered after the lapse of several months, he and the innkeeper furnishing the farmer with the needed bags. The farmer carts his produce to the yard of a firm he knows, and deposits it there, with full confidence that the firm will pay him the actual market price: he also orders his broker-friend to sell his grain to Russian merchants without troubling himself about the price the broker will obtain for him. The country broker consigns his grain to his broker at the station, and considers it a matter of fact that his interests will be well protected.[50]

The dependence on personal relationships, and the corresponding weakness of legal or financial structures, favored the fluid operation of small enterprises, while militating against the accumulation of capital and introduction of new technologies that might have led to higher levels of development.

[49]For a description of the Great Guild (in this case spelled Gild [*sic*]), and the transfer system, see Hosea Ballou Morse (1909), 49–52, and CIGC, *Returns of Trade* (1898), 1. The Chinese term for "transfer money" is *guoluyin*, or "money which has passed the furnace," meaning silver money cast in the form of an ingot, or "sycee." The "sycee hong" [*hang*], which carried out these "transfers," was called a *lufang* or "furnace shop."

[50]CER (1924), 99.

4. Flexibility

The last and most important feature of commerce in 19th-century Manchuria was the ability of enterprises in this region to shift their investments and change their functions in response to the market. There is
nothing unusual about businesses that seek to reduce losses and increase returns. What is striking about businesses in Manchuria, however, was their flexibility in shifting among various activities—buying,
selling, processing, shipping, money-lending, or real estate—to fit the
changing conditions. This behavior was driven by a determination to
minimize risk and maximize short-term returns, while avoiding large
commitments and long-term investments of the sort that in other con-
texts has led to higher levels of productivity and development.

Flexibility was a hallmark of the local grain dealerships, or *liangzhan*.
The function of the *liangzhan* was, as the name implies, to buy and sell
grain (or beans), but its underlying purpose was to make money for
the investors, so that a successful dealer was always ready to change directions in response to market demand. Grain-trading, bean-pressing,
flour-milling, wine-making, shipping, pawn-brokering, buying and
selling of real estate: all were fair game for the *liangzhan*, which moved
into and out of each opportunity with the rise and fall of its promise for
immediate returns. In practice, it was often difficult to distinguish the
grain trader who had decided to experiment with bean pressing from
the miller who had taken up the buying and selling of grain and beans.
Each was the flip side of the other.

The same was true of the innkeeper, who began as a host for farmers
or carters, who were taking their produce to market, and made the most
of his knowledge of local conditions by serving as an agent between
buyers and sellers. For a time, this side of the business might expand, as
the innkeeper sent his touts out to find suppliers and offered free lodging to customers in exchange for a commission on the sale of their
goods. Eventually, however, as the farmers grew familiar with the market, they began to bypass the innkeeper-agent and deal directly with
the merchants themselves. Then, the innkeeper might shift his investments, open a *liangzhan*[51] of his own, trade in beans and grain, or move
with the markets into whatever business promised the highest return.

[51] There is an interesting relationship between the term, *liangzhan*, and the role of the
innkeeper as agent and trader in produce. *Liang* means "grain," and the primary meaning of *zhan* is "warehouse" or "storehouse." This is curious, because few if any *liangzhan*
had facilities in which to store grain; they simply bought and shipped it to the next party
up the line. But the secondary meaning of *zhan* is "tavern" or "inn," which fits quite well

Bean mills, the enterprises that added value to Manchuria's most important cash crop, behaved in the same opportunistic way, rising and falling with the times. One cause of these fluctuations was climatic: Mills could receive the delivery of beans only in November, when the earth froze and the fall crop could be shipped by cart, or May, when the rivers thawed and the remainder of last year's crop arrived by junk. When these seasonal supplies were exhausted, the mill had to close until the next delivery. The second reason was financial and explains why the mills could not hold large stocks of beans to ensure the continuous use of expensive fixed capital. Mill owners had little working capital, even less means of obtaining credit, and faced volatile markets in beans and bean products, owing to causes beyond the miller's ken or control. Under these conditions, any miller who bought and pressed beans in hopes of finding a buyer willing to pay the right price was likely to fail. Instead, the smart miller kept his eye on the markets, and when he saw a sufficient gap between the prices of beans (low) and beancake (high), made time-contracts to purchase the former and sell the latter. Certain that the sale of the cake would cover the cost of the beans, the miller went to work, setting aside the oil for later sale, when the price was right. If successful, the miller pocketed his profits and waited for the next opportunity to repeat this exchange. If unsuccessful, he lost his capital and the mill closed.[52]

The same pattern is evident in Manchuria's second largest industry—the grinding of wheat to make flour. By the end of the 19th century, there were hundreds of small, old-style flour mills in Manchuria. Each mill had one or two millstones, which were driven by animal power and produced limited amounts of flour, primarily for local consumption. Most flour mills were auxiliary operations run by bean mills, breweries, sugar refineries, or other businesses. Milling took precedence when the price of wheat was low and the price of flour high. Otherwise, a flour mill was not a flour mill, but a bean mill, brewery, or factory-in-waiting.[53] Successful millers, like innkeepers, grain dealers, and investors in other fields, moved in and out of bean milling, flour milling, commodity trading, pawn-brokering, land speculation, and other lines as conditions warranted. They spread their risk by diversifying over space and time.

---

with the description of late-19th century Manchurian inns, whose courtyards were regularly filled with cartloads of grain and beans en route to market.

[52] CER (1924), 250–52; Kong Jingwei (1990), 405–6.

[53] Kong Jingwei (1990), 410–13. Ibid., 406–10, makes a similar point regarding the brewing industry.

In sum, this examination of the soybean industry shows that Chinese who moved to Manchuria continued to behave in much the same way as they did in China proper. Chinese farmers, merchants, and entrepreneurs used simple, traditional technologies, favored small organizations with limited financing, and moved their investments among various business activities based on a preference for short-term profits and low risks. Although the character of these activities remained unchanged, it is worth asking whether the performance of Chinese improved or the results of their efforts were different north of the Great Wall compared with similar activities in China proper. To answer this question we turn to an examination of the record of economic growth and development that occurred (or did not occur) in Manchuria during the period of Chinese ascendancy, prior to the introduction of the railroads in 1903.

C. Did the Economy of Manchuria Develop?

Recent scholarship in the field of Chinese economic history has reevaluated the performance of late-traditional China to recognize its "early modern" development. This interpretation follows the "classical" model of Adam Smith, according to which the commercialization of agriculture triggers a process that leads over time to higher productivity (output per unit of labor) and structural changes of the sort associated with development. The leading spokesmen for the early modern school, Thomas Rawski and Loren Brandt, argue that during the transition period from 1870 to 1930, the Chinese economy, including both the modern urban and traditional rural sectors, followed the path outlined by Smith.[54] If growth and development as described by these authors did occur, it is reasonable to look for evidence of these trends in Manchuria, where population and land under cultivation were expanding, foreign trade stimulated a demand for raw and semi-processed agricultural goods, the abundance of land relative to population made it possible to specialize in cash crops, and the clean slate of the frontier invited initiative and experimentation with new techniques.

Previous studies of the economic history of Manchuria present arguments for growth and development in agricultural production, processing and trade during the 19th century. Kungtu Sun (1969), Nai-Ruenn Chen (1970), and Alexander Eckstein et al. (1974) have all argued that

[54] The leading proponents of the "early modern" school are Thomas G. Rawski (1989) and Loren Brandt (1989). For accounts of their work, see also Ramon H. Myers (1991) and Philip C. C. Huang (1991).

after 1860, the growth of population, expansion in the area of land under cultivation, application of traditional agricultural techniques to new areas, and stimulus of external demand combined to trigger significant increases in agricultural output and exports of both raw and processed agricultural goods.[55] These studies are based on estimates of population and land under cultivation and figures on external trade through Shanhaiguan for the years 1777–80 and through the treaty port of Newchwang from 1867 on.

In the first of these studies, Kungtu Sun shows that the average annual growth in exports of beans and bean products from Manchuria increased sevenfold, from 0.7 percent during the period 1780–1867, to 4.9 percent from 1867 to 1890, and that after the opening of Newchwang as a treaty port in 1862, the average annual exports of beans and bean products increased in each successive decade—from 2.0 million piculs during 1867–76, to 3.7 million piculs in 1877–86, and 5.6 million piculs in 1887–96—reaching a peak of 8.2 million piculs per year in 1897–99.[56] Although there are no figures for the acreage or production of soybeans in Manchuria during the 19th century, Sun believes that the volume of exports can serve as "an estimate of annual bean production." Similarly, Eckstein et al. point out that during the period 1872–99, the value of Manchurian exports increased by 7.1 percent per year, while soybeans and bean products consistently accounted for 80 percent of the total.[57] Chen focuses on land and labor rather than production and trade, but his assessment is consistent with the others. All of the authors conclude that during the period in question the Manchurian economy exhibited "rapid development," "rapid agricultural expansion," "gather[ing] momentum" or "agricultural growth."[58]

Both the statistical analyses and the characterization of changes presented in these studies support the argument for the "early modern" development of the Manchuria economy. In fact, pursuing the evidence further, one could make an even stronger case for this thesis. In addition to the increases in exports, there was a change in their composition

---

[55] Kungtu Sun (1969), 16–18; Nai-Ruenn Chen (1970), 149; Alexander Eckstein (1974), 243, 251.

[56] Kungtu Sun (1969), 17.

[57] Alexander Eckstein (1974), 248. A comparison of the data in Tables I and III, 261–63, shows that in each of the years 1872–1903, beans and bean products accounted for between 70–88 percent of total exports. These numbers are consistent with the CIGC, *Returns of Trade* for the same years.

[58] Kungtu Sun (1969), 17; Nai-Ruenn Chen (1970), 151; Alexander Eckstein (1974), 240, 243.

from raw beans to processed goods, beancake, and bean oil. During the years 1868–77, beans accounted for more than 60 percent and bean products for less than 40 percent of exports within this category, whereas by 1901–03, the balance was reversed: 40 percent beans, 60 percent cake and oil. Meanwhile, the increase in exports, especially bean-cake, was due almost entirely to the growth of sales to Japan. After reaching a peak in 1891, the shipment of beans and bean products from Manchuria to China proper first stagnated, then declined, while Japan began importing vast quantities of beancake, as well as beans—first 2 million, then 3 million, finally 4 million piculs per year.[59] By 1903, the sale of beancake far exceeded raw beans, and nearly half of all such exports went to Japan. In sum, these numbers show that during the period, 1868–1903, there was a significant increase in the bean trade, Manchurian bean mills captured a larger share of the added value as beancake replaced raw beans as the leading category of exports, and the chief stimulus to these changes was foreign demand—all statements that fit neatly into the "classical" model of economic development and its application to "early modern" China.

But this analysis raises questions which must be addressed before drawing any final conclusion. First, is a question about the level of output at the point when the statistical series on Manchurian exports begins. Kungtu Sun calculates the growth of trade beginning in 1777–80, using figures from the Shanhaiguan customs office, which were reported in the traditional unit of measurement, the *shi*. Sun says that the *shi* was "roughly equivalent" to the picul and proceeds to compare these figures with later reports of the Inspectorate General of Customs, which adopted the picul as its standard.[60] In fact, several sources confirm that the *shi* (or *dan*) was equal to *three* piculs [*jin*] rather than one. If we apply this conversion rate, then the annual exports during the period 1777–80 were *not* in the vicinity of 1.2 million piculs as proposed by Sun, but around 3.7 million piculs. Any upward adjustment of the starting point flattens the slope of growth that might have been achieved in the course of the 19th century, and serves as a warning that there was less change during this period than previously proposed.[61]

[59] CIGC, *Returns of Trade* (1896–1903).

[60] Kungtu Sun (1969), 14.

[61] The standard unit of measurement adopted by the Inspectorate General of Customs in the 1860s, was the "picul," which was (and is) equal to 133.33 pounds. In the early 20th century, the traditional Chinese unit of weight, the *shi* (or *dan*), was made equivalent to the "picul," and the *jin*, or "catty," which was (and is) 1/100th of a *shi* was made equivalent to 0.01 picul. Thus, the relationship which was established at that time and remains in

TABLE 3
Average annual exports from Newchwang, beans and bean products, by value,
volume, and type of shipping, 1877–79 and 1901–3

	1877–79	1901–3	Increase (%)
Value (1,000,000 Haikwan taels)			
Foreign shipping	3,361	15,494	361
Native shipping	5,804	3,279	−44
Total shipping	9,165	18,773	105
Volume (1,000 piculs)			
Foreign shipping	3,329	8,171	145
Native shipping	3,909	987	−75
Total shipping	7,238	9,158	27

SOURCE: CIGC, *Returns of Trade.*

Second, the accounts of Sun and Eckstein are based entirely on trade returns from the Chinese Inspectorate General of Customs (CIGC), which include only goods carried on ships of a foreign type, excluding goods transported by native craft or junks. Kungtu Sun claims that the omission of native shipping is justified, because the portion of trade carried by junks "was not large and grew smaller as time went on."[62] But this statement is misleading. For while it is true that junk traffic declined over time, it was in fact very large at the beginning of the treaty port era, and in terms of understanding the nature and pace of development this makes all the difference.

Although we do not have a complete run of figures for the junk trade to go alongside the CICG series for foreign bottoms, the customs office at Newchwang did report on junk traffic for three years, 1877–79, and again consistently after 1900, making it possible to compare the performance of exports, measured by both the value and volume of beans and bean products, over this interval (Table 3). In their studies of Manchurian trade, Sun and Eckstein consider *only* foreign shipping: Figures for

---

force today, is: 1 *shi* = 1 picul = 133.33 pounds, and 1 *jin* = 1 catty = 1.33 pounds. Before this equivalence between the *shi* and the picul was decreed, however, the traditional *shi* was *not* equal to 133.33 pounds, but was apparently three times as great. According to the CICG, *Reports on Trade* (1877), 10, and (1886), 3, one *shih* [sic] equals 3 piculs or 300 catties (that is, 400 lb. or 181.5 kg). Similarly, CER (1924), 92–93, states that one *shi* was equal in weight to 8 bushels of wheat (@ 56 lb.) = 448 lb. (3.36 piculs). When the term *shi* appears in a Chinese text prior to 1860, we must assume that it refers to the traditional unit of weight that was equal to around 400 pounds. Thus, it is incorrect to assume, as does Kungtu Sun, that in 1780, the *shi* was "roughly equivalent" to the picul.
[62] Kungtu Sun (1969), 16.

this category show that the increases in exports from the former period to the latter were quite large and that the growth of foreign trade was correspondingly rapid; one might infer from these findings, along with Sun and Eckstein, an equally rapid growth in the Manchurian economy as a whole. However, after adding the figures for native shipping, the increases between these two periods appear much more modest. In one respect, Sun and Eckstein are correct: namely, exports to Japan, especially beancake, added decisively to Manchuria's external trade.[63] Yet, even with the addition of sales to Japan, the fact remains that during the quarter-century before the introduction of the railroad in 1903, when the potential for development under premodern conditions was greatest, exports of beans and bean products, which were by far Manchuria's leading trade goods, grew by only 1 percent per year. In sum, Manchurian exports did increase during the late 19th century, but the increases were smaller than suggested by the CIGC figures, and the reason for the discrepancy was that foreign ships, the units measured by the CIGC, were in part taking over an established trade previously carried by junks. When all forms of shipping are counted, the rise in exports and the shift from raw beans to processed goods are much more modest than proposed in earlier studies.

Finally, what do the figures on exports tell us about the production of beans in Manchuria? The "classical" model of economic development posits a direct connection between the two: that is, increases in exports of beans and bean products should trigger a decision by farmers to plant more land in beans and produce more of them. Kungtu Sun is confident that this connection existed, for he asserts that the volume of exports can serve as "an estimate of annual bean production." Eckstein and Chen decline to make such claims. In fact, no land use or production surveys were carried out in Manchuria during the 19th century, and there are no proxy data that can be used to estimate the area of land planted or output for any crop. The earliest figures for cultivated area by crop are for Fengtian in 1908, which show that 30 percent was planted in sorghum [*gaoliang*], 23 percent in soybeans, 18 percent in millet, and lesser amounts in corn, wheat, and other crops.[64]

[63] In 1890, Japan took only 2.5 percent by value of Manchurian exports in foreign bottoms; if junk trade (none of which went to Japan) were added, Japan's share would have been even lower. Exports to Japan began to grow in the early 1890s and took a big jump after the Sino-Japanese War (1895). In 1903, Japan received 40 percent of all Manchurian exports, by all carriers to all locations. In 1902–03, over 60 percent of Manchurian beancake exports went to Japan. See: CIGC, *Returns of Trade*.

[64] Fengtian, 1908: Kong Jingwei (1990), 357–58. I have found three estimates for the production of beans in Manchuria in the first decade of the 20th century: Alexander Hosie

In the absence of numbers, the best evidence for cropping patterns in 19th-century Manchuria comes from the reports of foreign travelers, which paint a rather surprising picture.[65] On one hand, many observers noted the long lines of great carts, moving mounds of produce through ice and snow, which seems to suggest that beans were grown virtually everywhere. "I have travelled in different parts of China," noted Alexander Hosie, the British consul at Newchwang, following his visit to Jilin in the winter of 1896. "I have seen the great salt and piece goods traffic between Ssu-ch'uan, Kwei-chow and Yunnan, but I never saw a sign which from its magnitude impressed me so much with the vast trade of China as the carrying trade from north to south in Manchuria." On a single day, Hosie saw "at least a thousand carts heavily laden with the produce of the interior, including beans, tobacco, abutilon hemp, dressed pigs, skins and large droves of black pigs all bound south. . . ."[66] At Tieling on the Liao River, where the overland traders were forced to halt their advance, he found "string after string of carts laden with beans," awaiting the thaw, when they would join the summer shipments by junk to Newchwang.[67]

In winter, when travel was confined to the frozen track between Newchwang and Jilin, the whole country seemed alive with the traffic in beans. During summer, however, as the same travelers passed fields of sorghum, millet, maize and wheat, the impressions of the previous season seem to change. Summer travelers do mention bean fields, but not nearly as often as they note the prevalence of sorghum, millet and cash crops, such as tobacco, indigo and hemp. In short, there is nothing in the travelogues of the 19th century to suggest that farmers in Manchuria were devoting vast areas to the production of beans or shifting in significant fashion from food to commercial crops. Beans were undoubtedly the leading commercial crop, but they occupied a relatively small portion of the cultivated area, probably less and perhaps much less than 25 percent, and there is no direct evidence that their share was increasing over time.

(1904), 243–44; CIGC, *Returns of Trade* (1908), 19; and SMR, *Report on Progress in Manchuria, 1907–1928*, 49. However, all are too low compared to the figures for exports during this period (>550,000 mt) to elicit confidence. *Manchoukuo Year Book (1934)*, 260–62, reports on area of cultivation and output of soybeans and other crops, 1924–33.

[65]See, for example: Henry James (1888), 11–12; Francis Younghusband (1904), 21, 24, 47–48; Alexander Hosie (1904), 180; J. A. Wylie (1893), 444.

[66]Alexander Hosie (1904), 15–16. For similar description, see Henry James (1888), 371.

[67]Alexander Hosie (1904), 15.

D. Conclusion

Study of the Manchurian bean industry prior to 1903 offers little support for the "early modern" thesis and suggests why change in this area was slow. The bean business, from cultivation through processing, sales and shipping, was the work of many small organizations with limited financing and simple, traditional technologies, run by entrepreneurs who moved into, around, and out of various activities in response to the prospects for short-term gain. None of the players—farmers, grain traders, innkeepers, millers, bankers, carters, or junkmen—was prone to invest in capital goods, technology, or management in ways that might raise the productivity of any particular venture. All seemed to agree that the object of the game was to avoid risk and make money and that the safest, and therefore best, strategy was to shift direction in response to changing conditions, rather than going for broke in one particular product, process, or enterprise. A winner-take-all strategy, which would have implied heavy investment in one or more of the bottlenecks of production and trade, raising the productivity of a particular enterprise, enabling it to survive a temporary downturn, drive out less effective competitors and dominate the industry during the next cycle, had no (or at least few) takers.

This account bears a striking resemblance to previous descriptions of textile handicrafts in late-traditional China and the explanation put forward by several scholars for the success of traditional handicrafts in withstanding the challenge of modern machine manufactures.[68] The spinning, weaving, and dyeing of cotton yarn and cloth in China were household industries, carried out by unskilled farm women and youth, using inexpensive equipment, working at home, alone and in their spare time, producing primarily for their own consumption and, as opportunity permitted, for the market. Even after the introduction of machine-made yarn, which was better and cheaper than homespun, household weaving persisted, thanks to an efficient distribution system in which suppliers provided yarn to and received cloth from rural households. In some ways, household handicrafts were unlike bean pressing, for the latter depended on wage workers who were employed by capitalist enterprises, worked cooperatively with others and continuously over sustained periods, used relatively (compared to household looms) expensive equipment, and produced for a large, distant, and impersonal

---

[68] For details on textile handicrafts, see: Kang Chao (1977); Mark Elvin (1972); and Philip Huang (1985).

market. In other respects, however, the two activities are similar: Both were based on small-scale organizations, with limited financing and simple technologies, and depended on a system that expanded or contracted in response to demand, while its individual components opened, closed, or transformed themselves into whatever opportunities promised the highest profits in the shortest time at the least risk. The individual farmer-textile worker picked up or laid down the hoe or the loom, changing from farmer to weaver and back again, in the same way that the Manchurian landowner, grain merchant, bean miller, flour miller, brewer, transporter, money-lender, or real estate tycoon shifted his investments and functions to keep pace with changing conditions.

This system, while apparently good for individual players, may have been bad for the development of the Manchurian economy as a whole. Mark Elvin makes a similar argument in describing Chinese textile handicrafts as a function of the "high-level equilibrium trap." Because traditional handicrafts relied on cheap, simple technology and flexible labor, Elvin argues, "there would be no great prospective rewards for investors in times of boom, and few penalties in times of slump would be severe enough to drive the inefficient permanently of business." Successful entrepreneurs favored trade over manufacturing and kept their capital in liquid form rather than fixed investments. This was good for investors, who made suitable profits with low risk, but yielded few innovations in productive technology or organization, because those with capital, skill, and a knowledge of market forces had no understanding or appreciation for how the goods were made, and no compelling interest in trying to make them in much larger volume or at a much lower price.[69] The same can be said of the bean business and other related businesses in Manchuria.

[69] Mark Elvin (1972), 162.

CHAPTER 8

A Tale of Two Cities:
Newchwang and Dairen (1903–22)

IN HIS HISTORY OF CHICAGO, *Nature's Metropolis*, William Cronon shows how the development of the American frontier was inextricably linked through an infrastructure of transportation, trade, and finance to the markets and centers of population that formed its opposite pole. The growth of Chicago was made possible by the lumber, grain, and meat produced within the great arc from Michigan to Nebraska. But it was the cities of the eastern seaboard and Europe that established the value of these commodities. And it was the railroads and harbors, grain elevators and stockyards, banks and commodity markets, located in and running through Chicago, that joined producer and consumer, making westward expansion possible. Cronon's point is that the frontier exists in relation to its metropole, and the development of each depends upon the channel between them. This observation applies with equal force to Manchuria, where the expansion of settlement and cultivation depended upon a system of transportation, trade, and finance that connected this region to markets in China, Japan, and beyond.

But why Chicago? Again, Cronon's answer sheds light on the story of Manchuria. During the first half of the 19th century, the center of commerce in the interior of North America was St. Louis, where goods produced along the great river system of the mid-continent were gathered and sent down the Mississippi to New Orleans. While St. Louis prospered, Chicago remained a small trading post, mired in a bog, with a shallow sandy harbor facing Lake Michigan to the east and meager prairie stream petering out to the west. Then came the railroad connecting Chicago to New York, the building of port facilities to accommodate

oceangoing ships on the Great Lakes, followed by a string of technological and organizational innovations that helped reorient trade along an
east-west rather than the old north-south axis. St. Louis survived. But
Chicago boomed: first, because the markets in and through New York
far outstripped those tied to New Orleans; second, because the methods
for reaching these markets favored the new technology of railroads over
the old riverboat transport; and third, because the spirit of innovation,
not only in material technologies, but also in organization, finance, and
trade, transformed Chicago more than any of its rivals.

   The parallels with Manchuria are striking. Newchwang emerged as
the first center of trade in this region, owing to its location on a reliable,
but slow-moving river and its ability to connect markets up- and down-
stream using traditional riverine transport. Meanwhile, Dairen languished, despite its oceanfront and excellent harbor, because it lacked
connections to the hinterland. Then, in the early 1900s came the railroad, the development of the harbor, innovations in technology, trade,
and finance, and the opportunity to reach a much larger market than
had been available under the old regime. In the space of five years,
Dairen bypassed Newchwang as the center of commerce for Manchuria
as a whole. There is an irony in both stories, for the advantages enjoyed
by the early leaders, St. Louis and Newchwang, discouraged these cities
from adopting changes required to maintain their leadership, while
what seemed to be the disadvantages of Chicago and Dairen became assets when new technologies appeared and the structure of external
markets changed.

A. A Tale of Two Cities

During the 19th century, Newchwang served as the principal link between agricultural producers in the Liao River basin and the port cities
of eastern China. Farmers along the Liao produced soybeans, cotton,
and grain that were transported down the river to Newchwang, where
seafaring junks picked up the produce and delivered manufactured
goods to exchange in return. The development of the textile industry in
north China and of commercial agriculture in sugar, silk, and tea on the
lower Yangzi created a demand for raw cotton, beancake, and grain that
fueled trade in both directions. Newchwang's location in the heart of
the Liao delta gave it direct access to the produce and markets of the
surrounding countryside, while shallow-draft junks could proceed up

river as far as Mukden, the center of Manchurian wealth and power. When, in the Treaty of Tientsin (1858), Britain and France demanded entry into northern China, they chose Newchwang as the first treaty port in Manchuria, leading to further increases in trade through that port.

As Newchwang developed, pressures on the geography underlying this system mounted, and its weaknesses became more evident.[1] Even in the best of times, the Liao is a shallow, meandering, silt-laden river that can be drained by a stretch of dry weather, leaving only the smallest boats with sufficient draft to sail upstream. In times of trouble, which were increasingly common at the end of the Qing, slow-moving junks were vulnerable to piracy and brigandage. The intensification of agriculture diverted water for irrigation, requiring that the river be dredged so that junks could reach the secondary markets and transit points located upstream. By the early 1900s, development along the Shuangtaizi River, which branches from the Liao several miles above Newchwang, threatened to divert the main channel and leave the harbor at Newchwang dry. At the turn of the century, the linked system of agriculture and transportation that had once breathed life into Newchwang was now strangling on its own success.

Meanwhile, Newchwang was also threatened from its seaward side. A sandbar, 15 miles below the city, prevented deep-draft oceangoing vessels from reaching Newchwang. Foreign ships, first sailing ships and by the late 19th century steamships, had to load and unload at Yingkou, located below the bar, leaving junks to ferry their goods back and forth to the main port. After 1861, when Newchwang was opened to foreign trade and the number of foreign bottoms calling at Yingkou increased, the burdens of this shuttle service became more onerous. Finally, the river both above and below Newchwang froze solid for four months each year. Freezing was a boon to the great carts that supplied Newchwang from the interior, but that was little solace to the captain whose ship sat in Yingkou, waiting for the river to thaw.

Despite its mounting problems, merchants, bankers, officials, and others responsible for the fate of Newchwang grew complacent, for this city enjoyed many advantages, while other Manchurian ports had even more serious handicaps. Dairen is a case in point. The problem with Dairen and its neighbor Lushun (Port Arthur) was not shipping. On the contrary, at the tip of the Liaodong promontory rocky cliffs plunge into

[1] The following account of the geography of Newchwang is based on CIGC, *Returns of Trade*: (1909), 70–71; (1910), 102; (1911), 114; (1912), 119; (1913), 202; (1915), 203; (1917), 214–15.

deep harbors that are immune from silting, while the surrounding hills protect the ships anchored there against the wind. Warm ocean currents keep the climate mild and the harbors free of ice all year round. For centuries, naval commanders (and pirates) had recognized these strengths: throughout the 19th century, the Chinese Peiyang (North Sea) Navy made its base at Lushun, while the British fleet assembled in Dairen in 1859, on the eve of its invasion of Beijing.

The virtues of Dairen and Lushun as harbors were their downfall as ports, however, for both locations lacked natural connections to the hinterland and indeed a hinterland of any value to connect to. Located at the end of the long spine of north-south trending mountains that form the Liaodong Peninsula, Dairen and Lushun are backed by hills and cliffs that block access to the surrounding territory. The Peninsula is rocky and barren, so that runoff from the mountains is rapid, seasonal, and cuts deep east-west trending gullies that obstruct travel from north to south. As late as the 19th century, cultivation on the Peninsula was limited and transportation difficult. Coastal trade was restricted to a handful of ports—Piziwo [Pikou] and Dagushan on the east coast and Gaizhou (Gaiping) on the west (Map 1). Few merchant vessels called on Dairen or Lushun, which offered little scope for trade.[2]

Given the wealth of the Liao basin and the relative poverty of the Liaodong Peninsula, the technologies then available for agriculture and transportation, and the already established networks of shipping and trade, it is understandable that few if any Chinese imagined a system based anywhere other than Newchwang. But it was possible to dream of other worlds. Following his visit to Manchuria in the 1860s, the missionary Alexander Williamson made a bold proposal, which, although ignored at the time, described with uncanny precision Manchuria's future:

I venture to suggest as the first and chief means towards the opening up of the country, that a railway be constructed, commencing at Ta-lien-wan [Dalian] Bay on the southern point of the promontory and proceeding northward via Kin-chow, Fu-chow, Kai-chow, Hai-ching, Liau-yang, Mouk-den and on to the pulse [bean] and indigo-producing districts in the North. This country being new, less densely peopled, and with fewer graveyards, seems a suitable place to open the railway-scheme in this empire. Nature would seem to have provided for railway operations in this quarter; Ta-lien-wan Bay has an excellent harbour,

[2]For conditions on the Liaodong Peninsula, see Alexander Hosie (1904), 76–81; and on the Liaodong ports in the 19th century, see Charles Gutzlaff (1834) 144, 417; Alexander Williamson (1870), 33–38; Henry James (1888), 403–5.

well sheltered, with deep water to nearly the edge, and is open all the year round. . . . For many reasons, the present port, Ying-tsze [Yingkou], would never do in the new order of things: the bar at the mouth of the river, the fact of its being frozen up for fully four months every year, independently of the apparent shallowing of the water, which must end in leaving that market, like its predecessors, high beyond navigable limits, would infallibly remove business to the more eligible spot.[3]

It is easy to feel admiration for Williamson and at the same time sympathy for the Newchwang Chinese, who realized that the river system was gradually decaying, but had no idea that it would be replaced by steam engines, steel bands, and the exchange of goods between producers and consumers on opposite sides of the globe. The Newchwang Chamber of Commerce tried to address the immediate problems, voting additional levies to deepen the bar that separated Newchwang from Yingkou, dredge the channel above and below the city, and rebuild the bulwarks and docks surrounding the harbor. But the government in Beijing, preoccupied with troubles of its own, failed to come up with the necessary funds. Attempts to construct a weir that would restrict the flow from the main channel of the Liao into the Shuangtaizi River above Newchwang were blocked by peasant mobs determined to extract water from the river for irrigation. In 1919, a decade after the Newchwang chamber called for action, some work had begun to improve the harbor and dredge the channel, but no steps had been taken to limit silting or ensure the flow of water from upstream. Over time, what first seemed like a brave and confident optimism degenerated into a blind and stubborn reaction. Promoters of Newchwang refused to admit that the railroads were winning the battle for trade with the interior, complained that the railroad's success was due to unfair and discriminatory freight rates, and clung to their faith in the dwindling river.[4]

B. The Rise of Dairen

It was the railroads more than any other factor that account for Dairen's (like Chicago's) sudden ascent. The backbone of the Manchurian rail system was the "T" built by the Russians between 1897–1903: the horizontal east-west line cut across Manchuria from Manzhouli to Suifenhe, creating a shortcut for the Trans-Siberian Railway, which ended in

[3] Alexander Williamson (1870), 48–50.
[4] CIGC, *Returns of Trade* (1905), 4; (1906), 1–2; (1909), 70.

Vladivostok; the vertical north-south line ran from Harbin to Dairen (called Dalny by the Russians and Dalian by the Chinese). The Chinese Eastern Railway (CER), including the east-west line and the southern spur from Harbin to Changchun, remained under Russian or Soviet control until 1949. The southern segment from Changchun to Dairen was transferred to Japan in 1905, following the Russo-Japanese War, after which it became known as the South Manchuria Railway (SMR). The Japanese upgraded the SMR with improved roadbeds, rolling stock, and mining and industrial developments and built branch lines from Changchun to Jilin (1912) and Dunhua (1928), from Mukden to Andong (1907), and from Siping to Zhengjiatun (1918) and Taonan (1923). During the same period, the Chinese also built railroads in Manchuria or took over lines built for them by the Japanese. The most important Chinese line, from Beiping to Mukden, was completed in 1907. During the 1920s, three more Chinese lines were opened: connecting Dahushan on the Beiping-Mukden line to Tsitsihar; through Mukden via Hailong to Jilin; and from Hulan to Hailun.[5] But it was the South Manchuria Railway, the golden spike of Japanese imperialism, that defined the economy of Manchuria during the first half of the 20th century.

Railroads, harbors, and docking facilities were concrete manifestations as well as gleaming symbols of how and why Japanese Dairen eclipsed Chinese Newchwang in the battle for Manchuria. But the shift from Chinese to Japanese leadership had as much to do with the organization of finance and trade as with material construction or new technologies. One of the chief reasons farmers and merchants were drawn away from the Liao River and Newchwang and toward the railroads and Dairen, was that the latter offered better methods and terms of financing. As noted in the previous chapter, during the Qing period and into the early 20th century, there was no banking system in rural Manchuria, organized money-lending was limited to a small number of wealthy and well-connected individuals, and pawnshops, which were the only credit institutions available to most people, charged prohibitively high interest. One reason Newchwang enjoyed an advantage in trade with the interior was the "transfer money" system, which operated as a monopoly of the Great Guild of Newchwang and provided interest-free credit to merchants in the interior. But scandals rocked the transfer system, forcing officials in Newchwang to outlaw the practice, after which goods passing through Newchwang had to be paid for at

[5] Harry L. Kingman (1932), 11–21; Owen Lattimore (1934), 281–86.

least partly in cash. As a result, Chinese merchants began to look to other channels, especially Dairen.[6]

The first crack in the transfer system appeared in the winter of 1906. With Manchuria flush with the cash that had flowed into the region during the Russo-Japanese War, importers in Newchwang shipped large stocks of merchandise up-country. Prices were high, and merchants in the provincial towns used cash receipts from the sale of these goods to buy beans and other produce, expecting to sell at a profit before the bills in Newchwang came due. When prices declined, however, the merchants were forced to hold onto their stock. Retailers in the interior could not pay wholesalers in Newchwang, who could not pay suppliers in Shanghai, and for several months trade came to a standstill. Finally, in May, banks in Kuanchengzi sent a shipment of cash to Newchwang, and the stalemate was broken.[7] In the end, this was only a minor glitch, caused by speculation on the part of small-town merchants and settled by the intervention of big-city bankers who knew, or thought they knew, how to keep the system solvent.

A more serious crisis occurred the following year, when it was revealed that enormous sums of money had been "transferred" back and forth without independent auditing to ensure the creditworthiness of the borrowers. One of the biggest businesses in Newchwang, Tung Sheng Ho, a Cantonese firm that was involved (as were most Chinese businesses) in all areas of commerce, including milling, shipping, importing, exporting, banking, and real estate, went bankrupt. In the aftermath, it was discovered that the firm had not squared its books for years, but the problem went undetected because of the lack of accountability among the sycee hongs and their largest customers. During this crisis, current obligations were recalled, no one would risk making further loans, and trade came to a halt. Finally, the Chinese guilds stepped in to guarantee the payment of import duties, and money began to arrive from the outside. But revelations of the underlying weakness of the transfer system began to dog Newchwang, and worse was yet to come.[8]

From the moment they entered Manchuria in 1905, the Japanese moved immediately to establish a system of banking and credit that extended up and down the South Manchuria Railway from Dairen to Changchun. Headquarters and branch offices of commercial banks were opened in the major cities, and agents were stationed in railway

[6]CIGC, *Returns of Trade* (1907), 36; (1913), 207.
[7]CIGC, *Returns of Trade* (1906), 1.
[8]CIGC, *Returns of Trade* (1907), 36.

towns, where merchants and farmers could obtain small loans on a commercial basis.[9] Even more important was the development of a system of futures contracts, which became the principal means of financing agriculture and agricultural trade in Manchuria.

The financing of futures originated in Tokyo and rippled outward to the smallest farmer in Heilongjiang. It began when an importer in Japan obtained a loan from a Japanese bank to purchase Manchurian beans or grain. The bank issued a letter of credit in the name of the importer through its affiliate in Dairen, and the importer notified a Manchurian export firm that it could draw on this credit to purchase produce. The export firm paid cash to a wholesaler for futures contracts, which guaranteed the delivery of a certain quantity and quality of grain on a specified date. The wholesaler in turn paid local grain dealers or farmers for secondary futures contracts that would ensure the wholesaler of the supplies he needed to meet his obligations in Dairen. Rich farmers with large holdings were attracted to this system, because they needed cash to pay workers before they sold their crop in the fall. Poor farmers whose food ran out before the next harvest were forced to sell their crop while it was still in the ground. The sellers received payment in paper or copper cash, which could be exchanged for silver. No comparable system of rural credit was available through either Chinese or Russian sources, making the Japanese option attractive to most farmers and essential to many.[10]

To facilitate the enormous volume of trade in futures, in 1913, the Governor General of Kwantung—the Japanese leased territory surrounding Dairen—established the Dairen Staple Produce Exchange. This government agency oversaw the buying and selling of futures contracts on beans, beancake, bean oil, sorghum, maize, and millet. To protect and regulate this market, only Japanese and Chinese companies were accepted as members, and trading in the six designated commodities was prohibited outside the Exchange.[11] Smaller private exchanges were set up in Changchun, Harbin, and Fujiadian, the last of which was the center for trade along the Russian-controlled Chinese Eastern Railway, but the Dairen Exchange was by far the largest market and established the price of beans and grain throughout the Far East.[12]

Futures sales were often a means of exploiting the vulnerability of small farmers and posed a risk to Chinese grain traders and middlemen

[9] CIGC, *Returns of Trade* (1913), 207.
[10] CER (1924), 90–93, 368–70.
[11] CIGC, *Returns of Trade: Dairen* (1913), 145.
[12] CER (1924), 106–12.

as well. Farmers who sold their crops on futures generally had to accept prices that were twenty to forty percent below market value at harvest time, making it impossible for them to accumulate capital for investment and often difficult to escape the cycle of debt. Japanese creditors, who held mortgages to farmland as collateral on futures contracts, could be quite ruthless when it came time to collect. "In winter, food prices increase and the peasants are unable to deliver the goods," reported the Chinese Governor of Fengtian in 1910. "The foreign merchants then either confiscate their land lease or go to the villages with interpreters to make forcible demands for payment."[13] Theoretically, a futures market could have enabled Chinese middlemen to accumulate capital and invest in trade and production, but that was rarely the case. Most traders bought and sold futures contracts as a form of moneylending or speculation, settling for cash when the due date approached, rather than actually delivering or accepting the grain. It was a risky business, subject to abuses, which often resulted in the ruin of the participants and sometimes disrupted the entire market.[14]

Because of the enormous profits that could be made by buying and selling futures, especially when it was done on margin and without an intention to consummate the deals, the Dairen exchange attracted opportunists and on more than one occasion risked collapse. In the early summer of 1917, for example, prospects for a poor bean harvest drove up the price of futures. Speculators entered the market, and by late summer the volume of produce promised in signed contracts was several times the amount that could possibly be delivered when the contracts came due in the fall. The Exchange, alarmed by this situation, suspended business, tried to persuade wholesalers and exporters to cancel outstanding deals, and required that buyers put up more cash to guarantee contracts. But to no avail: the sales continued, prices soared, and in August the Exchange closed. In October, after the arrival of the fall crop, prices stabilized and the Exchange reopened, although many sellers were still unable to deliver on their contracts, giving rise to conflicts, suits, and countersuits.[15] Although the Japanese financial

[13] *Jindai Dongbei renmin geming yundong shi* [The history of the people's revolutionary movement in the Northeast in modern times] (Changchun: Jilin renmin chubanshe, 1960), 156, cited in Herbert Bix (1972), 433. Bix, 431–32, argues that the peasants suffered most from a system that advanced credit through a succession of Chinese middlemen.

[14] CER (1924), 91, 94–96.

[15] CIGC, *Returns of Trade, Dairen* (1917), 155. William Cronon (1991), 127–32, describes how attempts to "corner" the market in Chicago produced similar risk for the traders and the commodity markets as a whole.

system was subject to volatility and abuse, it succeeded in draining both capital and customers away from the older Chinese systems centered in Newchwang.

Another innovation that drew farmers and merchants into the Japanese orbit was the mixed storage and shipment of beans. Traditionally, Chinese merchants in Manchuria bought and shipped beans in standard 189-lb bags. The ownership of an individual bag could be established at the time of purchase and remained under the control of the owner until it reached the next point of sale. This practice worked well, so long as the volume of trade remained modest. When the volume increased, however, it proved cumbersome to separate and track each individual bag. In 1922, the South Manchuria Railway, in cooperation with the Russian Chinese Eastern Railway, introduced mixed storage. Under this practice, following each harvest the bean crop was evaluated and the beans divided into three grades. On delivery at a warehouse, a shipment of beans was classified and a receipt issued for the appropriate quantity and quality of produce. From this point on, beans of a similar grade traveled in bulk, and the "owner" held a document which entitled him to reclaim the designated amount and grade of beans at a specified time and place. This practice had several advantages: The grading of beans created an incentive for producers to improve quality and rewarded successful farmers for adding to the value of their crop. Mixed storage made it easier to handle and transport beans in large quantities and gave all parties greater flexibility and efficiency in the movement of grain. And the warehouse receipt became a negotiable document that added to the volume and liquidity of money. In the same year, 1922, the Japanese and Russian railways also began shipping bean oil in tank cars, based on the same principle of mixed storage.[16]

C. Newchwang vs Dairen

As a result of these measures, commerce on the South Manchuria Railway and in Dairen quickly eclipsed the Liao River-Newchwang network. Reports by the customs offices in these two cities show contrasting patterns in the exports of beans and bean products during the first two decades of the 20th century: Exports from Newchwang declined during the Russo-Japanese War (1904–05), recovered by 1909 to

---

[16]CER (1924), 416–17. William Cronon (1991), 109–19, provides a similar account of bulk shipment of grain in Chicago.

their prewar peak, and then slid steadily downward, while Dairen's trade shot up from the opening of the customs office in 1907, and was still on the rise when East Asia entered the era of post-World War I expansion. In 1919, total exports of beans and bean products from Newchwang had fallen to 5 million piculs, about one-half the previous peak, while exports from Dairen were 28 million and rising. The volume of shipping and the value of imports, exports, and total trade followed the same pattern. Exports from Dairen were carried in increasing volume by foreign ships to foreign ports, while Newchwang continued to depend on a shrinking trade transported by junk to markets on the China coast.[17]

During the first two decades of the 20th century, global demand for soybeans and bean products increased exponentially, and Manchuria became the chief supplier of these commodities to the world. Beancake was the fertilizer of choice for rice farmers in Japan and a fertilizer and feed for farmers and livestock producers throughout Asia and as far away as Europe. The global market for beancake appeared first, while bean oil, which had long been favored in China, was demoted to the role of by-product. Then, with the outbreak of World War I, the demand for bean oil as a lubricant and raw material for the manufacture of munitions, soap, paint, and other products jumped dramatically. The chief beneficiary of these developments was Dairen, which was most propitiously located and best equipped for oceangoing trade. Newchwang merchants held on to an established market in China proper, where they had good connections and where junks had a record for reliable service, especially for the transport of delicately packaged oil. But that success damns the Newchwang merchants with faint praise, for their skill in holding onto the market in China is the reason they missed out on much greater opportunities elsewhere.

Chinese and Japanese were not the only actors in this drama. The other major railroad operating in Manchuria during the early 20th century, the Russian Chinese Eastern, presents a striking contrast to the South Manchuria Railway and helps explain the success of the Japanese against their chief rival for imperialist power on the mainland of Asia. The Chinese Eastern Railway (CER) was designed in the 1890s as a bridge between Siberia and the Pacific port of Vladivostok. Russian engineers chose the path dictated by topography and other natural

[17] Data on all aspects of trade to and from Dairen, Newchwang, and other Manchurian ports comes from CIGC, *Returns of Trade*, for various years.

conditions and acceded to the Chinese request that this route avoid the intervening cities, whose graveyards and *fengshui* might otherwise have been defiled by iron tracks. The result was a railroad that touched none of the existing centers of population and trade—Tsitsihar, Petuna, Hulan, Jilin, and Ninguta—while at the junction where the CER crossed the Sungari, a wholly new city, Harbin, was established. This architecture suited Moscow, because the purpose of the railroad was to facilitate trade between Russia and the Pacific, not to develop production or commerce in the intervening territory. At the time, the Chinese, blind to the significance of the railroads, agreed.[18]

Freight rates on the Chinese Eastern, designed to promote trade with Russia, also discouraged the development of Manchuria. At first (1903–05), rates between Siberia and the ports at Vladivostok and Dairen were kept low, while those to or from Manchurian stations were high. Then, after the loss of the South Manchuria Railway to Japan, the rates to Vladivostok were reduced further, while those from Harbin to Changchun (the southern spur of the CER that remained in Russian hands) were raised to discourage traffic on the Japanese (SMR) line from Changchun to Dairen. This rate structure became highly dysfunctional, however, as merchants in northern Manchuria abandoned the Chinese Eastern Railway entirely, moving goods by cart to and from Changchun and relying on the South Manchuria Railway with its more efficient operations and commercially competitive rates to channel trade through Dairen. The only Manchurian industry that received support from the Russians was flour milling, which gained temporary favor during the Russo-Japanese War, when bread was needed to supply Russian troops, but was abandoned shortly thereafter, as demand declined and Russian mills stepped in to fill the gap. In addition to these economic factors, the operations of the Chinese Eastern Railway were disrupted by World War I, the Russian Revolution, and the Siberian Intervention (1918–20), when rolling stock was diverted to military needs and conflict wreaked havoc all along the line. Finally, in 1922, when the new Soviet regime introduced the liberal New Economic Policies, the Chinese Eastern was reorganized on a commercial basis, and Manchurian merchants began to use it for shipments to Vladivostok, Changchun, and ultimately Dairen.[19]

[18]CER (1924), 269–70, 397–99.
[19]CER (1924), 18–19, 275–78, 380–83, 399–403. Shipping on the CER reached a peak of 2.1 million metric tons (mmt) in 1916, fell to 1.3 mmt in 1918, recovered to 2.0 mmt in 1921 and soared to 2.8 mmt in 1923. Ibid., 421.

The Russian and Japanese railroads present a contrast in imperial styles and practical results. The Chinese Eastern Railway, a government enterprise, operated on the assumption that the pattern of trade could be dictated by the state and that the facility could be commandeered as required for military purposes. The South Manchuria Railway, a joint public-private venture, was run on a more (one cannot say purely) commercial basis, and its operations were not disrupted (at least during this period) by the movement of troops. A comparison of the value of goods exported from Manchuria through the southern outlets of the South Manchuria Railway, Dairen and Andong, with shipments on the Chinese Eastern Railway that exited via Siberia (through Manzhouli) and the Russian Far East (Suifenhe) testifies to the results of these two approaches. In 1910, the first year for which comparable figures are available, the SMR carried about 60 percent more exports than the CER; by 1917, its lead had grown to over 300 percent; and from that point on, the gap widened.[20] The difference between a modern industrial infrastructure centered around Dairen, on one hand, and both the traditional system around Newchwang and the technologically modern but commercially dysfunctional system anchored in Vladivostok, on the other, continued to grow during the 1920s and 1930s, until Japanese-controlled Dairen became a major center of commerce in Northeast Asia, while the Russian port languished and Chinese Newchwang receded into oblivion.

D. Conclusion

The historical irony by which the advantages of geography, technology, and organization that had favored the rise of Newchwang became the source of its undoing, while the apparent handicaps imposed on Dairen made it suitable for modern solutions introduced from abroad, lend support to Mark Elvin's theory of the "high-level equilibrium trap." Elvin argues that water transportation was one of two areas (the other was agriculture) where traditional Chinese technology had reached an advanced level of such efficiency that it discouraged both further evolution from within and the introduction of novel solutions from without.[21] Rational economic analysis showed that where well-developed systems of water transport existed, further improvements in traditional

[20] CIGC, *Returns of Trade.*
[21] Mark Elvin (1972), 172.

techniques were either too expensive or produced narrow gains, while the high cost of modern alternatives could not be recouped by the marginal increases in efficiency. Not that such analysis was always considered, for other factors, such as the impact of railroads on grave sites or just plain conservatism, were often sufficient to discourage change. Nonetheless, the principle prevailed: The old ways of moving on water were cheap and ingrained, and the new ways of moving on land expensive and disruptive, so that nothing changed—until the introduction of the railroads and modern shipping, when everything changed and the old world was passed by.

If Elvin is correct, that the reluctance of Chinese to reach for new solutions was due to the "high level" of their traditional methods, then the creation of a modern infrastructure of trade and transportation should have removed this obstacle and enabled them to evolve in new and more productive directions. With access to railroads, steamships, commercial banks, and other conveniences, Chinese farmers, merchants, and entrepreneurs were free to take the next steps along the road to development. However, Elvin and others have argued, there was another structural impediment—the imbalance between (too few) resources and (too many) people—which also prevented the Chinese from advancing from a productive but still traditional economy to the much higher level of growth achieved in the West. The final chapter will explore the question raised by the Elvin thesis: namely, whether conditions in Manchuria enabled men with abundant assets of land, labor, and capital to overcome the constraints imposed by population and resources in China proper and put this region on the road to development and growth.

CHAPTER 9

Agriculture: Innovation and Development?

AFTER 1903, MANCHURIAN FARMERS were linked to global markets through an infrastructure of railroads, shipping, banking and other facilities that had not existed before this time. If during the 19th century, the persistence of traditional Chinese technologies, organizations, and financial practices imposed limits on the growth and development of the Manchurian economy, then the 20th century offered new opportunities, symbolized by the ascendance of Dairen over Newchwang and of the South Manchuria Railway over the Liao River. In addition to the advantages provided by the new infrastructure, Manchuria, especially northern Manchuria, enjoyed an abundance of fertile land, adequate wage labor, and concentration of capital, all of which contrasted with conditions in China proper. Wealthy landowners had an opportunity unavailable elsewhere in China to produce cash crops and reinvest the profits in a manner that might lead to the development that had been lacking in previous times and other places. In this chapter we ask: Whether large Chinese landowners in Manchuria took advantage of these changes? Whether their efforts, if any, led to development and growth of a sort absent in this region during the 19th century? And what this says about the economic history of Manchuria and by extension of modern China?

A. The Big Landowners

The evidence for this analysis comes from the Kotoku surveys, which were introduced in Chapter 4. In the following tables, the households in each of the survey villages are divided into four classes—the two biggest landowners, other landowners, tenants, and wage-workers, the last of which includes a small number of miscellaneous households—and households of each class are aggregated by region (see Map 7). The reason for separating out the largest landowners is to compare the resources and strategies of this class with those of other households and to consider whether conditions in Manchuria encouraged or made possible economic behavior on the part of the most advantaged households that distinguish them from their counterparts in China proper. The reason for identifying the two largest owners within each village (rather than taking the largest owners in whatever location) is to highlight the behavior of those who had a relative advantage over their neighbors and the opportunity to expand their market share, invest the earnings, and launch the process of agricultural development that was lacking in China proper. Finally, the aggregation of this data by region will reveal variations related to geographic factors and to the progressive history of migration, settlement, and cultivation as Chinese moved from south to north.

Table 4 gives details on land tenure and land use—the area of land owned, rented out, rented in, and cultivated—per household for each class of households in each region, and the percentage of households, land owned, and land cultivated by region and household class. (In this table, "land owned" refers to "land owned that is actually under cultivation" [*shizhi di suoyou shudi*] rather than the broader category of "land owned" [*suoyou di*], which includes wasteland and other land that might or might not be arable or under cultivation.) For example, on average the 16 biggest landowners in Region 1 owned 459.77 *mu* of land, rented out 42.23 *mu*, rented in 17.84 *mu*, and cultivated a balance of 433.99 *mu*, while together these 16 households constituted 2.86 percent of all households in this region and owned 38.02 percent and cultivated 34.05 percent of the land in each of these categories.

The most striking fact demonstrated by Table 4 is the dominance of the landowners, and especially the biggest owners, throughout Manchuria. As shown by the totals at the bottom of this table, the 74 biggest landowners, who made up just over 4 percent of the 1,776 households in the Kotoku surveys, owned 50 percent of the land under cultivation and cultivated nearly 30 percent of all farmland themselves. The other 793 landowners (45 percent) owned almost all the remaining land and farmed more than 42 percent of the land under cultivation. The majority of the households were landless tenants (21 percent)

TABLE 4

Area of land owned, rented, and cultivated per household, and percentage of households, land owned, and land cultivated, by region and household class

Household Class	Number of Households	Percentage of Households	Land Owned (mu/ household)	Percentage of Land Owned	Land Rented Out (mu/ household)	Land Rented In (mu/ household)	Land Cultivated (mu/ household)	Percentage of Land Cultivated
Region 1								
Biggest owners	16	2.86%	459.77	38.02%	42.23	17.84	433.99	34.05%
Other owners	380	67.98%	31.50	61.86%	4.23	5.91	33.14	61.75%
Tenants	34	6.08%	0.36	0.06%	0.09	29.72	23.36	3.90%
Wage workers	129	23.08%	0.09	0.06%	0.04	0.43	0.48	0.31%
Total	559	100.00%	34.61	100.00%	4.10	6.43	36.48	100.00%
Region 2								
Biggest owners	12	4.80%	150.94	28.62%	118.29	20.67	52.90	7.54%
Other owners	92	36.80%	48.71	70.80%	23.57	16.75	41.82	45.69%
Tenants	95	38.00%	0.38	0.57%	0.69	41.06	41.37	46.68%
Wage workers	51	20.40%	0.02	0.02%	0.00	0.14	0.15	0.09%
Total	250	100.00%	25.32	100.00%	14.62	22.79	33.68	100.00%
Region 3								
Biggest owners	18	4.66%	632.49	38.70%	227.12	69.17	473.77	26.96%
Other owners	134	34.72%	134.19	61.12%	79.22	41.54	98.90	41.90%
Tenants	88	22.80%	0.56	0.17%	0.19	112.79	111.26	30.96%
Wage workers	146	37.82%	0.03	0.01%	0.00	0.00	0.39	0.18%
Total	386	100.00%	76.22	100.00%	38.14	43.36	81.94	100.00%

Region 4								
Biggest owners	26	5.02%	1,608.00	61.71%	889.57	46.22	802.46	32.77%
Other owners	153	29.54%	169.40	38.26%	70.64	49.64	144.81	34.79%
Tenants	154	29.73%	0.00	0.00%	0.14	135.83	132.71	32.10%
Wage workers	185	35.71%	0.13	0.03%	0.00	0.20	1.18	1.24%
Total	518	100.00%	130.79	100.00%	65.56	57.44	122.92	100.00%
Region 5								
Biggest owners	2	3.17%	356.00	21.56%	0.00	0.00	356.00	21.24%
Other owners	34	53.97%	74.76	76.97%	1.21	1.12	74.09	75.16%
Tenants	5	7.94%	1.60	0.24%	0.00	14.20	15.80	2.36%
Wage workers	22	34.92%	1.84	1.22%	0.00	0.05	1.89	1.24%
Total	63	100.00%	52.42	100.00%	0.65	1.75	53.20	100.00%
All Regions								
Biggest owners	74	4.17%	852.33	50.00%	396.11	40.27	509.22	29.56%
Other owners	793	44.65%	79.31	49.85%	31.83	21.42	68.56	42.65%
Tenants	376	21.17%	0.28	0.08%	0.29	95.28	93.17	27.48%
Wage workers	533	30.01%	0.15	0.06%	0.01	0.19	0.72	0.30%
Total	1,776	100.00%	71.03	100.00%	30.78	31.47	71.77	100.00%

SOURCE: *Kotoku gannendo*, Table 1, and *Kotoku sannendo*, Table 1.

TABLE 5
Cultivated area per farm household, and percentage of small, medium, and large farms, by province, 1918

| Province | Cultivated Area per Household (*mu*) | FARM SIZE (%) | | | Total |
		Small (<27 *mu*)	Medium (27–102 *mu*)	Large (>102 *mu*)	
Jehol	37.5	57.7	31.4	10.9	100
Fengtian	45.0	22.3	43.8	14.9	100
Jilin	88.5	32.5	45.7	21.8	100
Heilongjiang	130.5	15.6	39.2	45.2	100

SOURCE: *Manchoukuo Year Book, 1934,* 295.

or wage-workers (30 percent). The former rented and cultivated a little over a quarter of the land, whereas the latter supported themselves by wages and had access only to small garden plots. In this case, as elsewhere, rental produced a more equitable distribution of cultivated land (or what others have called "operational holdings"), thus moderating the extreme inequality of land ownership. On the other hand, the large number of wage workers, who had access to only minuscule plots (0.3 percent of cultivated land), constituted a much larger share of village society in Manchuria (30 percent) than the 1.6 percent of rural households classified as "landless laborers" in a 1937 survey covering all of China *except* Manchuria, which was then under Japanese control.[1]

The second feature demonstrated by this table is that the area of cultivated land per household and the concentration of land in the hands of the biggest owners increased along a gradient from south to north. In Regions 1 and 2, the area of cultivated land per household was in the range of 34–36 *mu*, in Region 3 nearly 82 *mu* and in Region 4 nearly 123 *mu*. Meanwhile, once beyond the Liao basin (Region 1), the percentage of land owned by the two biggest owners in each village increased from less than 30 percent in Region 2 to more than 60 percent in Region 4. In sum, as one moved from south to north, more land was available, and more of it was owned and farmed by a small number of very rich households. Nor was this an entirely new phenomenon: Statistics compiled in 1918 by the Ministry of Agriculture and Commerce (Table 5) show the same gradient in cultivated area per household and distribution of land from Jehol in the south to Heilongjiang in the north.

[1] See National Land Commission [*tudi weiyuanhui*] survey, cited in Loren Brandt and Barbara Sands (1990), 813–15.

Finally, Table 4 describes what the biggest owners did with their land. Again the totals at the bottom of the table show that on average the largest landowners owned 852 *mu*, of which they rented out 396 *mu* (46 percent) and, after renting in a small amount of additional land, cultivated 509 *mu* (or the equivalent of 60 percent of their holdings) on their own. In other words, the biggest landowners had both a significant stream of income from the rental of land and a significant amount of land left to farm. And they were surrounded by a large number of landless workers who were available for hire.

The brief histories of villages in the Kotoku surveys provide additional information on the process by which the distribution of landownership within and between these villages occurred. In most villages, the earliest settlers and their immediate offspring amassed large holdings in the range of hundreds or even thousands of *mu* (10s to 100s of *shang* or *tiandi*), and attracted friends, relatives, and acquaintances to farm this land as their tenants or workers. The manner by which the first settlers obtained land varied. In southern Manchuria, which was settled in the early Qing, they generally began as tenants or workers on banners or estates and gradually assumed control of the land by methods described in Chapter 2. Later, and in areas further north, most settlers bought land that had been "surveyed and released"[2] by government agencies, often after it had passed through the hands of a "monopolist" or "speculator." In some instances, villages were founded by squatters who took control of a substantial area of wasteland and succeeded in holding onto it after the authorities arrived. Whatever the process, it invariably began with a high concentration of ownership or inequality between large landowners, landlords, or farm managers on one side and landless tenants or workers on the other. This pattern was established in the villages of southern Manchuria during the 17th and 18th century, and repeated as later generations of migrants settled areas further north.

Over time, these initial large holdings fragmented and ownership devolved to numerous moderate, small, or even minuscule family farms that measured in the scores of *mu* or less. The growth in population by immigration and natural increase, the buying and selling of land that followed the rise and fall of individual fortunes, and the persistent splintering of family holdings by partible inheritance broke up large

[2] Chinese sources refer to the process by which land was "released" [*fang*] for sale. The Kotoku texts describe this process using the Chinese characters, "*fuxia*."

family farms and created a society of smallholders. By the 1930s, the oldest villages, which were located in southern Manchuria, resembled their counterparts in Hebei and Shandong. These villages had few or no large landowners, the majority of peasants were owners or owner-tenants whose holdings were too small to fully employ or support their large households, and they survived by producing as much as possible, while sending their surplus workers to the surrounding villages, cities, or more distant locations to work for wages. Survey villages in Jilin and Heilongjiang, on the other hand, which were settled in the late-19th or early-20th century, retained a higher concentration of landownership associated with an earlier stage of development. The data from these northern villages provides a basis for judging whether and how the big landowners in this region were able to exploit the advantages offered by land, labor, and other resources.

B. Farm Labor

How much labor and of what types was available to farmers, including landowners, large and small, and landless tenants? Table 6 shows the number of persons and workers (i.e., those who were engaged in full-time farm work or other productive occupations) per household and the amount of labor (measured in man-days per year) within the household, the amount hired in and hired out, and total labor per household for each region and household class. Since the wage workers listed in Table 4 did not control farmland, they do not appear as a separate category in this or subsequent tables, which are designed to describe the management of farming, although these households did supply much of the labor that was hired in by others. Man-days of labor have been calculated as follows: A yearly worker, who normally worked for eight to ten months,[3] has been counted as 9 months times 30 days or 270 man-days; a monthly worker as 30 man-days for each month worked; and a daily worker as one man-day per day. In this table, each household member described as a worker is counted as the equivalent of one yearly worker, or 270 man-days, for the reason that it is hard to know what other standard to employ. (The reader should note, however, that it may be misleading to equate household workers with hired workers, a topic that will be discussed further below.)

[3] See explanatory notes to Table 4 in introduction to *Kotoku sannendo*.

TABLE 6

Persons, workers, and labor resources per household, by region and household class

Household Class	House-holds	Persons per House-hold	Workers per House-hold	Labor (man-days per year per household)	Hired out	Hired in	Total
Region 1							
Biggest owners	16	13.63	3.81	1,029.38	0.00	2,009.56	3,038.94
Other owners	380	6.27	2.40	648.00	43.29	73.13	677.84
Tenants	34	5.56	1.97	532.06	72.38	18.32	478.00
Total	430	6.49	2.42	653.02	43.98	140.85	749.89
Region 2							
Biggest owners	12	9.17	2.25	607.50	0.00	252.92	860.42
Other owners	92	7.87	2.41	651.52	39.36	139.73	751.90
Tenants	95	7.05	2.66	719.05	47.63	45.94	717.36
Total	199	7.56	2.52	681.11	40.93	101.78	741.95
Region 3							
Biggest owners	18	17.22	3.89	1,050.00	0.00	1,250.94	2,300.94
Other owners	134	7.16	2.27	612.54	45.03	176.65	744.16
Tenants	88	6.86	2.56	690.34	77.64	133.17	745.88
Total	240	7.80	2.50	673.88	53.61	241.28	861.55
Region 4							
Biggest owners	26	17.35	3.81	1,028.08	12.15	2,737.73	3,753.66
Other owners	153	8.01	2.48	668.82	35.13	278.84	912.53
Tenants	154	7.49	2.73	738.12	97.10	117.83	758.84
Total	333	8.50	2.70	728.92	62.00	396.36	1,063.29
Region 5							
Biggest owners	2	13.00	3.50	945.00	0.00	945.00	1,890.00
Other owners	34	6.29	2.06	555.88	26.35	100.06	629.59
Tenants	5	2.80	1.60	432.00	109.80	0.00	322.20
Total	41	6.20	2.07	559.76	35.24	129.07	653.59
All Regions							
Biggest owners	74	15.07	3.58	963.24	4.27	1,767.24	2,726.22
Other owners	793	6.94	2.38	642.48	40.83	139.19	740.85
Tenants	376	6.99	2.59	699.41	77.98	92.69	714.13
Total	1,243	7.44	2.51	678.80	49.89	222.05	850.96

SOURCES: *Kotoku gannendo*, Table 1, and *Kotoku sannendo*, Table 1.

At first glance, the data in Table 6 is unsurprising. Households that owned the most land had substantially more members and more workers than other households. This is what one should expect, given the evidence that the size of rural Chinese households varied directly with landholdings.[4] The figures also show that the biggest owners hired more labor than other households and that once outside the Liao basin,

[4]See, for example, John Lossing Buck (1937A), 277–79, for comparable figures relating household size to landholdings in north China.

the numbers of persons and workers per household and the amount of labor (man-days per year) both within the household and hired in increased from south to north. Thus, the total amount of labor controlled by the biggest households in Region 4 (3,754 MD/yr) was more than four times as great as in Region 2 (860 MD/yr). These trends are consistent with the parallel increases in the availability and concentration in ownership of land and in incomes from rent over the same gradient (Table 4). In other words, proceeding from south to north, the biggest farms became bigger, the biggest landlords were able to rent out more land, earn more income from rents, and hire more workers to farm the still very large areas of land remaining under their control. The degree of inequality and the ability of the biggest landowners to take advantage of their landless neighbors increased as one approached the frontier.

C. Productivity

How did farm households of various size use the land, labor, and other resources under their control? Table 7 compares the household classes and regions in terms of labor (including both household and hired labor, in man-days per year) per household (from Table 6), labor (MD/yr) per unit (*mu*) of cultivated land (from Table 4), and output (*piculs*) of the five major crops—soybeans, sorghum, corn, millet, and wheat—per unit of labor (1000 MD/yr). The figures in column one show, as already indicated, that the biggest landowners used the most labor. The figures in column three, however, point in the opposite direction, showing that the biggest owners used *less* labor per unit of cultivated land than either smaller landowners or tenants. Finally, the figures in column five show that the biggest owners achieved much *higher* levels of productivity, or output per unit of labor (113 *piculs* per 1,000 MD/yr), than the other two classes.[5]

These numbers (Table 7) indicate: first, that labor productivity for all classes of households was higher in the north (Regions 3 and 4) than in the south (Regions 1 and 2); and second, that the productivity of the biggest farms was much higher than that achieved by other landowners

[5] The ratio of output per unit of labor used here, although not a direct representation of reality, provides a fair basis for comparison. Total labor contributed to products other than the five major crops, so that total output was greater than the amounts given in Table 7. Also, different crops with different weights and volumes are measured in *piculs* and lumped together in one number. However, since the cropping pattern adopted by all classes of households within each region and the percentage of land planted in the five crops in all regions were approximately the same, these figures are valid for comparing the levels of productivity among the various categories.

TABLE 7

Labor per mu *of cultivated land, and output of five major crops per household and per 1,000 man-days per year of labor, by region and household class*

Household Class	Labor (man-days per year per household)	Cultivated Land per Household (*mu*)	Labor per *Mu* of Cultivated Land (man-days per year)	Output per Household (*piculs*)	Output per 1,000 Man-days per Year of Labor (*piculs*)
Region 1					
Biggest owners	3,038.94	433.99	7.00	311.18	102.40
Other owners	677.84	33.14	20.45	20.46	30.19
Tenants	478.00	23.36	20.46	16.54	34.60
Total	749.89	47.28	15.86	30.97	41.30
Region 2					
Biggest owners	860.42	52.90	16.26	46.70	54.27
Other owners	751.90	41.82	17.98	34.28	45.59
Tenants	717.36	41.37	17.34	39.76	55.43
Total	741.95	42.27	17.55	37.65	50.74
Region 3					
Biggest owners	2,300.94	473.77	4.86	327.65	142.40
Other owners	744.16	98.90	7.52	57.25	76.93
Tenants	745.88	111.26	6.70	64.82	86.90
Total	861.55	131.54	6.55	80.30	93.21
Region 4					
Biggest owners	3,753.66	802.46	4.68	424.29	113.03
Other owners	912.53	144.81	6.30	75.93	83.20
Tenants	758.84	132.71	5.72	64.48	84.97
Total	1,063.29	190.56	5.58	97.83	92.01
Region 5					
Biggest owners	1,890.00	356.00	5.31	143.07	75.70
Other owners	629.59	74.09	8.50	31.37	49.82
Tenants	322.20	15.80	20.39	8.20	25.46
Total	653.59	80.73	8.10	33.99	52.01
All Regions					
Biggest owners	2,726.22	509.22	5.35	307.49	112.79
Other owners	740.85	68.56	10.81	39.45	53.25
Tenants	714.13	93.17	7.66	53.23	74.54
Total	850.96	102.24	8.32	59.58	70.01

SOURCES: *Kotoku gannendo*, Tables 1 and 12, *Kotoku sannendo*, Tables 1 and 12.

or tenants. In other words, big landowners on or near the frontier were using income derived from the rental of nearly half of their land to pay wage-workers to farm the remainder of their land, and in this way achieved a higher output per unit of labor than any of the other households in these regions or elsewhere in Manchuria.

In fact, the apparent differences in productivity between the biggest owners and other owners and tenants are so great that they require some explanation. The chief reason for the difference may be that the biggest owners employed mostly (65 percent) wage labor, whereas other owners and tenants employed mostly (81 and 87 percent respectively) household labor (Table 6), and there was considerable difference between these two types of workers. Japanese researchers in north China during the 1930s reported that the schedule of a year-laborer was fixed by custom and extremely demanding. The wage laborer typically worked from the crack of dawn until early evening, with 12 hours of actual work and three hours of breaks. In the course of the work-year, which was 8–10 months long, the wage-worker's only holidays were the three-day Dragon Boat Festival [*Duanwujie*], in the fifth month of the lunar calendar, and a ten-day summer vacation, during the slack between planting and harvest. By any measure, paid laborers worked long and hard. By contrast, self-employed middle peasants in north China during the 1930s confided that they had a habit of slacking off, going to the market, and looking for diversions from the drudgery of farm work. Philip Huang, who interviewed such men, believes that farmers with less land may have concluded that the marginal returns on their labor were not worth the effort and therefore did only the minimum.[6]

Did these differences between household and hired labor also apply in Manchuria? Perhaps even more so. The high concentration of landownership and large number of landless peasants in Jilin and Heilongjiang gave landowners considerable leverage over labor. When hiring out, poor families had to send those members of the households who commanded the highest wages, primarily adult males, leaving women, children, and old people to farm whatever land was available to them.[7] The result was to put the most productive workers under the most demanding conditions on the farms of the biggest owners, and leave the least productive workers, with perhaps less incentive to work, on the farms of other owners and tenants. Recall that in Table 6, "household workers" were counted as equal to hired "yearly workers" (270 mandays of labor each), for the sole reason that there was no other standard available. But it is clear from this discussion that household workers contributed *less* and hired workers *more* than the norm. Whether this was because the hired workers were more productive (i.e., produced more per unit of time worked), or because they worked longer hours, or both

[6]Philip Huang (1985), 165–66.
[7]In the 21 villages covered in the *Kotoku sannendo* survey, 72 percent of household members described as "workers" and 91 percent of those hired out as day-laborers were male. *Kotoku gannendo* does not provide a breakdown of workers by gender.

cannot be determined on the basis of available evidence. The point is that the largest owners got the best workers who produced the best results.

D. Investment Strategies

The biggest owners had by far the most land, they had a substantial stream of income from renting nearly half of this land to tenants, they used a portion of this income to hire the most productive workers from among the large number of landless households in the village, and they deployed these workers on their remaining farmland. Surprisingly, however, this small number of very large landowners, who were in the best position to accumulate capital, invest in new or additional technologies, engage in more commercialized agriculture, and by these means increase their own wealth (while coincidentally advancing the cause of agricultural development), chose not to do so. Rather than leverage land, labor, and capital to increase output and sales, the biggest owners seemed more inclined to reduce costs, while producing and marketing at the same level as their neighbors.

Logic dictates that if the largest landowners sought to maximize their income from agriculture, they would adopt a cropping pattern different from their neighbors. Wealthy households with large holdings could satisfy their subsistence needs by planting a relatively small area in food and devote the balance to income-producing crops. Conversely, small landowners and tenants would presumably plant more land in a wider variety of food crops as a hedge against flood, drought, or famine. Large landowners could afford the risk and reap the benefits of planting more cash crops, whereas small owners and tenants, who were more vulnerable to risk, should have planted more food.

Yet, despite this logic, the evidence indicates that in selecting crops the practices of rich and poor were essentially the same.[8] Table 8, reporting the percentage of land planted in the five major crops by each class of household in each region, shows that there was little variation in the cropping patterns of large landowners, small landowners, and tenants within each region, although there were significant variations from one region to the next. The only notable difference between classes was in the planting of corn—tenants were about 2.5 times more likely to plant this crop than were the largest landowners. But corn was the least popular of the five crops, while the differences among classes in

[8]Loren Brandt (1987), 676, reports similar findings for farms of various sizes but almost identical cropping patterns in villages of Hebei during the 1930s.

TABLE 8
Percentage of cultivated land sown in five major crops, by region and household class

Household Class	Soybeans	Sorghum	Corn	Millet	Wheat	Total
Region 1						
Biggest owners	10.02	49.60	0.48	20.21	0.00	80.31
Other owners	8.52	49.74	1.62	17.09	0.80	77.77
Tenants	7.87	43.89	1.80	17.75	0.29	71.60
Total	9.00	49.39	1.24	18.18	0.50	78.32
Region 2						
Biggest owners	24.56	24.89	8.26	7.21	0.00	64.91
Other owners	19.05	24.37	6.26	12.05	0.00	61.73
Tenants	30.21	24.69	13.21	8.78	0.00	76.90
Total	24.64	24.56	9.64	10.17	0.00	69.01
Region 3						
Biggest owners	17.78	15.61	7.67	18.98	16.90	76.94
Other owners	17.81	13.47	9.31	20.13	11.85	72.58
Tenants	13.66	17.92	14.00	23.03	3.63	72.24
Total	16.50	15.44	10.33	20.73	10.65	73.65
Region 4						
Biggest owners	27.66	7.04	6.28	15.28	18.78	75.04
Other owners	24.15	9.74	9.80	16.75	16.03	76.47
Tenants	24.52	7.37	12.77	18.00	8.98	71.63
Total	25.42	8.09	9.60	16.67	14.66	74.44
Region 5						
Biggest owners	15.45	0.00	1.83	14.04	26.69	58.01
Other owners	16.28	0.00	3.98	18.46	22.43	61.15
Tenants	12.66	0.00	5.70	51.90	12.66	82.91
Total	16.01	0.00	3.56	18.31	23.11	60.99
All Regions						
Biggest owners	21.90	16.97	5.48	16.86	14.74	75.95
Other owners	18.30	20.39	7.29	17.39	10.68	74.05
Tenants	21.61	13.28	12.82	18.45	6.25	72.41
Total	20.29	17.40	8.29	17.53	10.65	74.16

SOURCES: *Kotoku gannendo*, Table 12, and *Kotoku sannendo*, Table 12.

planting the more prevalent soybeans, sorghum, and millet, were minuscule. Taken together, the five crops occupied about the same portion of farmland (72–76 percent) planted by all classes in all regions. What changed was the mix among these crops. In southern Manchuria, farmers devoted most of their land to sorghum and millet, put less in soybeans and none at all in wheat. In northern Manchuria, the cooler, drier conditions favored soybeans and wheat, while less area was planted in sorghum. Corn did best in the middle latitudes, tapering off to both north and south. Within each region, however, all farmers, large and small, planted the same crops in roughly the same proportions.

Similarly, large landowners declined to invest more than their neighbors in capital and technology. The two most important forms of capital on these farms were draft animals (oxen, horses, donkeys, and mules) and large machinery (carts and plows). Draft animals were virtually the only source of nonhuman power in Manchuria and of manure for fertilizer, which was highly valued and in short supply.[9] The great cart described in Chapter 7 was essential for hauling produce and other farm tasks. A wealthy landowner with horses and carts could monopolize the transport and sale of grain in markets located some distance from his village.[10] Plows were perhaps an even more important measure of wealth. Only the long plow pulled by two or three oxen could break through the heavy sod of Heilongjiang. According to peasants in this region, "when wealthy families with many plows met and talked about production, they always asked about the number of plows."[11] Table 9 shows the number of draft animals, carts, and plows per household and per 1,000 *mu* of cultivated land, aggregated by region and household class. As we would expect, the largest landowners had the largest numbers of animals and farm tools. But measured in terms of the cultivated area, the big owners in fact owned *less* capital than their neighbors. If the big owners were getting more productivity from labor, it was *not* through the substitution of capital. And if they had a more productive workforce, they were not inclined to raise output higher by investing more in animal power or equipment.

Of all the challenges facing Manchurian farmers, none was more compelling than the need for fertilizer. The same was true in China proper, where four out of five farmers said that they needed more fertilizer to raise outputs, but could not afford or obtain it.[12] And the problem was even more serious in Manchuria, where yields were perceptibly declining and the application of fertilizer, manure, and night soil (chemical fertilizer was unavailable at this time[13]), was only about 60 percent of the average amount used in north China.[14] Nonetheless,

[9] During this period, only natural fertilizer, *tufen*, a mixture of soil and animal manure or human waste, was used in Manchuria. The chemical fertilizer, ammonium sulfate, was first manufactured in this region in the 1940s.

[10] For one such example see: *Kotoku sannendo*, site 2.

[11] *Heilongjiang waiji* [External Notes of Heilongjiang] and *Heilongjiang zhigao* [Heilongjiang Gazette], cited in Sun Zhanwen (1981), 97; and CER (1924), 52–54.

[12] John Lossing Buck (1937A), 260.

[13] The Japanese began making ammonium sulfate in Dairen in 1935, but most farmers in Manchuria had no access to chemical fertilizer until after 1949. See: James Reardon-Anderson (1986), 215–19.

[14] John Lossing Buck (1937A), 259, reports that the average farm in the "winter wheat-kaoliang" area of north China used 685 pounds of fertilizer (manure plus night soil) per *mu* of cropland compared with 409 pounds in Manchuria (Table 10). Buck's data show that the use of fertilizer in north China varied inversely with farm size. (NB: Buck reports in

TABLE 9

Number of draft animals, carts, and plows per household and per 1000 mu *of cultivated land, by region and household class*

Household Class	PER HOUSEHOLD			PER 1,000 MU OF CULTIVATED LAND		
	Draft Animals	Carts	Plows	Draft Animals	Carts	Plows
Region 1						
Biggest owners	7.06	1.44	2.38	16.27	3.31	5.47
Other owners	0.87	0.28	0.40	26.20	8.58	12.07
Tenants	0.44	0.09	0.15	18.88	3.78	6.29
Total	1.07	0.31	0.45	22.46	6.57	9.56
Region 2						
Biggest owners	1.00	0.33	0.83	18.90	6.30	15.75
Other owners	1.28	0.32	0.84	30.67	7.54	20.01
Tenants	1.06	0.32	0.65	25.70	7.63	15.77
Total	1.16	0.32	0.75	27.44	7.48	17.70
Region 3						
Biggest owners	9.89	1.11	2.78	20.87	2.35	5.86
Other owners	1.86	0.32	0.99	18.79	3.24	10.04
Tenants	1.77	0.35	0.83	15.93	3.17	7.46
Total	2.43	0.38	1.07	18.43	2.85	8.09
Region 4						
Biggest owners	15.73	2.19	5.23	19.60	2.73	6.52
Other owners	3.20	0.46	1.30	22.07	3.20	8.98
Tenants	1.91	0.34	0.95	14.39	2.59	7.14
Total	3.58	0.54	1.44	18.72	2.84	7.55
Region 5						
Biggest owners	30.00	5.00	5.00	84.27	14.04	14.04
Other owners	3.97	1.24	1.38	53.59	16.67	18.66
Tenants	1.00	0.60	0.20	63.29	37.97	12.66
Total	4.88	1.34	1.41	59.68	16.41	17.31
All Regions						
Biggest owners	10.43	1.54	3.30	20.49	3.03	6.48
Other owners	1.67	0.37	0.77	24.30	5.39	11.18
Tenants	1.52	0.32	0.76	16.30	3.43	8.19
Total	2.14	0.42	0.92	20.90	4.10	8.94

SOURCES: *Kotoku gannendo,* Tables 1 and 8, and *Kotoku sannendo,* Tables 1 and 9.

the largest Manchurian landowners chose not to invest in fertilizer or fertilizer producing livestock. Data from the *Kotoku* surveys (Table 10) show that although landowners as a whole had more fertilizer per cultivated area than their tenants, the biggest owners had *less* than all other owners. Moreover, if the older settlements in southern Manchuria (Region 1) represented the future, then one could expect that over time the

pounds per crop acre, which have been converted at the rate of 1 acre = 6 *mu*.) Philip Huang (1985), 150–51, found that in Shandong and Hebei the application of fertilizer was about the same in large managerial and small family farms.

TABLE 10
Fertilizer, manure, and night soil, per mu *of cultivated land, by region
and household class*

Household Class	Manure (lbs./*mu*)	Night soil (lbs./*mu*)	Total fertilizer (lbs./*mu*)
Region 1			
Biggest owners	285	32	317
Other owners	410	115	525
Tenants	409	135	544
Total	366	87	453
Region 2			
Biggest owners	434	116	550
Other owners	503	119	622
Tenants	402	101	503
Total	450	110	560
Region 3			
Biggest owners	374	29	403
Other owners	326	47	373
Tenants	260	38	298
Total	318	39	357
Region 4			
Biggest owners	338	22	360
Other owners	406	38	444
Tenants	264	34	298
Total	337	31	368
Region 5			
Biggest owners	1,256	29	1,285
Other owners	886	53	939
Tenants	1,216	86	1,302
Total	962	48	1,010
All Regions			
Biggest owners	355	27	382
Other owners	417	64	481
Tenants	284	44	328
Total	361	48	409

SOURCES: *Kotoku gannendo*, Tables 1 and 8, and *Kotoku sannendo*, Tables 1 and 9.

largest landowners would invest *still less* in maintaining the fertility of their soil.[15] The chief constraint on increasing farm animals in China

[15] The figures for manure and night soil in Table 10 were calculated as follows. Manure: number of "animal units" was calculated using the conversion rates in John Lossing Buck (1937A), 473: ox, horse, and mule = 1.0, donkey = 0.5, pig = 0.2, chicken = 0.01, counting adult animals as 100 percent and juveniles as 50 percent; then, following Buck (1937A), 258, the amount of manure was calculated at the rate of 15,983 lbs. per year per animal unit. Night soil: number of household members and FTE of hired labor were added to get a total FTE of individuals in each class of households and regions; this number was multiplied by 0.6 to produce average number of adult male equivalents; following Buck (1937A), 258, the amount of night soil was calculated at the rate of 992 lbs. per adult male equivalent.

TABLE 11

Pigs per household and per mu *of cultivated land, by region and household class*

Household Class	Pigs	Pigs per Household	Pigs per *Mu*
Region 1			
Biggest owners	270	16.88	0.04
Other owners	492	1.29	0.04
Tenants	49	1.44	0.06
Total	811	1.89	0.04
Region 2			
Biggest owners	35	2.92	0.06
Other owners	138	1.50	0.04
Tenants	124	1.31	0.03
Total	297	1.49	0.04
Region 3			
Biggest owners	153	8.50	0.02
Other owners	318	2.37	0.02
Tenants	143	1.63	0.01
Total	614	2.56	0.02
Region 4			
Biggest owners	477	18.35	0.02
Other owners	664	4.34	0.03
Tenants	496	3.22	0.02
Total	1637	4.92	0.03
Region 5			
Biggest owners	34	17.00	0.05
Other owners	121	3.56	0.05
Tenants	11	2.20	0.14
Total	166	4.05	0.05
All Regions			
Biggest owners	969	13.09	0.03
Other owners	1733	2.19	0.03
Tenants	823	2.19	0.02
Total	3525	2.84	0.03

SOURCES: *Kotoku gannendo*, Tables 1 and 8, and *Kotoku sannendo*, Tables 1 and 9.

proper, which was the shortage of grazing land, did not apply in northern Manchuria, where the largest farms had more land than they could cultivate and wasteland surrounding many of these farms went unclaimed and unused. Yet the big landowners did not invest disproportionately in grazing livestock. Similarly, the favored Chinese farm animal, the hog, is also the most efficient producer of high quality fertilizer, but measured in terms of cultivated area (Table 11), the biggest landowners declined to invest in hogs. Perhaps the market for pork did not make it profitable to raise hogs, despite their contribution of fertilizer, although it is striking that there was no effort on the part of any of the large Manchurian landowners to explore an integrated animal-and-crop agriculture.

TABLE 12

Yield of five major crops, by region and household class (piculs per mu*)*

Household Class	Soybeans	Gaoliang	Corn	Millet	Wheat	Total
Region 1						
Biggest owners	0.58	1.04	1.00	0.68	n.a.	0.89
Other owners	0.47	0.94	0.59	0.61	0.29	0.80
Tenants	0.48	0.90	0.38	0.56	0.72	0.76
Total	0.51	0.98	0.63	0.63	0.30	0.83
Region 2						
Biggest owners	0.98	1.81	1.45	0.93	n.a.	1.35
Other owners	1.12	1.58	1.86	0.76	n.a.	1.31
Tenants	1.07	1.49	1.44	0.90	n.a.	1.25
Total	1.08	1.56	1.56	0.82	n.a.	1.28
Region 3						
Biggest owners	1.13	0.84	0.93	0.83	0.76	0.90
Other owners	0.75	0.87	0.77	0.89	0.66	0.80
Tenants	0.63	0.94	0.82	0.81	0.56	0.80
Total	0.83	0.89	0.82	0.85	0.69	0.83
Region 4						
Biggest owners	0.68	0.87	1.00	0.60	0.65	0.70
Other owners	0.69	0.83	0.79	0.59	0.67	0.69
Tenants	0.61	0.88	0.80	0.69	0.58	0.69
Total	0.66	0.86	0.84	0.63	0.64	0.70
Region 5						
Biggest owners	0.64	n.a.	0.00	0.84	0.69	0.69
Other owners	0.68	n.a.	0.00	0.83	0.71	0.69
Tenants	0.68	n.a.	0.00	0.64	0.78	0.63
Total	0.67	n.a.	0.00	0.82	0.70	0.69
All Regions						
Biggest owners	0.76	0.98	0.98	0.68	0.68	0.79
Other owners	0.71	0.97	0.82	0.70	0.66	0.78
Tenants	0.69	1.03	0.87	0.74	0.58	0.79
Total	0.72	0.98	0.87	0.71	0.66	0.79

SOURCES: *Kotoku gannendo*, Tables 1 and 12, and *Kotoku sannendo*, Tables 1 and 12.

Unwilling to adopt a more aggressive cropping strategy or to invest more in draft animals, farm equipment, or fertilizer, it is hardly surprising that the biggest owners failed to achieve higher yields than their neighbors. Table 12 reports on the yields (piculs per *mu*) of the five major crops, aggregated by household class and region. These figures show that the highest yields for all crops occurred in Region 2, suggesting that yields were a function more of geography and proximity to markets than to choices exercised by producers. Meanwhile, within each region the yields of all crops by all classes of households were approximately the same. Regions 3 and 4, which had the highest levels of productivity (output per unit of labor), did not have especially high

TABLE 13

Sales of two largest cash crops, per household and per 100 mu *of cultivated land,
by region and household class*

Household Class	Sales per Household (yuan)	Sales per 100 *Mu* (yuan)
Region 1		
Biggest owners	420.74	96.95
Other owners	24.95	75.29
Tenants	3.07	13.13
Total	37.95	80.01
Region 2		
Biggest owners	141.95	268.32
Other owners	76.57	183.10
Tenants	28.68	69.33
Total	57.65	136.26
Region 3		
Biggest owners	457.74	96.62
Other owners	93.54	94.58
Tenants	45.17	40.60
Total	103.16	78.29
Region 4		
Biggest owners	623.13	77.65
Other owners	101.03	69.77
Tenants	36.66	27.63
Total	112.03	58.59
Region 5		
Biggest owners	37.50	10.53
Other owners	53.30	71.95
Tenants	0.00	0.00
Total	46.03	56.32
All Regions		
Biggest owners	445.28	87.44
Other owners	58.42	85.22
Tenants	33.11	35.54
Total	73.81	71.97

SOURCES: *Kotoku gannendo*, Tables 1 and 14, and *Kotoku sannendo*, Tables 1 and 13.

yields (output per unit of land). Overall, the largest owners obtained the same yields as their neighbors. Presumably, they could have achieved higher yields by investing more in capital and labor, but they chose not to do so.

Finally, even if they invested roughly the same amount in capital goods, adopted the same cropping pattern and achieved the same yields, perhaps the biggest owners were able to use their more abundant land and more productive labor to produce more marketable goods per unit of land ? Again, the evidence indicates that this was not the case. Table 13 shows the sales (in yuan) of the two largest cash crops within each village, per household and per 100 *mu* of cultivated land, aggregated by region and household class. The main cash crops were soybeans and wheat in the north and beans and sorghum in the south, although in some instances millet, tobacco, or some other crop might rise to the top. In every village, one or two crops accounted for most (sometimes nearly all) sales, so that for comparative purposes figures for the top two crops serve as a fair approximation of the whole. Again, the numbers show that whereas the largest landowners accounted for most sales, when compared in terms of sales per unit of cultivated land, the big owners were *not* more inclined than other owners to use their land for commercial purposes — or if inclined, they were not more successful. The widest differences in this regard are between all landowners and tenants, presumably because owners could afford to devote less land to food and more to cash crops than was possible for less well endowed tenants, and between Region 2, which had the right combination of favorable land-to-man ratio and proximity to markets, and less endowed regions to the north or the south. In sum, the biggest landowners did not convert their superior assets into a higher degree of commercialization compared to landowners as a whole.[16]

E. The Flexibility Factor

If the largest landowners in Manchuria, households with extensive holdings, abundant capital and access to wage labor, chose not to invest more heavily than their neighbors in the production of cash crops, or indeed any crops at all, then what did they do with their money? The answer seems to be the same one given in Chapter 7 to describe the behavior of merchants, manufacturers, and entrepreneurs: that is, they diversified their investments in fields that relied on simple technologies, small organizations, and limited capital, and they moved these investments quickly from one opportunity to the next. Chinese farmers and owners of farmland, like other Chinese, preferred to shift their time, talent, and money among areas that promised the highest return in the shortest time with the least risk, rather than concentrate their resources on capital-intensive, high-technology, complex-organization, high-risk, long-term investments that might (or might not) yield exceptional profits and, coincidentally, move the economy toward development and growth.

[16]Loren Brandt (1987), 676–77, reports that farms of various sizes in Hebei during the 1930s had similar "marketing ratios" (percentage of farm output marketed).

The histories of villages in Jilin and Heilongjiang are filled with examples of large landowners who secured their initial capital from non-agricultural activities and invested the profits in land, or who, after purchasing land, used the income from it to go into sideline ventures. Thus, we find among the farmers and landlords of these villages operators of bean mills, gristmills, drugstores, general stores and pawnshops, innkeepers, grain traders, and moneylenders, and people who were ready to do business in whatever field seemed most immediately promising.[17] This approach was not limited to the village elite. Even an ordinary peasant could hook up the cart and team of horses that he normally used for farmwork and for a time assume the role of shipping agent. He might join a caravan of six or eight carts, traveling together for safety, and make the round-trip of a few days or a few weeks from his home village to a regional market and back. If he was especially enterprising, he could get current information on market conditions, buy grain in the village, sell it in the city, and use the proceeds to purchase sundries for sale back home. In this way, the peasant-carter-grain dealer-goods merchant made his living in competition with larger, better financed and more professional shippers and merchants.[18]

Still another example of this flexibility and its effects on the economy of the northern territories is the breeding and raising of livestock. As Chinese farmers reclaimed land and expanded cultivation onto the Mongolian steppe, different forms of animal husbandry emerged, each in its own environmental niche. Stud farms established during the early Qing along the boundary between Manchuria and Inner Mongolia disappeared, as Chinese farmers converted these areas to agriculture, which was more productive per unit of land and supported a denser population than herding. Meanwhile, Mongol herders were forced to retreat to the colder, drier steppe west of the Daxing'anling Mountains, where they carried on the breeding of horses, sheep, and cattle, using traditional methods of nomadic pastoralism. Chinese farmers in Manchuria, like those in China proper, raised pigs, purchased horses and cattle as draft animals, and bred donkeys and mules for use on their farms. But they did not cross the divide that separated farming from pastoralism. In contrast to the Europeans, who invented whole new

[17] Bean mills: *Kotoku sannendo*, sites 3, 15, 17. Gristmill: *Kotoku gannendo*, site 2. Drugstores: *Kotoku gannendo*, site 3. General stores: *Kotoku gannendo*, sites 4 and 6. Pawnshops: *Kotoku gannendo*, site 6. Innkeeper: *Kotoku gannendo*, site 4. Grain traders: *Kotoku gannendo*, sites 5 and 10. Moneylenders: *Kotoku gannendo*, sites 3 and 5.

[18] This example is based on evidence from *Kotoku gannendo*, site 10.

economies and ways of life on the plains of North and South America, Chinese were reluctant to reinvent themselves as gauchos or cowboys.[19]

One exception was the cattle business. The expansion of farming westward drove Mongol herders onto the high plateau, where they raised cattle, horses, and sheep by grazing on the open range and remained, throughout this period, the chief suppliers of livestock to markets in Manchuria, northern China, and Siberia. Meanwhile, the growth in demand for beef in Russia and among the foreign residents of Manchurian cities persuaded Chinese farmers in adjacent areas to fatten cattle by stall-feeding. Following World War I, cattlemen of the Northeast entered the global market for beef: the municipalities of Harbin, Hailar, and Manzhouli built slaughterhouses; the Chinese Eastern Railway offered free storage facilities and refrigerator cars and reduced its rates on the shipment of meat through Vladivostok; and the British Produce Export Company operated a large refrigerating plant in Harbin and exported beef to Japan on a large scale.[20]

What this record shows, however, is that in this field as in others Chinese were more adept at diversifying into profitable sideline businesses than in creating whole new industries. Chinese farmers who adopted stall-feeding generally fattened retired work animals, using traditional techniques, to produce beef that was of low quality and suitable only for local consumption. A few Chinese processing firms fattened younger animals with special feeds to produce higher quality meat for export. But these operations were invariably linked to distilleries or oil mills, where the animals were fed mash or beancake, and thus share the small scale, low technology, minimal financing, and flexibility that made Chinese enterprises in Manchuria profitable in the short run, but limited their ability to achieve higher levels of productivity and a larger market share over time. Absent from this story are attempts to invest large sums of money, adopt new technologies, or take on a whole new approach to production in the quest for exceptional wealth or some other measure of success.[21]

Based on interviews they conducted in the 1980s, anthropologists Burton Pasternak and Janet Salaff reached similar findings about Han farmers who migrated, beginning in the 1930s, from southern and central Manchuria to Hulunbuir, a Mongol herding region in the northwest

[19]CER (1924), 125–31. For additional details on changes in the Mongol livestock industry during this period, see Xing Yichen (1987).

[20]CER (1924), 133–34, 144.

[21]CER (1924), 140–41.

corner of Heilongjiang. These migrants had come from relatively moist, warm areas, where they engaged in rain-fed agriculture, and intended to continue these practices in the drier, colder north. What is striking is not that they found crop farming under these conditions difficult, but that they persisted so long without change. Only after 1949, when the government introduced dairy cows, which the Chinese could manage as a sideline without going to the extreme of extensive pastoralism, did they make the switch. When they did change, many Han herders found their new way of life both easier and more profitable than farming. But the change came (and apparently had to come) from official direction above, rather than by the spontaneous choice of those below.[22]

F. Material Constraints?

In analyzing the behavior of Manchurian landowners, one cannot overlook the unfavorable conditions that prevailed at the time of the Kotoku surveys. By all accounts, the early 1930s were hard on Manchuria and Manchurian farmers. Following the clash between Chinese Nationalist and Soviet forces over the Chinese Eastern Railway in 1929, Moscow blocked the shipment of goods by rail from northern Manchuria to the port of Vladivostok.[23] The Manchurian Incident of 1931 undermined local authorities and encouraged banditry, disrupting production and trade, driving down the value of land, and forcing many farmers to abandon their fields. The Great Depression shrank the world market for agricultural goods, especially soybeans, which had been the leading Manchurian export.

Nature was also unkind. Owing to the continuous cultivation of farmland and the shortage of fertilizer, the yields on agricultural crops throughout Manchuria were declining. Virtually all of the northern Kotoku sites reported reductions in yields, often by as much as 40–50 percent, from the time the land was first reclaimed in the late-19th or early-20th century, until the mid-1930s. Most peasants responded by increasing the application of fertilizer, but no one succeeded in restoring production to previous levels.[24] Several villages reported declines in the output of soybeans, owing to drought.[25] And in 1933 and 1934,

[22] Burton Pasternak and Janet Salaff (1993), 18–19, 54–55, 148–49.
[23] SMR, *Fifth Report*, 80.
[24] Generally, the use of fertilizer was limited only by its availability. In one case, however, tenant farmers refused to fertilize their fields for fear that the following year the landlord would confiscate the land. See *Kotoku gannendo*, site 10.
[25] See, for example, *Kotoku gannendo*, sites 9, 10, and 14.

severe flooding destroyed crops in much of the north. In contrast to the 1920s, when sales of agricultural goods were booming and the future of Manchuria seemed bright, everything about the early 1930s was depressing and depressed.

Statistics on agricultural production and trade confirm what Manchurian farmers already knew — that their business was in trouble. After rising steadily during the 1920s, the planted area and output of soybeans and other agricultural crops in Manchuria declined after 1931, reaching their nadir in 1934.[26] For a time, the volume and price of bean and bean product exports remained steady, but prices for these commodities also fell by 20 percent between 1931 and 1933.[27] And in 1935, following the disappointing harvest of the previous year, the volume of exports of beans and bean products dropped by one-third from their previous high.[28]

Finally, the villages of northern Manchuria were subject to the same systemic forces that had broken up large holdings and persuaded big landowners to shift their investments from agricultural to other pursuits in the south. In some villages, landlords held onto their land and exercised considerable power over their tenants, but in others they lost control over both land and labor, as ownership was dispersed.[29] Speculators and large landowners were often forced to sell some of their land to pay the costs of reclamation and the taxes on the resulting farmland. Large landowners tended to have large families, while the practice of partible inheritance fragmented family farms at the turn of each generation. Finally, the increase in population and difficulty of managing large farms chipped away at individual holdings.[30]

These factors help explain why large landowners in Jilin and Heilongjiang were reluctant to invest in farming and preferred to diversify rather than concentrate their holdings. Still, there is no reason to believe that they acted differently in the mid 1930s, when the snapshot of the Kotoku surveys was taken, than either before or afterward. In some villages, the cropping pattern may have changed somewhat to keep pace with the rise and fall of prices. But it was more common for cropping

[26] SMR, *Fifth Report*, 162–63.

[27] *Manchoukuo Year Book, 1934*, 284, shows that the average prices of soybeans, beancake and bean oil, based on spot deal quotations at the Dairen Staple Produce Exchange, remained steady from 1926 to 1931, then dropped by 20 percent between 1931–33.

[28] Exports of beans and bean products declined from 4.3 million metric tons in 1931 and 1932 to 2.9 mmt in 1935. See: SMR, *Fifth Report*, 160.

[29] For an example of concentrated ownership and a powerful landlord, see *Kotoku gannendo*, site 16; and for the opposite case, see *Kotoku gannendo*, site 4.

[30] For a discussion of the causes for dispersion of landownership, see: *Kotoku gannendo*, site 15.

to remain the same or to change gradually in response to climatic or environmental conditions. Moreover, none of the Kotoku village histories indicates that large landowners planted different crops than their neighbors or responded in different ways to the market.[31] It is also unlikely that, under conditions of general hardship, the largest owners suddenly found buyers for their draft animals and farm equipment, so that their capital stock was abnormally low at the time of the Kotoku surveys. On the contrary, the fact that land sales declined in the early 1930s suggests that there was probably little demand for other goods and that the distribution of capital was about the same at the time of the survey as before. Finally, there is every reason to believe that even during the 1920s, when farming and farm prices were at their peak, large landowners shifted their investments among activities inside and outside of agriculture. In sum, although the conditions of the 1930s were unfavorable, the behavior of the big landowners was probably not significantly different then as compared to any other time.

G. Conclusion

While the actions of tenants, workers, and even small farmers might be explained as a response to misfortune or hedge against future disaster, large landowners could afford a higher level of risk. Agriculture is an inherently volatile business. Changes in market and natural conditions make it impossible to guarantee high outputs and high prices every year. Yet, over time, successful farmers are those who can survive the lows and capitalize on the highs. The figures for crop areas and output, both of which rebounded after 1935, show that patience and persistence would be rewarded.[32] With the restoration of order and the return of refugees, land prices in virtually all of the survey villages, which had declined after 1931, were back up by 1934. Those farmers who held on, and if they had money, took advantage of the downturn to buy additional land, equipment, and fertilizer-producing livestock, would find themselves better off than before. There is, however, little reason to believe that many Chinese farmers on the Manchurian frontier, who could afford to take the long view, did so. Chinese landowners, like Chinese pioneers generally, it seems, were reluctant to change.

[31] For details on cropping patterns, see especially the village histories for *Kotoku gannendo*, sites 6–9.
[32] In 1934, Manchurian crop area and output fell to their lowest point since 1927. By 1938, agricultural outputs had regained most of their losses, while total crop area reached a new high. See: SMR, *Fifth Report*, 162–63.

Analysis

THIS ACCOUNT OF THE MANCHURIAN ECONOMY provides an opportunity to test current theories and debates about the course of Chinese economic history and the degree to which China changed both before and after the arrival of western imperialism and the integration of China into the world market. The discussion of modern Chinese economic history takes place against the backdrop of classical economic theory of Adam Smith and Karl Marx, which posits a "normal"course of development, following the model of 17th-century England. According to this theory, commercialization and the discipline of the marketplace force a series of adaptations, including the commodification and specialization of production, separation of capital and labor, increase in investment, and improvement in technology, culminating in the emergence of capitalism in agriculture, industry, and commerce. The classical theory has been used to explain the rise of capitalism in Europe, North America, and other parts of the world. How, one might ask, does it apply to China? And if, as we shall find, it does *not* apply, then why is this so?

A. "Classical" Economic Theory and "Early Modern" China

During the 1950s and 1960s, most historians both within China and abroad agreed that the classical model did not apply to China. Marxist scholars described imperial China as "feudal," Western scholars called it "Confucian," and both agreed that it was stagnant, lacking the capacity for change from within, especially of the type that would lead to capitalism as described by Smith and Marx. In recent years, however, scholarship on China has changed. Proponents of the "sprouts of capitalism" school in China and some economic historians in the United States have argued that the economy of late-imperial China was growing, both in total output and in the degree of commercialization, pointing the way to a reassessment of the prevailing orthodoxy and its replacement with a view of traditional China as dynamic and capable of further change. Today, most scholars accept the first part of this argument—that the economy of late-imperial China was marked by growth and commercialization—although they differ on the question of whether this meant that China was on the road to development.

One school, represented by Thomas Rawski (1989) and Loren Brandt (1989), argues that commercialization and growth propelled China toward "early modern" development, which they identify as an increase in productivity, or output per unit of labor, in all sectors, including agriculture and rural handicrafts. Lacking figures for agricultural labor and output, Rawski and Brandt make their case using proxy data on population, wages, and the production of handicrafts. They concede that some features of the classical model, such as increases in capital investment and improvements in technology, were absent in China, but conclude that during the early modern period, roughly 1870 to 1930, China achieved higher productivity by increasing the degree of specialization in the production of cash crops (especially cotton), adapting crops to their most suitable environments, and using the best available techniques. The result was not just more production and more commerce, but more output per unit of labor.

In the conclusion to Chapter 7, we analyzed the performance of Manchurian bean production during the 19th century and concluded that it does not support the argument for early modern development or the assumptions of the classical thesis. Now, after considering the evidence for the early 20th century, we return to the same questions. There is no doubt that during the period 1870–1930, the economy of Manchuria was both growing and commercializing. The production and trade of soybeans and other crops increased steadily and, after the opening of the railroads in 1903, dramatically. But did these changes lead to higher levels of productivity and restructuring of the sort associated with modern development? And if not, then how are we to understand the changes that did occur during this period?

There are no reliable figures for calculating the yields (output per unit of land) or productivity (output per unit of labor) of Manchurian

TABLE 14
Agricultural yields and productivity, Manchuria, 1924–38

	Crop Output (1000 mt)	Crop Area (1000 ha)	Yield (mt/ha)	Population (thousands)	Productivity (mt per capita)
1924	13,182	8,148	1.62		
1925	14,873	10,143	1.47	25,508	0.58
1926	13,727	10,267	1.34	26,133	0.53
1927	17,892	11,887	1.51	26,783	0.67
1928	18,167	12,901	1.41	28,033	0.65
1929	18,062	13,124	1.38	29,198	0.62
1930	18,672	13,063	1.43	29,575	0.63
1931	18,484	13,733	1.35	29,959	0.62
1932	15,395	12,665	1.22	30,930	0.50
1933	18,477	13,241	1.40		
1934	13,432	11,891	1.13	32,869	0.41
1935	15,704	12,709	1.24		
1936	16,830	13,328	1.26		
1937	16,853	13,839	1.22	36,933	0.46
1938	16,827	14,089	1.19		

SOURCES: Crop area and output: SMR, Reports 5:163–64; 6:156. Population: *Manchoukuo Year Book*, 1934, 27; SMR, Reports 4:13; 5:151; 6:146.

agriculture prior to 1924, when the Japanese began to collect data on population, production, and crop area. Even after this date, most reports give totals for the three provinces of the Northeast or Manchukuo as a whole, while it is often unclear how the data were collected, what areas they cover, and how they vary by region or sector. Despite these limitations, however, the rough dimensions and general trends are clear. The most complete data, reported by the Manchukuo government (Table 14), show that during the period 1924–38, agricultural yields declined by more than 26 percent, while agricultural productivity, after rising to a peak in the late 1920s, declined over the period 1925–37 by more than 20 percent. That agricultural yields in Manchuria fell during the 1920s and 1930s is beyond question: The reported drop of 26 percent in 15 years is too large to discount or explain away. The physical parameters, crop area and output, do not depend on the distribution of population or other variables that might skew these findings. And farmers in several of the Kotoku survey villages confirmed that the decline in yields was one of their most serious problems. The estimates of productivity, on the other hand, deserve further comment: The population figures in Table 14 are totals for Manchuria as a whole, not the rural sector alone, much less agricultural labor, which is the proper measure of productivity. Is it possible that, owing to the growth of

Manchuria's cities and factories, a smaller number of farmers were producing equal or greater amounts of food for a larger number of workers—that is, the very definition of higher productivity?

When the economist Nai-Ruenn Chen set out to answer this question, he thought that with abundant untapped farmland, the best practices of existing agricultural technology, and time to find a proper fit with the new environment, Chinese farmers in Manchuria would achieve higher levels of productivity. His first study (1970) made this claim, challenging the theory of T. W. Schultz (1964), which holds that, absent capital investment and technological change, traditional agriculture must remain stagnant, while gains in productivity can come only with the introduction of modern techniques.[1] To Chen's surprise, however, further research showed that along with the growth of cities and factories, the population of rural Manchuria was also increasing—in fact, during the 1920s, rural population grew faster than the area of cultivated land![2] And in the end, he found that during both the Republican (1914–31) and Manchukuo (1932–34) periods, agricultural output per unit of labor declined.[3] "No matter how abundant the land," Chen concluded (conceding to Schultz), "as long as the state of arts in agriculture remained unchanged, the expansion of labor input through immigration and other means could only push agricultural production of the newly settled region from a lower level of stagnation to a higher level of stagnation."[4]

These findings, although based on limited data, indicate that Manchuria fits the profile of growth or commercialization without development, which in the view of some economic historians typifies China as a whole, distinguishing it from classical economic theory and the assertions of the "early modern" school. If this is the case, then we must ask: What theories do the "growth without development" skeptics offer to explain changes in the Chinese economy? And do these theories fit the Manchurian case?

B. Growth without Development

The leading spokesmen for the "growth or commercialization without development" thesis have been Philip Huang (1985, 1990, 1991) and more recently Sucheta Mazumdar (1998). Huang and Mazumdar agree

[1] Nai-Ruenn Chen (1970), 149–51.
[2] Nai-Ruenn Chen (1970), 152.
[3] Nai-Ruenn Chen (1972), 94.
[4] Nai-Ruenn Chen (1972), 92.

that the economy, including the traditional agricultural sector, of late-19th and early-20th century China was growing and becoming more commercialized, but reject the notion that this led to higher productivity or structural change of the sort implied by the term "development." They offer complementary, albeit distinct explanations for this outcome. Huang's theory of "involution" is based on an analysis of material conditions: namely, the concentration of too many people on too little land. During the first two centuries of the Qing, Huang notes, a significant increase in the population of China was accompanied by a corresponding expansion in the area of farmland and intensification of farming, so that the balance between population and resources was maintained, while growth in agricultural output and perhaps even output per capita was achieved. During the late-19th and early-20th centuries, however, neither the expansion of farmland nor the marginal utility of labor could keep pace with the continued growth of rural population. The result, in Huang's words, is that "at a given level of technology, population pressure will sooner or later lead to diminished marginal returns for further labor intensification, or what I, following Clifford Geertz (1963), term involution."[5]

Mazumdar points to a different cause. Drawing on the work Karl Polonyi and Robert Brenner, she argues that secular trends, such as the commercialization of agriculture, act through preexisting social structures that limit and shape their outcomes. Brenner calls these structures "property relations" and maintains that given any particular set of "relations," there is a "best strategy" for each individual or group to protect and reproduce its material interests. The rural society of south China during the Qing and Republican periods, the case examined by Mazumdar, was dominated by small producers, including both owner-cultivators and tenants. All the forces and events of history—the growth of population, commercialization of agriculture, political revolution, and so forth—had to be filtered through the existing structures of ownership and control, which prevented fundamental change of the sort envisioned by Smith and achieved in the West. "Even with the growth of world markets," Mazumdar concludes, "the economic arrangements resulting from these social property relations were incompatible with the requirement of growth and development."[6]

While identifying different drivers or causes, Huang and Mazumdar reach similar conclusions about the implications for China's

[5] Philip Huang (1990), 11–12.
[6] Sucheta Mazumdar (1998), 406.

development, or the lack thereof, and the effects of these drivers on the factors of production: land, labor, and capital. First, both authors note the difficulties wealthy elites faced in accumulating large tracts of land, such as would be required to create plantations or other forms of capital-intensive agriculture. Mazumdar focuses on sociological or organizational factors: local restrictions on the buying and selling of land, the preference or right of first refusal accorded to family and friends, and the role of lineage or village associations in enforcing local privileges and preventing outsiders from buying up and consolidating farmland. Huang's explanation, rooted in "involution" theory, reflects market forces: Wealthy landlords succeeded in building up "managerial farms" in the range of 100–200 *mu*. Beyond this size, however, the costs of management became prohibitive and the alternative of renting land to tenants and investing the income in nonagricultural activities more appealing. In either case, agricultural production was left to the small family farm, which had limited capacity to accumulate capital or introduce new techniques.

The same logic applied to labor, which remained under the control of peasant households rather than separate out into a class of landless wage workers on the model of the English rural, and later urban, proletariat. Again, Mazumdar's argument relies on socioeconomic factors: Peasant households controlled the production and consumption of their members, who were assigned to work either inside or outside the household in accordance with short-term opportunities and demands. Seasonal labor shortages were met by cooperative arrangements. Decisions were made by the household head, so that workers were trapped within the web of family and village obligations. Huang's analysis, based on market considerations, leads to the same conclusion: Given the surplus of population, shortage of land and quest of the peasant family for self-sufficiency, each household assigned its workers to farming, handicrafts, or wage work, whichever promised the highest return—*even though* that return might be *below* the subsistence level. By driving wages to below subsistence, this practice prevented the rise of a class of independent rural wage-workers who could maintain and reproduce themselves by selling their labor on the open market.

Finally, Huang and Mazumdar argue, since land was not consolidated into large holdings and a class of wage-workers was not available to provide labor to plantations or commercial estates, capital flowed to investments *other than* agriculture. Rather than engage in production themselves, most large landowners preferred to extract the agricultural surplus from small household producers through rents, money-lending, tax-farming, trade in futures contracts, control of transportation and markets, the threat or use of violence, and other mechanisms. And they chose to transfer the profits derived from agriculture to higher-status and potentially more lucrative pursuits, such as commerce, education, public office, or political influence. It was less common for men with capital to invest in irrigation, fertilizer, seed, machinery, or other aspects of agriculture that would lead to higher outputs per unit of land or labor, while requiring their direct engagement in production. The point, according to these authors, is not that the system failed, but that it worked only too well in satisfying the needs and interests of the participants without transforming the means or relations of production.

C. The Case of Manchuria

The evidence presented in Part Three supports the finding that Manchurian agriculture experienced growth without development, but not for the reasons proposed by Philip Huang or Sucheta Mazumdar. Manchuria in general and northern Manchuria in particular were subject neither to the material constraints, which according to Huang led to "involution," nor to the defining "social relationships" of the small producer household identified by Mazumdar. Far from suffering from an imbalance between (too much) population and (too little) farmland, Manchuria enjoyed abundant arable land, an adequate supply of wage labor without an excess of population, and a gradient that made more land available to fewer people the further one moved north. But these conditions failed to prompt large landowners in Manchuria to pursue strategies different from their neighbors or to induce behavior among any segment of Manchurian society different from that described by Philip Huang in north China. In both regions, large landowners achieved higher levels of productivity than small holders or tenants and did so without adopting different cropping patterns, investing more in capital goods, or achieving higher yields.[7] Thus, whether or not "involution" was the cause of underdevelopment in China proper, this condition cannot be used to explain the performance of Chinese agriculture north of the Great Wall.

Evaluating the social and economic structures of rural Manchuria as proposed by Mazumdar is more complicated. Agricultural production

[7] Philip Huang (1985), 140–45, 155–59.

in Manchuria began in the early Qing with the manorial system, which, according to classical economic theory, forestalled progress toward development by obstructing the creation of markets in land and labor. As shown in Parts One and Two, however, Chinese migrants transformed the manors into a system of free markets and imported social structures, the small family farm and associations based on lineage or locale, all of which conform to practices previously established in China proper. Thus, it might be argued that rural society in the densely settled areas of southern Manchuria resembled the small producer economy observed by Mazumdar (and Huang) and credited by them for obstructing the development of Chinese agriculture. However, as late as the 1930s, these conditions had not been reproduced in northern Manchuria. On the contrary, several of the Kotoku survey villages in Jilin and Heilongjiang were established by individual settlers who obtained large tracts of land and brought in friends and relatives to farm the land as tenants or wage workers, while decades later their successors still held on to large landholdings, employed numerous wage workers, and operated without noticeable interference from village associations or clansmen. There is no indication that these villages resembled the small producer economy described by Mazumdar, nor that the largest and most powerful families that dominated these villages were subject to control by local organizations of the sort Mazumdar found in south China.

The distribution of land and disposition of labor in northern Manchuria were quite different from the conditions described by Mazumdar and Huang. As noted (Table 4), in the Kotoku survey sites, 4 percent of the households owned 50 percent and farmed 30 percent of the land. The size of the farms increased from south to north, with the largest spreads in Heilongjiang (Region 4) averaging more than 800 *mu*. Meanwhile, large landowners had access to wage workers, who accounted for more than one third of the villagers in the northern Kotoku sites (Regions 3 and 4). The separation between large, centrally owned and centrally managed farms on one side and large numbers of landless wage laborers on the other—both features of the 17th-century English revolution and the classical model that followed from it—were the rule rather than the exception in northern Manchuria during the 1930s.

This brings us to the final factor of production: capital. One of the defining features of the cases studied by Mazumdar and Huang was the propensity of landowners and other elites to invest in areas *other than* agriculture. In this regard—and in contrast to the differences described

above—Chinese men of means in Manchuria behaved like their counterparts in China proper. Large landowners identified in the Kotoku
survey villages, along with entrepreneurs associated with the soybean
trade and with commerce in Newchwang, declined to concentrate their
investments in agriculture or any other single enterprise. Instead, they
diversified, spread the risk, and kept their commitments short-term and
mobile. This strategic choice, rather than the material constraints of involution or the social constraints of small producer economy, guided
the Manchurian elite toward stable and profitable investments, but *not*
toward the higher levels of productivity or structural changes associated with development.

Why, if they were constrained neither by the imbalance between
population and resources (à la Huang) nor the structure of the small
producer economy (Mazumdar), did investors in Manchuria behave in
this way? No doubt, environmental factors—the fear of bandits and the
need to keep assets dispersed and mobile; the volatility of agricultural
markets and higher returns to be had in other areas; and concern that
officials, warlords, or imperialists could seize wealth that grew too large
and visible—may have influenced or conditioned their choice. It has
been the consistent theme of this study, however, that Chinese migrants
reproduced in Manchuria the habits of mind and practices inherited
from China proper, and their economic behavior seems to fit that
model. Chinese of the late-19th and early-20th centuries had learned
that the best way to manage capital was to diversify their investments
in small-scale, short-term, low-risk opportunities and to move into, out
of and around these opportunities in response to changes in the marketplace. The fact that they faced different circumstances in Manchuria—
that they had moved from an area where land was scarce and labor was
tied to the household, to an area with abundant land and a large class
of wage-workers, or that they were no longer trapped in a society of
small household producers—did not cause them to unlearn the lessons
of the past or to adopt new strategies, which might have been more appropriate to their new conditions, and might coincidentally have
moved the Chinese economy in new and more productive directions. In
this regard as in others, they were simply reluctant to change.

Conclusion

IN THE END, THE MEASURE of any society—whether frontier, colony, "middle ground," or something else entirely—lies in its cultural expressions, which establish and make known the identity of its inhabitants. This is a point on which both Frederick Jackson Turner and his critics agree. For Turner, who portrayed the frontier as the generator of new cultures and values, the identity of American frontier society lay in the "intellectual traits" that distinguished it from its precursors and from its counterparts in the eastern United States and Europe:

> that coarseness and strength combined with acuteness and inquisitiveness; that practical, inventive turn of mind, quick to find expedients; that masterful grasp of material things, lacking in the artistic but powerful to effect great ends; that restless, nervous energy; that dominant individualism, working for good and for evil, and withal that buoyancy and exuberance which comes with freedom—these are the traits of the frontier. . . .[1]

These traits, which grew out of the pioneers' engagement with nature, defined the culture of the frontier and in turn influenced the development of the United States as a whole.

The "middle ground," described by Richard White—or more precisely each middle ground—also had its own identity and culture. Several new Western historians have shown how the interactions among peoples and landscapes produce distinct regions and regional cultures, although few have said precisely what "culture" is or how it should be defined. Patricia Limerick describes the West as a place

[1] Frederick Jackson Turner (1963), 57.

undergoing a "contest for cultural dominance."[2] William Cronon speaks of the process of "self-shaping," which helps to transform frontiers into regions and subregions with "special cultural identities."[3] Unfortunately, neither has much to say about how culture in any context can be identified, measured, or distinguished from its neighbors. In the epilogue to his book, *The Middle Ground*, White himself suggests that the culture of a particular region is revealed in the stories that are told by and about the people who shape its history. The identity of the Great Lakes region of the 17th and 18th century, the middle ground studied by White, was expressed in stories of the Shawnee Indian chief Tecumseh and his brother Tenskwatasta and in the stories and dreams Tenskwatasta told to others. In White's account, this region—at one time, a "middle ground"—existed both in reality as a physical landscape and in the imagination of its people as a dreamscape. And when the landscape changed and the inhabitants ceased to dream the old dreams, the middle ground withered and died.[4] In similar fashion, Elliott West shows how the stories of the American Great Plains varied with the storytellers and changed over time, from the generation of pioneers who viewed the West as "placeless," without history, a blank slate on which they could write their own stories, to the Indians and later settlers who embraced the West as their "place," and if they left home for a time, realized their mistake and hastened to return.

Borrowing a page from these new Western historians, we might look to the culture of Manchuria for guidance on how to think about this region, its formative experiences and ultimate fate. This is not a simple matter, for as the examples just cited remind us, culture can be thought of in many different ways. Each cultural expression, moreover, applies only to the time and place in which it was produced and thus cannot be taken to represent an entire region or its historical experience as a whole. Thus, if we are to describe Manchurian culture and connect it some way to the character and identity of human settlement in this region, we must choose our examples carefully. One place to start, following the examples of White and West, is with the storytellers. And in the case of 20th century Manchuria, the most prominent storytellers and best guide to the identity of this region might be Northeastern Writers Group.

[2] Patricia Nelson Limerick (1987), 27.
[3] William Cronon et al. (1992), 18.
[4] Richard White (1991), 518–23.

A. The Northeastern Writers Group

The Northeastern Writers were a group of young authors from this region who were active during the 1930s, including two whose work enjoyed great popularity throughout China: Xiao Jun, and his common-law wife, Xiao Hong. Xiao Jun's first major work, *Village in August* [*Bayue di xiangcun*], published in 1935, was the most widely read novel in China during the prewar era, and the first contemporary Chinese novel to be translated into English and published abroad. Xiao Hong's *The Field of Life and Death* [*Shengsi chang*], which appeared the same year, also reached a large audience. Both works are set in rural Manchuria and describe the struggle of Chinese guerrilla forces against the Japanese. By combining realistic descriptions of peasants and villages with the anti-Japanese cause, these books gave voice to an emerging regional identity, while at the same time striking a chord among Chinese students and intellectuals who embraced the current of Chinese nationalism.[5]

Both Xiao Jun (1908–??) and Xiao Hong (1911–42) were genuine products of Manchurian rural society, and their works were infused with a strong regional character. Xiao Hong came from a landlord family of Hulan County, Heilongjiang. Xiao Jun was born in a mountain village of northern Manchuria, located at some distance from the nearest city, to a family whose members slipped in and out of farming, commerce, soldiery, and organized crime. When asked to provide accounts of their early lives, neither of the Xiaos mentioned his or her family's "origin" [*chushen*] in China proper, as was common among Chinese whose forebears had migrated to this region, indicating that they identified to an unusual degree with the Northeast. Both grew to young adulthood by way of personal hardships that exposed them to the wide range of people and experiences. Xiao Jun served as a soldier, secretary, apprentice to a professional boxer, waiter, and millstone pusher, and by his own testimony aspired to life as a "mountain bandit." Xiao Hong, although from a family of greater means, suffered psychological abuse that drove her through abandonment, hunger, prostitution, and drug addiction, before she began her youthful and short career as a writer. Neither received any formal education beyond middle school. They met in Harbin in 1932, and lived together in a community of impoverished writers and artists, whose bohemian existence revolved around art,

[5] For English translations of these novels, see: Hsiao Chun (1942), and Hsiao Hung (1979). Other members of the Northeast Writers Group included: Duanmu Hongliang, Li Huiying, Lo Feng, and Shu Qun.

politics and finding their next meal. The Xiaos moved, in 1934, to Shandong, then Shanghai, Wuhan, and Xi'an and, after splitting up, to the wartime capitals of Chongqing (Xiao Hong) and Yanan (Xiao Jun). Xiao Hong died in Hong Kong in 1942. Xiao Jun returned to the Northeast with the Communists in 1946, after which his fate again became entwined with his native land.[6]

The writings of both Xiaos are highly autobiographical, set among the peasants and villages of the Northeast, and filled with details on the landscape, people, and customs of their homeland. Their first novels, although received by an admiring public for their nationalistic and anti-Japanese themes, in fact portray Manchurian society with an uncompromising realism that disowns political correctness. Xiao Hong's translator and biographer, Howard Goldblatt, says of *The Field of Life and Death*, that the anti-Japanese theme is secondary to the grim and powerful portrait of village life, which shows peasants to be conservative and fatalistic and prone to mistreat one another as much as they are mistreated by the Japanese.[7] Edgar Snow sounds a similar note in his introduction to Xiao Jun's *Village in August*. "Here is no black-and-white tale of villainy and bestiality on one side and saintly perfection on the other," Snow observes, "but a realistic report written by a soldier, filled with enthusiasm for the whole story of . . . ordinary mortals."[8]

Xiao Jun, although committed to the nationalist cause and increasingly immersed in the politics of China, retained a passion for his homeland. "I was born and brought up in Northern Manchuria, for whose pure boundless snowy plains I have an abiding love," he wrote while in Shanghai in 1936.

I love the endless depths of her blue sky, her ink-dark forests of pines and cypresses, her straight branches and maples thrusting into the clouds, shining with silver; I love the herds of cattle wandering over the plains like the waves of a sea; and above all I love her fearless honest people. The whirling snowflakes, the roaring winds, may cut my face like knives, but I love them all. And now I feel to the depths of my heart a great loneliness, for I no longer have that frozen and refreshing air against my face, and my lungs are numbed. They say that the spring in the south of China is like poetry, but it means nothing to me since I have lost my home.[9]

[6]Biography of Xiao Jun: Leo Lee (1973), 223–41. Biography of Xiao Hong: Howard Goldblatt (1976).

[7]Howard Goldblatt (1976), xx–xxiii.

[8]Edgar Snow, "Introduction," in Hsiao Chun (1942), xiii.

[9]Hsiao Chun (1936). The translation is from Yuan Chia-hua and Robert Payne, (1946), 12.

Even after spending the war years in Yanan, Xiao Jun continued to identify with Manchuria. Returning to Harbin in 1946, he broke with the Party over its alliance with the Soviet Union, the prosecution of the Civil War, excesses of land reform, and abuses of power, which he considered harmful to the region and people for whom he spoke.[10] Xiao Jun was a Manchurian first, and a Communist a distant second. Xiao Hong, who was never deeply committed to politics, returned again and again to recollections of her homeland, nostalgic portraits of its natural beauty, hard but engaging looks at its people, and realistic descriptions of the villages and villagers that populated her memory world.

Notwithstanding the strong regional character of their work, it is striking that the Xiaos appear during the 1930s as typical, even quintessential Chinese writers and intellectuals and that they gained such ready acceptance in China proper. In his autobiographical account of their flight from Manchuria to Shandong in 1934, Xiao Jun looks forward to the moment when they would "stand on *our beloved native soil* on the other side of the sea, where everything would come to my rescue." And on seeing, for the first time, the green mountains above the port of Tsingtao, he cries, "Oh, *my own country!*"[11] "We had made up our minds to leave Manchukuo," Xiao Hong recalls, "and be part of *our own country* again."[12] (Italics added.) The Xiaos' flight from the Northeast requires no apology: What had once been their homeland was now a Japanese colony; their work was proscribed by Japanese authorities; one of their friends had been arrested; and they were under suspicion. It was natural that they should seek a safe haven for themselves and a base from which to carry on their literary work and their struggle against Japan. What is telling, however, is how seamlessly they moved, physically and psychologically, from Manchuria to China proper and into the mainstream of Chinese literary society.

The Xiaos' sojourn in Shandong lasted only a few months, for they were anxious to move to Shanghai, meet the foremost writer of the age, Lu Xun, on whom they pinned their personal and professional hopes, and join the community of writers whose self-appointed mission was to chart the future of Chinese art and society. Their quest succeeded in storybook fashion, for they were soon attached as friends and disciples to Lu Xun, won fame and, if not fortune, at least a livelihood from writing, and became recognized figures in China's literary elite. It was in

[10] Merle Goldman (1967), 73–79.
[11] Tian Jun, "Aboard the S.S. Dairen Maru," Edgar Snow (1937), 207–11.
[12] Hsiao Hung (1986), 109.

this context that their first novels, which were written in Shandong and published in Shanghai in 1935, took on a decidedly nationalistic tone. Xiao Hong grew especially close to Lu Xun, whose death, in 1936, came as a crushing blow. Thereafter, the lives and writings of the Xiaos took different turns, although both continued to operate within the familiar terrain of the modern Chinese literary movement.

How is it that these writers, who began life in villages of the Northeast, lived and worked in Harbin as young adults, wrote about this region, both while they were there and after they left, and in the case of Xiao Jun returned to take up the cause of Manchuria and its people after the war—how is it that at the same time they also fit so neatly into Shanghai, Yanan, and Chongqing? And how is it that their most popular works, while rooted in the countryside of a remote province, gained such a wide audience in China proper? The answer is clearly *not* that the Northeastern writers skated on the thin veneer of a modern national elite. The Xiaos were not from wealthy, educated, urban, or professional families. They did not attend one of the leading universities in Beijing, Shanghai, or Canton—or indeed any university at all. Except for Xiao Hong's sorry visit to Beijing as the mistress of a man who eventually abandoned her and their unborn child, neither of the Xiaos set foot outside Manchuria until 1934, when they were in their mid-twenties and had already begun their careers as writers. They had no friends or relatives to ease the move from Manchuria to China proper. All their ties were to Heilongjiang and a world of peasants, peddlers, prostitutes, and pimps, soldiers on the march, villages and earthy villagers, and the city of Harbin, whose bohemian subculture of self-styled actors, artists, and writers became their home. Yet they fit easily into China, and Chinese of their generation embraced them with a passion.

The explanation for this irony and the connection between the worlds of Shanghai and Heilongjiang was forged by the process described throughout this book: that is, by Chinese who had moved to Manchuria during the previous centuries and reproduced there the society and culture of their native land. Chinese villages in Manchuria were not creations, inventions, or even adaptations to new circumstances, as much as they were transplants of whole organisms that had grown to maturity down below. There is no more compelling testimony to this fact than the works of Xiao Jun and Xiao Hong themselves, which describe the villages of the Northeast with all of the detail and local color that convince the reader of their authenticity, and at the same time make them virtually indistinguishable from villages in Shandong or many other parts of

China. Xiao Hong's *Tales of Hulan River* contains vivid descriptions of agricultural crops and farm animals, peasants, merchants, gentry and officials, holidays, festivals and traveling operas, priests, sorcerers and soothsayers, gods, ghosts and spirits, the ceremonies and rituals surrounding birth, marriage, and death, and countless other aspects of village life. Xiao's purpose is to portray the villages and villagers of her childhood, and she succeeds both as a reporter and as a creative writer. Yet, it is striking how similar these accounts are to equally careful and convincing anthropological works, such as Martin Yang's description of his hometown in Shandong in *A Chinese Village*, or Arthur Smith's account of *Village Life in China*, based on material gathered in the same province during the 19th century. In making their way from Heilongjiang to Shanghai, Xiao Jun and Xiao Hong had to bridge the gaps between countryside and city, province and metropolis, uneducated peasants and university-trained intellectuals, but the distance from region to region was not very wide, and the reason for the similarities lies in the way Manchuria had been incorporated into Greater China.

B. The Chinese Western

Would the reality or the portrayal of this reality be different, if we were to consider Chinese writings from different times and places? If we captured the pioneers at the moment of their arrival, when they were still coping with their new surroundings and had less time to settle in? Or if we found them on a more distant frontier, where they were forced to adapt to powerful outside influences? It is difficult to say. Unfortunately, but also significantly, there is little Chinese writing of any type describing life in Manchuria during the 19th or early-20th centuries, much less before. Most migrants and travelers in this region were probably illiterate. Those who could write may have had little inclination to record what they considered an unfortunate and hoped would be short-lived chapter of their lives. They were sojourners, passing their time temporarily and grudgingly in an unfamiliar locale and apparently did not feel compelled to describe this interlude. Nor presumably was there a huge audience in China awaiting their reports. For most Chinese, both at home and abroad, life on the frontier was neither interesting nor significant.

In the absence of a broader Manchurian literature, one way to gain insight into the questions posed above is by examining Chinese literature from other border regions or newly settled frontiers. *The Chinese Western*, a collection of short stories first published in China in the wake of the Cultural Revolution (1976–88) and translated by the American scholar, Zhu Hong, offers an opportunity to do just that. In assembling this volume, Ms. Zhu made a special effort to identify Chinese stories that share key characteristics with their American counterparts: sweeping landscapes, the independence of individuals in an open and unregulated space, and the interplay among people of different backgrounds. Western China, like the western United States, Zhu notes, is a region marked by "its bleakness and barbarity on one hand, its native strength and unsullied beauty on the other," and by stories that depict the Chinese differently than they appear in China proper—"vital, resilient men and women, committed to survival." Chinese westerns, like American westerns, Zhu avers, "are national genres—in epic dimensions— that register a moment of change in historic significance, and both ponder the meaning of that change."[13]

Ironically—and this is the point—what is most striking about the stories Zhu has selected is precisely their lack of sweeping landscapes, rugged individuals, frontier settlements, encounters with nature and natives, or any other features prominent in the stories of the American West. Rather, these stories are typical of Chinese literature from the post-Cultural Revolution period, which feature village society, conflicts with political authority, tense relations between urban intellectuals "sent down" to the countryside and their peasant hosts, and the righting of wrongs committed under previous campaigns. With one or two exceptions, none of these Chinese "Westerns" fastens on subjects unique to western China. The authors, whether natives of this region or former sent-down youth, all moved back east or chose to publish their work in Beijing and Shanghai and to associate or identify with the literary communities of these metropolises. In short, what these stories tell us is that when fate puts literate Chinese on the fringes of the empire, they remain more interested in the shared political, economic, and cultural experience of the center than in the strange peoples, novel landscapes, challenges and opportunities of life on the edge. If these stories shed any light on our subject, it must be that the Northeastern writers were equally comfortable writing about their homeland as they were living and working in China, because there were so few differences socially and psychologically between the two.

The Chinese occupation of Manchuria was not devoid of adventure, of engagements between man and nature on a receding frontier or among peoples whose identities intertwined for a time on some

[13] Zhu Hong (1988), xi.

"middle ground." Nor should we view this experience as typical of Chinese behavior on the borders of the empire in all times and places. Several features of Manchuria—the abundance of land and a climate suitable for intensive farming of the sort practiced in China proper, the shortage of population in an area adjacent to the densely populated north China plain, the proximity to global trade routes, and the special attention accorded to this region by the Manchus, the Russians, and the Japanese—make this region unusual, perhaps even unique, and explain much of its modern history. But the manner in which Chinese migrated to, settled in, and eventually incorporated this region into the empire distinguishes this account from the expansion of peoples and formation of nations in other times and places. Despite all of the reasons that this story might have turned out differently, in the end, Manchuria emerges more as an extension of the old than a harbinger of the new.

C. Coda

The purpose of this book has been both to describe the events by which Chinese occupied and incorporated Manchuria into their empire and to explore the meaning and significance of this experience. Most striking in this story has been the degree to which the Chinese expanded by the replication of existing forms and practices rather than the creation or invention of something new. This stands in contrast to the experience of Russians in the Far East and Americans in the West and to historical accounts of areas on the margins of other empires or civilizations that have been characterized as "frontiers" and more recently as a "middle ground."

There are at least two reasons that the experience of China, or the Chinese, should be different from Russia and the United States. First, is geography. When Chinese left the core of their empire, the Yellow River Plain and the Yangzi Valley, the environments that greeted them were less hospitable than the one they left behind and became more so the further they moved from home. The north, Manchuria, and west, Inner Mongolia, Xinjiang, and Tibet, were colder, dryer, and harsher, while the south, Yunnan, was hotter, wetter, and denser than the land that had for millennia nurtured an intensive agriculture and Chinese way of life. When Chinese cast their glance to the distant frontier, they saw no pot of gold, literally or figuratively, comparable to California and Oregon, no great ocean like the Pacific, no world that they could imagine might be better than their own. To most Americans, the idea of moving to Siberia suggests oppression, punishment, and cold, but the Russian peasants who migrated to this region in the 19th century thought of Siberia as a land of opportunity so promising that they abandoned their homes in the Black Earth region and took a one-way ticket to the east. None of China's borderlands held out comparable promise.

In the absence of an appealing frontier, a California or Siberia, Chinese edged slowly, grudgingly, and by necessity into areas immediately adjacent to home and to regions that were already densely populated and developed. They had no incentive to leap over an intervening desert, taiga, or steppe in hopes of finding a significantly better way of life. This pattern of expansion, which Lattimore calls a "reluctant, eddying backwash,"[14] was unlikely to invite adventure, reward risk, or produce the same independence and creativity that we find in Russians of the Far East or Americans of the Far West. Chinese geography encouraged gradual drift rather than dramatic expansion and conquest.

It was not entirely a matter of environment, however, for Chinese social and cultural patterns also discouraged innovation and change. The organization of the village, strength and cohesion of the family, inheritance system that divided the property of the household with each generation, religious ideals rooted in the ancestors and in a particular locale, and persistence of practices favoring small-scale organization, simple technology, limited credit, and shifting, short-term investments—all these habits of mind and manner placed a premium on continuity and posed an obstacle to change. In all these ways, Chinese were reluctant pioneers.

[14]Owen Lattimore (1932), 100.

Glossary of Chinese Terms

Acheng	阿城	Changchun	長春
Aihui	瑷琿	Changling	長嶺
Alachuke	阿勒楚喀	Changning	長寧
Alukeerqin	阿魯科爾沁	Changtu	昌圖
Anda	安達	changzu	長祖
Andong	安東	Chaoyang	朝陽
Anguang	安廣	Chengde	承德
anjiafei	安家費	chi (foot)	尺
Aohan	敖漢	Chifeng	赤峰
		chuanchang	船廠
Bagou	八溝	chufang	出放
Baiquan	拜泉	chushen	出身
Balin	巴林	chushendi	出身地
baojia	保甲		
baoken	報墾	dache	大車
baoyi	包衣	dadou	大豆
Baqi	八旗	Dagushan	大孤山
Bayan	巴彥	Dahushan	大虎山
beile	貝勒	daidi touchong	帶地投充
Benqi	本溪	Dalai	大賚
bianshen	辨審	Dalian	大連
bing	兵	dan	石
Binzhou	賓州	dangpu	當鋪
Bohai	渤海	danshen touchong	單身投充
Buteha	布特哈	Danyu	聃榆
		Daxing'anling	大興安嶺
Chahar	察哈爾	Dehui	德惠
Changbaishan	長白山	dian	典

dianmai	典賣	guanzhuang	官莊
dianya	典押	guoluyin	過爐銀
diao	吊		
ding	丁	Haicheng	海城
Dongbei	東北	haijin	海禁
Duanwujie	端午節	Hailar	海拉爾
duanzu	短祖	Hailong	海龍
duimai	兌賣	Hailun	海倫
Dunhua	敦化	hang	行
Durbet	土伯特	Hanjun	漢軍
		Harbin	哈爾濱
Emu	額穆	Heilongjiang	黑龍江
enchangdi	恩償地	Heishan	黑山
		Heishui	黑水
Faku	法庫	hongce	紅冊
fang	放	honghuzi	紅鬍子
fangdi	方地	Huachuan	樺川
Fangzheng	方正	Huaide	懷德
Fengcheng	鳳城	huangdou	黃豆
Fenghua	奉化	huangzhuang	皇莊
Fenghuang	鳳凰	Huanren	桓仁
fengjin	封禁	Hubu	戶部
Fengning	豐寧	Hulan	呼蘭
fengshui	風水	Hulin	虎林
Fengtian	奉天	Hulunbuir	呼倫貝爾
fu	府	Hunchun	琿春
Fujiadian	傅家店		
Fujin	富錦	Jalait	扎賚特
Fushun	撫順	jasagh	札薩克
fuxia	拂下	Jehol	熱河
Fuxin	阜新	jialing huzhu	價領戶主
Fuyu (Jilin)	扶餘	Ji'an	輯安
Fuyu (Heilongjiang)	富裕	Jianchang	建昌
Fuzhou	復州	jiangjun	將軍
		Jianping	建平
Gaiping	蓋平	jiedi yangmin	借地養民
Gaizhou	蓋州	Jilin	吉林
Gannan	甘南	jimi	羈縻
gaoliang	高粱	jin	斤
gong	公	Jingqi	京旗
Gorlos	郭爾羅斯	Jingxing	景星
Guandi	關帝	Jin Xian	錦縣
Guangning	廣寧	Jinxian	金縣
guanhuang	官荒	Jinzhou	錦州
guantie	官帖	Jurchen	女真

kaifang	開放	Manchukuo	滿洲國
Kailu	開魯	Manzhouli	滿洲里
Kaitong	開通	Mergen	墨爾根
Kaiyuan	開原	mindi	民地
Kalahetun	喀喇河屯	Mingshui	明水
Kalaqin (Kharchin)	喀喇沁	minren	民人
Kangping	康平	minren qi dongdi	民認旗東地
Kangxi	康熙	Mishan	密山
Kedong	克東	Moho	漠河
Keerqin (Khorchin)	科爾沁	mu	畝
kenwuju	墾務局	muchang	牧場
Keshan	克山	Mudan River	牧丹江
Keshiketeng	克什克騰	Mulan weichang	木蘭圍場
Kuandian	寬甸	Muleng River	穆稜河
Kwantung	關東		
		Nahe	訥河
landou	攬斗	Naiman	奈曼
Lanxi	蘭西	Neiwufu	內務府
Laoha River	老哈河	Nenjiang (Nonni) River	嫩江
liangzhan	糧站	Newchwang	牛莊
Liao River	遼河	Ning'an	寧安
Liaodong	遼東	Ningcheng	寧城
Liaoning	遼寧	Ninguta	寧古塔
Liaoyang	遼陽	Ningyuan	寧遠
Liaoyuan	遼源	niulu	牛彔
Liaozhong	遼中	Nong'an	農安
Libu	禮部	nupu	奴僕
Lifanyuan	理藩院	Nurhaci	努爾哈赤
Lindian	林甸		
Lindong	林東	Panshan	盤山
Linjiang	臨江	Panshi	磐石
Linxi	林西	paotui'erdi	跑腿兒地
Liquan	醴泉	Petuna	伯都訥
Lishu	梨樹	Pikou	皮口
Liuhe	柳河	Pingquan	平泉
Liutiaobian	柳條邊		
Longzhen	龍鎮	qi 旗	
Luan River	灤河	qi shengke di	旗升科地
Luanping	灤平	Qian'an	乾安
Lubei	魯北	qiangken	搶墾
lufang	爐坊	Qianlong	乾隆
Lushun	旅順	qianpu	錢鋪
		qidi	旗地
machang	馬場	Qingcheng	慶城
mai	賣	Qinggang	青岡

qingzhang	清丈	Tieling	鐵嶺
qiren	旗人	ting	廳
qiyudi	旗餘地	Tonghua	通化
qizhu	旗主	Tongken River	通肯河
Quanning	全寧	Tongliao	通遼
		Tsitsihar	齊齊哈爾
Raohe	饒河	tudi shen	土地神
		tufen	土糞
Sanxing	三姓	tuiling	退領
Sanzuota	三座塔	Tumet	土默特
shachuan	沙船	tuntian	屯田
shang	晌		
Shanhaiguan	山海關	Ussuri River	烏蘇里江
shengjidi	生計地		
Shengjing	盛京	wang	王
shengkedi	升科地	Wangkui	望奎
shi 石		wangzhuang	王莊
shizhi di suoyou shudi	實質的所有熟地	Weichang	圍場
		wen	文
Shuangcheng (bao)	雙城 (堡)	Wengniute	翁牛特
Shuangshan	雙山	Wuchang	五常
Shuangtaizi River	雙臺子河	Wudan	烏丹
Shunzhi	順治	Wulanhada	烏蘭哈達
Siping	四平		
Siqi	四旗	xian	縣
Solun	索倫	xiexiang	協餉
Suidong	綏東	Xifeng	西豐
Suifenhe	綏芬河	Xifengkou	喜峰口
Suihua	綏化	Xilamulun River	西喇木倫河
Sungari River	松花江	Xilingele	錫林郭勒
suoyou di	所有地	Xingcheng	興城
		Xingjing	興京
taiji	台吉	Xinmin	新民
Taikang	泰康	Xiuyan	岫岩
Tailai	泰來		
Taining	泰寧	Yalu River	鴨綠江
Tangyuan	湯源	Yanji	延吉
Tao'an	洮安	Yanshan	燕山
Tao'er River	洮爾河	yaqian	押錢
Taonan	洮南	Yi'an	依安
taoqi	逃旗	Yilan	依蘭
taorenfa	逃人法	yimin shibian	移民實邊
Tazigou	塔子溝	Yingkou	營口
tiandi	天地	Yitong River	伊通河
Tianshan	天山	Yongji	永吉

Yongzheng 雍正
Yushu 榆樹

Zhalute 扎魯特
zhangfang 丈放
zhangkan 丈勘
zhangliang 丈量
Zhangwu 彰武
Zhaodong 肇東
Zhaowuda (Jo-oda) 昭烏達
Zhaozhou 肇州

Zhelimu (Jerim) 哲里木
Zhendong 鎮東
Zhengjiatun 鄭家屯
zhidi jieqian 指地借錢
zhou 州
zhuandian 轉佃
zhuangding 壯丁
Zhuanghe 莊河
zhuangtou 莊頭
Zhuosuotu (Josoto) 桌索圖

Works Cited

1. PRIMARY SOURCES

Baqi tongzhi [Gazetteer of the Eight Banners]. 1739. Compiled by E'ertai 鄂爾泰 et al. Changchun: Dongbei shifan daxue chubanshe. 1986.
China, Inspectorate General of Customs (CIGC). Various Years. *Statistics of Trade at the Port of Newchwang, 1863–1872; Reports on Trade at the Treaty Ports* (1865–81); *Returns of Trade and Trade Reports* (1882–1919); *Annual Trade Report and Returns* (1920–); *Foreign Trade of China* (1920–31). Shanghai: Inspectorate General of Customs.
Jilin Tongzhi [Jilin gazetteer]. 1965. 10 vols. Zhongguo bianjiang congshu, di 1 ji, 2.
Kotoku gannendo noson jittai chosa [A survey of actual village conditions in 1934]. 1936. 3 vols. Changchun: Manzhouguo shiyebu linshi chanye diaochaju.
Kotoku sannendo noson jittai chosa [A survey of actual village conditions in 1936]. 1936. 4 vols. Changchun: Manzhouguo shiyebu linshi chanye diaochaju.
Manshu nogyo tokei [Annual statistics of Manchurian agriculture]. 1935 and 1938. Dairen.
Noson jittai chosa hokokusho [Report on a survey of actual village conditions]. 1937. 3 vols. Changchun: Manzhouguo shiyebu linshi chanye diaochaju.
Qinding Shengjing tongzhi (SJTZ) [Imperial Shengjing Gazetteer]. 1736. Wang He 王河 et al., comps. 3 vols. Reprint: Wenhai chubanshe, 1965.
———. 1784. A Gui 阿桂 et al., comps. 2 vols. Reprint: Shenyang: Liaohai chubanshe, 1997.

2. CHINESE

Chen Yuning 陳育寧. 1986. "E'erduosi diqu shamohua di xingcheng he fazhan shulun" [Account of the formation and development of the desertification of the Ordos region]. *Zhongguo shehui kexue*, 2:69–82.
Cheng Chongde 成崇德. 1990. "Qingdai qianqi Menggu diqu di nongmuye fazhan ji Qingchao di zhengce" [Development of agriculture and pastoralism

in the Mongol areas and government policies of the Qing dynasty during the early Qing period]. *Qingdai bianjiang kaifa yanjiu.*

———. 1991. "Qingdai qianqi dui Menggu di fengjin zhengce yu renkou, kaifa ji shengtai huanjing di guanxi" [The relationship between population, land reclamation and ecological environment and the closure policy toward the Mongols during the Early Qing Dynasty]. *Qingshi yanjiu,* 2:26–31.

Chifeng shi [History of Chifeng]. 1991. Suhemiaopo 蘇赫苗潑, Wang Deyuan 王德源 and Zhang Jianhua 張建華, eds. Beijing: Wenwu chubanshe.

Diao Shuren 刁書仁, ed. 1993. *Dongbei qidi yanjiu* [Research on bannerlands in the Northeast]. Jilin: Jilin wenshi chubanshe.

Gao Wangling 高王凌. 1992. "Ming-Qing shiqi di gengdi mianji" [Cultivated area during the Ming and Qing periods]. *Qingshi yanjiu,* 3:61–66.

Guo Songyi 郭松義. 1985. "Qingdai di renkou zengzhang he renkou liuqian" [Population movement and population circulation during the Qing Dyansty]. *Qingshi luncong,* 5:103–38.

Guo Songyi 郭松義. 1990. "Qingdai renkou liudong yu bianjiang kaifa" [Population movement and border development during the Qing Dynasty]. *Qing bianjiang kaifa yanjiu.*

He Yaozhang 何耀彰, ed. 1978. *Man Qing zhi Meng zhengce zhi yanjiu* [Research on Manchu Qing policies for controlling Mongolia]. National Taiwan Normal University, Institute of History, Special Issue Number 2. Taipei.

Heilongjiang tongji nianjian [Heilongjiang statistical yearbook]. 1995. Beijing: Zhongguo tongji chubanshe.

Hu Zhiyu 胡智育. 1984. "Ke'erqin nanbu caoyuan shamohua di yanbian guocheng ji qi zhengzhi tujing" [The process of desertification in the southern Keerqin grasslands and methods of controlling it]. *Zhongguo caoyuan jikan,* 2:66–69.

Jilin tongji nianjian [Jilin statistical yearbook]. 1995. Beijing: Zhongguo tongji chubanshe.

Jin Qicong 金啓孮. 1981. *Manzu di lishi yu shenghuo: Sanjiazitun diaocha baogao* [History and life of the Manchus: Report on an investigation of Sanjiazi village]. Harbin: Heilongjiang renmin chubanshe.

Kong Jingwei 孔經緯, ed. 1990. *Qingdai Dongbei diqu jingji shi* [Economic history of the Northeast region during the Qing]. Harbin: Heilongjiang renmin chubanshe.

Kuang Haolin 況浩林. 1985. "Pingshuo Qingdai Neimenggu diqu kenzhi di deshi" [Evaluation of the gains and losses in the colonization of the Inner Mongolian region during the Qing Dynasty]. *Minzu yanjiu,* 1:46–53.

Liang Bing 梁冰. 1991. *Yikezhao meng di tudi kaiken* [Opening of land to cultivation in Yikezhao League]. Hohhot: Neimenggu daxue chubanshe.

Liaoning tongji nianjian [Liaoning statistical yearbook]. 1995. Beijing: Zhongguo tongji chubanshe.

Liu Xuanmin 劉選民. 1936. "Dongsansheng Jingqi tunken shimo" [Survey of land reclamation by Capital banners in the Northeast]. *Yugong* (October 1936), 6.3–4:81–91.

———. 1938. "Qingdai Dongsansheng yimin yu kaiken" [Migration and land reclamation in the Northeast during the Qing Dynasty]. *Shixue nianbao* (December 1938), 2.5:67–120.

Lu Minghui 盧明輝, ed. 1994. *Qingdai beibu bianjiang minzu jingji fazhanshi* [Economic history of the peoples of the northern border during the Qing Dynasty]. Harbin: Heilongjiang jiaoyu chubanshe.

Ma Dongyu 馬東玉. 1985. "Qingdai tuntian tantao" [Investigation of military colonies during the Qing]. *Liaoning shifan daxue xuebao: shehui kexue ban*, 1:62–67.

Ma Ruheng 馬汝珩 and Cheng Chongde 成崇德. 1990. "Kang Qian shiqi renkou liudong yu changcheng bianwai kaifa" [Population movement during the Kangxi and Qianlong eras and development of the areas outside the Great Wall]. *Qingshi yanjiu*, 2:10–20.

Ma Yongshan 馬永山 and Zhao Yi 趙毅. 1992. "Qingchao guanyu Neimenggu diqu jinken fangken zhengce di yanbian" [Evolution of policies regarding land reclamation in the region of Inner Mongolia during the Qing Dynasty]. *Shehui kexue jikan*, 5:86–91.

Ma Yueshan 馬越山. 1986. "Qingdai Dongbei di fengjin zhengce" [Closure policy in the Northeast during the Qing]. *Shehui kexue jikan*, 3:44–49.

Manzu jianshi [Short History of the Manchus]. 1979. Beijing: Zhonghua shuju.

Manzu shehui lishi diaocha [Investigation into the social history of the Manchus]. 1985. Shenyang: Liaoning renmin chubanshe.

Neimenggu tongji nianjian [Inner Mongolia statistical yearbook]. 1995. Beijing: Zhongguo tongji chubanshe.

Qingdai bianjiang kaifa yanjiu [Research on the development of border regions during the Qing Dynasty]. 1990. Ma Ruheng 馬汝珩 and Ma Dazheng 馬大正, eds. Beijing: Zhongguo shehui kexue chubanshe.

Song Naigong 宋迺工, ed. 1987. *Zhongguo renkou: Neimenggu fence* [China's Population: Inner Mongolia]. Beijing: Zhongguo caizheng jingji chubanshe.

Sun Zhanwen 孫占文. 1981. "Qing chu, zhong qi Heilongjiang sheng di tudi kaifa" [Land reclamation in Heilongjiang Province during the early and mid-Qing]. *Beifang luncong*, 1:89–100.

Sun Zhanwen 孫占文 and Wu Wenxian 吳文銜. 1982. "Qing chu Heilongjiang diqu tudi kaifa gaishu" [Summary of land reclamation in the Heilongjiang region during the early Qing]. *Dongbei kaogu yu lishi*, 1:65–71.

Tian Zhihe 田志和. 1982. "Qingdai Ke'erqin Mengdi kaifa shulue" [Brief account of the development of Mongol territories of the Keerqin during the Qing dynasty]. *Shehui kexue zhanxian*, 2:187–92.

———. 1984A. "Qingdai Dongbei Mengdi kaifa shuyao" [General account of land reclamation in the Mongol regions of the Northeast during the Qing Dynasty]. *Dongbei shida xuebao, zhexue shehui kexue ban*, 1:87–94.

———. 1984B. "Qingdai Dongbei Mengdi di zudian ji qi xiang mindi di zhuanhua" [Transformation of rented land to private land in the Mongol areas of the Northeast during the Qing]. *Jilin daxue shehui kexue xuebao*, 4:85–90.

———. 1986. "Qingdai Dongbei Mengdi kaifa zhong di maodun he douzheng" [Contradictions and struggles in the reclamation of the Mongol lands in the Northeast during the Qing Dynasty]. *Dongbei shida xuebao, zhexue shehui kexueban,* 4:56–61.

———. 1987. "Lun Qingmo dongbu Mengqi diqu di yimin shibian wenti" [On the problem of "Moving population to strengthen the border" in the eastern Mongol banner region during the late Qing]. *Beifang wenwu,* 2:84–90.

Wang Bingming 汪炳明. 1990. "Qingmo xinzheng yu beibu bianjiang kaifa" [The New Policies of the late Qing and development of the northern border]. *Qingdai bianjiang kaifa yanjiu.*

Wang Shangyi 王尚義. n.d. "Lishi shiqi E'erduosi gaoyuan nongmuye di jiaoti ji qi dui ziran huanjing di yingxiang" [Alternation of agriculture and pastoralism on the Ordos Plateau in historical times and its influence on the natural environment]. *Lishi dili,* 5:11–24.

Wang Wenhui 王文輝, ed. 1990. *Neimenggu qihou* [Climate of Inner Mongolia]. Beijing: Qixiang chubanshe.

Wang Yaoyu 王藥雨. 1938. "Shandong nongmin licun di yige jiantao" [Investigation into the departure from villages of Shandong peasants]. *Zhongguo jingji yanjiu.* Vol. 1. Fang Xianting, ed. Shangwu yinshuguan.

Wang Yuhai 王玉海. 1990. "Qingdai Kalaqin di nongye fazhan he tudi guanxi" [Agricultural development and land relations in Kalaqin during the Qing dynasty]. *Qingdai bianjiang kaifa yanjiu.*

Wang Yuquan 王毓銓, et al. 1991. *Zhongguo tunken shi* [History of military colonization and cultivation in China]. Vol. 3. Beijing: Nongye chubanshe.

Weichang Manzu Mengguzu zizhixian zhi. 1997. [Gazetteer of the Weichang Manchu-Mongol Autonomous County]. Shenyang: Liaohai chubanshe.

Wengniuteqi wenshi ziliao [Historical Materials on Wengniute Banner]. 1986. *Zhengxie Wengniuteqi weiyuanhui wenshi ziliao gongzuo weiyuanhui,* ed. Wengniuteqi weisheng xitong yinshuachang.

Wu Chengming 吳承明. 1983. "Lun Qingdai qianqi woguo guonei shichang" [On China's domestic market in the early Qing]. *Lishi yanjiu,* 1:96–106.

Xiao Jun 蕭軍. 1936. *Luye di gushi* [Story of green leaves]. Reprint: Lanxi: Gansu renmin chubanshe, 1983.

Xie Guozhen 謝國楨. 1948. *Qingchu liuren kaifa Dongbei shi* [A history of the development, by exiles, of Manchuria during the early Qing dynasty]. Shanghai: Kaiming shudian.

Xing Yichen 邢亦塵. 1987. "Jindai Mengguzu xumuye shengchan di shangpinhua qushi" [Trend toward commodity production in modern Mongol animal husbandry]. *Mengguzu jingji fazhanshi yanjiu,* 1:182–93.

Xu Dixin 許滌新 and Wu Chengming 吳承明, eds. 1985. *Zhongguo zibenzhuyi fazhan shi* [History of the development of capitalism in China]. Vol. 1. *Zhongguo zibenzhuyi di mengya* [Sprouts of capitalism in China]. Beijing: Renmin chubanshe.

Xu Shuming 許淑明. 1988. "Qing qianqi Heilongjiang diqu di san zuo xincheng—Aihui, Mo'ergen he Qiqiha'er" [Three new cities in Heilongjiang during the early Qing—Aihui, Mergen, and Tsitsihar]. *Qing shi yanjiu tongxun,* 3:17–22.

———. 1990. "Qingdai Dongbei diqu tudi kaiken shulue" [Account of land reclamation in the Northeast region during the Qing dynasty]. *Qingdai bianjiang kaifa yanjiu.*

Yang Xuechen 楊學琛. 1963. "Qingdai qidi di xingzhi ji qi bianhua" [The nature of and changes in Qing bannerlands]. *Lishi yanjiu* (June 1963), 3:175–94.

———. 1988. "Qingdai di baqi wanggong guizu zhangyuan" [Eight Banner imperial and noble estates during the Qing period]. *Manzu shi yanjiu ji* [Researches on Manchu history]. Wang Zhonghan 王鍾翰, ed. Beijing: Zhongguo shehui kexue chubanshe.

Yuan Senpo 袁森坡. 1986. "Saiwai Chengde senlin lishi bianqian di fansi" [Reflections on historical changes in the forests of Chengde outside the Great Wall]. *Hebei xuekan*, 2:26–31.

Zhang Qizhuo 張其桌. 1984. *Manzu zai Xiuyan* [Manchus in Xiuyan]. Shenyang: Liaoning renmin chubanshe.

Zhang Xuanru 張琁如. 1983. "Qingchu fengjin yu zhaomin kaiken" [Closure and recruitment of people to reclaim land during the early Qing]. *Shehui kexue zhanxian*, 1:182–88.

Zhang Yaomin 張耀民. 1990. "Chengzhen xingqi yiji shougongye, jinrongye, he shangye" [The revival of market towns and handicrafts, finance, and trade]. *Qingdai Dongbei diqu jingji shi.* Kong Jingwei 孔經緯, ed. Harbin: Heilongjiang renmin chubanshe.

Zhang Zhihua 張植華. 1987. "Qingdai Hetao diqu nongye ji nongtian shuili gaikuang chutan" [Preliminary discussion of the conditions of agriculture and agricultural water control in the Hetao region during the Qing period]. *Neimenggu daxue xuebao* (1987), 4:85–93.

Zhao Yongfu 趙永復. 1981. "Lishi shang Maowusu shadi di bianqian wenti" [The question of change in the Maowusu sandland during historical times]. *Lishi dili*, 1:34–47.

Zhao Zhongfu 趙中孚. 1971. "1920–30 niandai di Dongsansheng yimin" [Migration to the Three Northeastern Provinces during the period 1920–30]. *Zhongyang yanjiuyuan jindaishi yanjiusuo jikan* (June 1971), 2:325–43.

———. 1972. "Yimin yu Dongsansheng beibu di nongye kaifa, 1920–30" [Migration and the agricultural development of Northern Manchuria, 1920–30]. *Zhongyang yanjiuyuan jindai shi yanjiusuo jikan* (December 1972), 3.2:347–63.

———. 1974. "Jindai Dongsansheng yimin wenti zhi yanjiu" [Research on the migration question in the Northeast in modern times]. *Zhongyang yanjiuyuan jindai shi yanjiusuo jikan* (December 1974), 4.2:613–64.

———. 1981. "Qingdai Dongsansheng di diquan guanxi yu fengjin zhengce" [Land ownership and closure policy in the three provinces of the Northeast during the Qing]. *Zhongyang yanjiuyuan jindaishi yanjiusuo jikan*, 10:283–302.

Zhongguo nonye nianjian [China agricultural yearbook]. Various years. Beijing: Zhongguo nongye chubanshe.

Zhongguo tongji nianjian [China statistical yearbook]. Various years. Beijing: Zhongguo tongji chubanshe.

Zhongguo ziran dili: Lishi ziran dili [China's Natural Geography: Historical Natural Geography]. 1982. Beijing: Kexue chubanshe.

3. ENGLISH

Adachi, Kinnosuke. 1925. *Manchuria: A Survey.* New York: Robert M. McBride & Co.

Andrews, Roy Chapman. 1932. *The New Conquest of Central Asia: A Narrative of the Explorations of the Central Asiatic Expeditions in Mongolia and China, 1921–1930.* New York: The American Museum of Natural History.

Arseniev, V. K. 1941. *Dersu the Trapper.* Translated by Malcolm Burr. New York: E. P. Dutton & Co.

Bartlett, Beatrice S. 1991. *Monarch and Ministers: The Grand Council in Mid-Ch'ing China, 1723–1820.* Berkeley: University of California Press.

Bawden, C. R. 1989. *The Modern History of Mongolia.* London: Kegan Paul International.

Binsteed, Lieutenant G. C. 1913. "The Tribal and Administrative System of Mongolia." *The Far Eastern Review,* 10(2): 41–48, 70.

Bix, Herbert. 1972. "Japanese Imperialism and the Manchurian Economy 1900–1931." *China Quarterly,* 51:425–43.

Bohr, Paul Richard. 1972. *Famine in China and the Missionary: Timothy Richard as Relief Administrator and Advocate of National Reform, 1876–1884.* Cambridge, MA: Harvard University Press.

Borei, Dorothy V. 1992. "Beyond the Great Wall: Agricultural Development in Northern Xinjiang, 1760–1820." *To Achieve Security and Wealth: The Qing Imperial State and the Economy, 1644–1911.* Jane Kate Leonard and John R. Watt, eds. Ithaca: Cornell University East Asia Program.

Brandt, Loren. 1987. "Review of Philip C. C. Huang, *The Peasant Economy and Social Change in North China.*" *Economic Development and Cultural Change,* 35.3:670–82.

———. 1989. *Commercialization and Agricultural Development in East-Central China, 1870–1937.* Cambridge: Cambridge University Press.

Brandt, Loren, and Barbara Sands. 1990. "Beyond Malthus and Ricardo: Economic Growth, Land Concentration, and Income Distribution in Early Twentieth-Century Rural China." *The Journal of Economic History,* 1.4:807–27.

Bray, Francesca. 1984. *Science and Civilisation in China.* Vol. 6, Part 2. *Agriculture.* Cambridge: Cambridge University Press.

Brown, Shannon R. 1981. "Cakes and Oil: Technology Transfer and Chinese Soybean Processing, 1860–95." *Comparative Studies in Society and History* (July 1981), 23.3:449–63.

Buck, John Lossing. 1930. *Chinese Farm Economy.* University of Nanking. Reprint: Taipei: Southern Materials Center, Inc., 1978.

———. 1937A. *Land Utilization in China.* Chicago: University of Chicago Press.

———. 1937B. *Land Utilization in China: Statistics.* Chicago: University of Chicago Press. Reprint: New York: Garland Publishing, 1982.

Buxton, L. H. Dudley. 1923. "Present Conditions in Inner Mongolia." *The Geographical Journal* (June 1923), 61.6:393–413.

Chan, Sucheng. 1990. "European and Asian Immigration into the United States in Comparative Perspective, 1820s to 1920s." *Immigration Reconsidered: History, Sociology and Politics*. Virginia Yans-McLaughlin, ed. New York: Oxford University Press.

Chao, Kang. 1977. *The Development of Cotton Textile Production in China*. Cambridge, MA: Harvard University Press.

———. 1986. *Man and Land in Chinese History: An Economic Analysis*. Stanford: Stanford University Press.

Chen Nai-Ruenn. 1970. "Labor Absorption in a Newly Settled Agricultural Region: the Case of Manchuria." *Economic Essays [Jingji lunwen congkan]*. The Graduate Institute of Economics, National Taiwan University. 1:139–54.

———. 1972. "Agricultural Productivity in a Newly Settled Region: The Case of Manchuria." *Economic Development and Cultural Change* (October 1972), 21.1:87–95.

China, Inspectorate General of Customs (CIGC). 1911. *The Soya Bean of Manchuria*. Special Series No. 31. Shanghai: Inspectorate General of Customs.

Chinese Eastern Railway Company (CER). 1924. *North Manchuria and the Chinese Eastern Railway*. Harbin: C.E.R. Printing Office.

Christiansen, Flemming. 1992. "New Land in China, 1900–1937: State Intervention and Land Reclamation." Leeds East Asia Papers, No. 10. Department of East Asian Studies, University of Leeds.

Cronon, William. 1987. "Revisiting the Vanishing Frontier: The Legacy of Frederick Jackson Turner." *Western Historical Quarterly* (April 1987), 157–76.

———. 1991. *Nature's Metropolis: Chicago and the Great West*. New York: Norton.

———, George Miles, and Jay Gitlin, eds. 1992. *Under an Open Sky: Rethinking America's Western Past*. New York: Norton.

Crossley, Pamela Kyle. 1990. *Orphan Warriors: Three Manchu Generations and the End of the Qing World*. Princeton: Princeton University Press.

———. 1997. *The Manchus*. Cambridge: Blackwell Publishers.

Du Halde, Jean-Baptiste. 1741. *The General History of China, Containing a Geographical, Historical, Chronological, Political and Physical Description of the Empire of China, Chinese Tartary, Corea and Thibet*. 4 vols. 3rd Edition. London: J. Watts.

Eckstein, Alexander, Kang Chao, and John Chang. 1974. "The Economic Development of Manchuria: The Rise of a Frontier Economy." *Journal of Economic History* (March 1974), 34.1:239–64.

Edmonds, Richard L. 1979. "The Willow Palisade." *Annals of the Association of American Geographers* (December 1979), 69.4:599–621.

———. 1985. *Northern Frontiers of Qing China and Tokugawa Japan: A Comparative Study of Frontier Policy*. University of Chicago, Department of Geography, Research Paper No. 213.

Elliott, Mark C. 2001. *The Manchu Way: The Eight Banners and Ethnic Identity in Late Imperial China*. Stanford: Stanford University Press.

Elvin, Mark C. 1972. "The High-Level Equilibrium Trap: The Causes of the Decline of Invention in the Traditional Chinese Textile Industries." *Economic*

Organization in Chinese Society. W. W. Wilmott, ed. Stanford: Stanford University Press.

———. 1973. *The Pattern of the Chinese Past: A Social and Economic Interpretation.* Stanford: Stanford University Press.

Esherick, Joseph W. 1981. "Number Games: A Note on Land Distribution in Prerevolutionary China." *Modern China,* 7.4:387–411.

———. 1987. *The Origins of the Boxer Uprising.* Berkeley: University of California Press.

Gamble, Sidney D. 1954. *Ting Hsien: A North China Rural Community.* Institute of Pacific Relations. Reprint: Stanford: Stanford University Press.

Goldblatt, Howard. 1976. *Hsiao Hung.* Boston: Twayne Publishers.

Goldman, Merle. 1967. *Literary Dissent in Communist China.* Cambridge, MA: Harvard University Press.

Gottschang, Thomas R., and Diana Lary. 2000. *Swallows and Settlers: The Great Migration from North China to Manchuria.* Ann Arbor: Center for Chinese Studies, University of Michigan.

Grousset, Rene. 1970. *The Empire of the Steppes: A History of Central Asia.* Translated by Naomi Walford. New Brunswick: Rutgers University Press.

Gutzlaff, Charles. 1834. *Journal of Three Voyages Along the Coast of China in 1831, 1832, and 1833.* London: Frederick Westley and H. H. Davis.

Guy, Donna J., and Thomas E. Sheridan, eds. 1998. *Contested Ground: Comparative Frontiers on the Northern and Southern Edges of the Spanish Empire.* Tucson: University of Arizona Press.

Hedin, Sven. 1933. *Jehol: City of Emperors.* Translated by E. G. Nash. New York: E. P. Dutton & Company.

Hedley, John, F.R.G.S. 1910. *Tramps in Dark Mongolia.* New York: Charles Scribner's Sons.

Ho, Franklin L. 1931. "Population Movement to the North Eastern Frontier in China." *Economic Trends and Problems in the Early Republican Period.* China Institute of Pacific Relations, ed. New York: Garland Publishing, 1980.

Ho, Ping-ti. 1959. *Studies on the Population of China, 1368–1953.* Cambridge, MA: Harvard University Press.

Hosie, Alexander. 1904. *Manchuria: Its People, Resources and Recent History.* New York: Charles Scribner's Sons.

Howard, Harvey J. 1926. *Ten Weeks with Chinese Bandits.* New York: Dodd, Mead and Company.

Hsiao Chun. 1942. *Village in August.* Translated by Evan King. New York: Smith and Durrell.

Hsiao Hung. 1979. *The Field of Life and Death and Tales of Hulan River.* Translated by Howard Goldblatt and Ellen Yeung. Bloomington: Indiana University Press.

———. 1986. *Market Street.* Translated by Howard Goldblatt. Seattle: University of Washington Press.

Huang, Philip C. C. 1985. *The Peasant Economy and Social Change in North China.* Stanford: Stanford University Press.

———. 1990. *The Peasant Family and Rural Development in the Yangzi Delta, 1350–1988*. Stanford: Stanford University Press.

———. 1991. "The Paradigmatic Crisis in Chinese Studies: Paradoxes in Social and Economic History." *Modern China* (July 1991), 17.3:299–341.

Huc, Evariste-Regis, and Joseph Gabet. 1987. *Travels in Tartary, Thibet and China, 1844–1846*. Translated by William Hazlitt. New York: Dover.

Isett, Christopher Mills. 1998. "State, Peasant and Agrarian Change on the Manchurian Frontier, 1644–1940." Ph.D. dissertation, University of California at Los Angeles.

Jagchid, Sechin, and Paul Hyer. 1979. *Mongolia's Culture and Society*. Boulder: Westview Press.

James, Henry E. M. 1888. *The Long White Mountain, or A Journey in Manchuria*. London: Longmans, Green and Co. Reprint: New York: Greenwood Press, 1968.

Kingman, Harry L. 1932. *Effects of Chinese Nationalism Upon Manchurian Railway Developments, 1925–1931*. Berkeley: University of California Press.

Lattimore, Owen. 1932. *Manchuria: Cradle of Conflict*. New York: Macmillan.

———. 1934. *The Mongols of Manchuria*. New York: John Day.

Lee, James Z., and Cameron D. Campbell. 1997. *Fate and fortune in rural China: Social organization and population behavior in Liaoning, 1774–1873*. Cambridge: Cambridge University Press.

Lee, James Z., and Robert Y. Eng. 1984. "Population and Family History in Eighteenth Century Manchuria: Preliminary Results from Daoyi, 1774–98." *Ch'ing-shih wen-t'i* (June 1984), 5.1:1–55.

Lee, Leo Ou-fan. 1973. *The Romantic Generation of Modern Chinese Writers*. Cambridge, MA: Harvard University Press.

Lee, Robert H. G. 1970. *The Manchurian Frontier in Ch'ing History*. Cambridge, MA: Harvard University Press.

Li, Lillian. 1982. "Food, Famine and the Chinese State." *Journal of Asian Studies*, 61.4:687–707.

Limerick, Patricia Nelson. 1987. *The Legacy of Conquest: The Unbroken Past of the American West*. New York: W. W. Norton & Co.

Mallory, Walter H. 1928. *China: Land of Famine*. American Geographical Society. Special Publication No. 6. New York: American Geographical Society.

Manchoukuo Year Book, The. 1934. Tokyo: Toa-Keizai Chosakyoku.

Mazumdar, Sucheta. 1998. *Sugar and Society in China: Peasants, Technology, and the World Market*. Cambridge, MA: Harvard University Press.

McIntyre, Rev. John. 1886. "Roadside Religion in Manchuria." *Journal of the North-China Branch of the Royal Asiatic Society*, 21:43–66.

McKeown, Adam. 1999. "Conceptualizing Chinese Diasporas, 1842 to 1949." *Journal of Asian Studies* (May 1999), 58.2:306–37.

McNeill, William H. 1964. *Europe's Steppe Frontier, 1500–1800*. Chicago: University of Chicago Press.

———. 1983. *The Great Frontier: Freedom and Hierarchy in Modern Times*. Princeton: Princeton University Press.

Michie, A. 1863. "Narrative of a Journey from Tientsin to Moukden in Manchuria in July 1861." *The Journal of the Royal Geographic Society of London* (1863), 33:153–66.

Millward, James A. 1998. *Beyond the Pass: Economy, Ethnicity, and Empire in Qing Central Asia, 1759–1864*. Stanford: Stanford University Press.

Morse, Hosea Ballou. 1909. *Gilds of China, with an Account of the Gild Merchant or Co-Hong of Canton*. London: Longmans, Green and Co.

Myers, Ramon H. 1970. *The Chinese Peasant Economy: Agricultural Development in Hopei and Shantung, 1890–1949*. Cambridge, MA: Harvard University Press.

———. 1976. "Socioeconomic Change in Villages of Manchuria During the Ch'ing and Republican Periods: Some Preliminary Findings." *Modern Asian Studies*, 10.4:591–620.

———. 1991. "How Did the Modern Chinese Economy Develop?—A Review Article." *Journal of Asian Studies* (August 1991), 50.3:604–28.

National Agricultural Research Bureau, Ministry of Industry. 1936. *Crop Reports* [Nong qing baogao], 4.7:171–80.

National Research Council. 1992A. *China and Global Climate Change: Opportunities for Collaboration*. Washington, D.C.: National Academy Press.

———. 1992B. *Grasslands and Grassland Sciences in Northern China*. Washington, D.C.: National Academy Press.

Needham, Joseph. 1965. *Science and Civilisation in China*. Vol 4, Part II. *Mechanical Engineering*. Cambridge: Cambridge University Press.

Newman, Robert P. 1992. *Owen Lattimore and the "Loss" of China*. Berkeley: University of California Press.

D'Orleans, Père Pierre Joseph. 1971. *History of the Two Tartar Conquerors of China, Including the Two Journeys into Tartary of Father Ferdinand Verbiest, in the Suite of the Emperor Kang-Hi*. New York: Burt Franklin.

Pasternak, Burton, and Janet W. Salaff. 1993. *Cowboys and Cultivators: the Chinese of Inner Mongolia*. Boulder: Westview Press.

Perdue, Peter C. 1987. *Exhausting the Earth: State and Peasant in Hunan, 1500–1850*. Cambridge, MA: Harvard University Press.

———. 1996. "Military Mobilization in Seventeenth- and Eighteenth-Century China, Russia, and Mongolia." *Modern Asian Studies* (October 1996), 30.4:757–93.

Perkins, Dwight. 1969. *Agricultural Development in China, 1368–1968*. Chicago: Aldine.

Perry, Elizabeth J. 1980. *Rebels and Revolutionaries in North China, 1845–1945*. Stanford: Stanford University Press.

Pruitt, Ida. 1945. *A Daughter of Han: The Autobiography of a Chinese Working Woman*. New Haven: Yale University Press. Reissue: Stanford: Stanford University Press, 1967.

Rawski, Evelyn S. 1998. *The Last Emperors: A Social History of Qing Imperial Institutions*. Berkeley: University of California Press.

Rawski, Thomas G. 1989. *Economic Growth in Prewar China*. Berkeley: University of California Press.

Reardon-Anderson, James. 1986. "Chemical Industry in China, 1860–1949." *Osiris* (1986), 2:177–224.

Rhoads, Edward J. M. 2000. *Manchus & Han: Ethnic Relations and Political Power in Late Qing and Early Republican China, 1861–1928*. Seattle: University of Washington Press.

Richardson, H. E. 1962. *A Short History of Tibet*. E. P. Dutton & Co.

Rigger, Shelley. 1995. "Voices of Manchu Identity, 1635–1935." *Cultural Encounters on China's Ethnic Frontiers*. Stevan Harrell, ed. Seattle: University of Washington Press.

Roth, Gertraude. 1979. "The Manchu-Chinese Relationship, 1618–36." *From Ming to Ch'ing: Conquest, Region, and Continuity in Seventeenth-Century China*. Jonathan D. Spence and John E. Wills Jr., eds. New Haven: Yale University Press.

Rowe, William T. 1984. *Hankow: Commerce and Society in a Chinese City, 1796–1889*. Stanford: Stanford University Press.

Sakatani, Baron Y. 1932. "Manchuria: A Survey of Its Economic Development." Unpublished report, revised by Grover Clark. New York: Carnegie Endowment for International Peace.

Schultz, T. W. 1964. *Transforming Traditional Agriculture*. New Haven: Yale University Press.

Sebes, Joseph, S.J., 1961. *The Jesuits and the Sino-Russian Treaty of Nerchinsk (1689): The Diary of Thomas Pereira, S.J.* Rome: Institutum Historicum, S.I.

Serruys, Henry. 1959. "Chinese in Southern Mongolia during the Sixteenth Century." *Monumenta Serica* (Journal of Oriental Studies), 18:1–95.

Shepherd, John Robert. 1993. *Statecraft and Political Economy on the Taiwan Frontier,1600–1800*. Stanford: Stanford University Press.

Shirokogoroff, S. M. 1924. *Social Organization of the Manchus: A Study of the Manchu Clan Organization*. Shanghai: Kelly & Walsh, Ltd.

———. 1926. "Northern Tungus Migrations in the Far East." *Journal of the North-China Branch of the Royal Asiatic Society* (1926), 57:123–83.

Siu, Paul C. P. 1952. "The Sojourner." *American Journal of Sociology* (1952), 50:34–44.

Smith, Arthur H. 1899. *Village Life in China*. Fleming H. Revell. Reprint: Boston: Little, Brown, 1970.

Snow, Edgar, ed. 1937. *Living China: Modern Chinese Short Stories*. Reprint: Westport, CT: Hyperion Press, 1989.

South Manchuria Railway Company (SMR), The. Various years. *Report on Progress in Manchuria*. Dairen: The South Manchuria Railway Company.

Sowerby, Arthur de Carle. 1919. "The Exploration of Manchuria." *The Geographical Journal* (August 1919), 54.2:73–92.

———. 1922. *The Naturalist in Manchuria*. Vol. I. *Travel and Exploration*. Tientsin: Tientsin Press.

Staunton, Sir George. 1797. *An Authentic Account of an Embassy from the King of Great Britain to the Emperor of China*. London: W. Bulmer and Co.

Stebelsky, I. 1983. "Agriculture and Soil Erosion in the European Forest Steppe."

Studies in Russian Historical Geography, James H. Baker and R. A. French, eds. London: Academic Press.

Sun, Kungtu C. 1969. *The Economic Development of Manchuria in the First Half of the Twentieth Century*. Cambridge, MA: Harvard University Press.

Sung Ying-Hsing. 1966. *T'ien-Kung K'ai-Wu: Chinese Technology in the Seventeenth Century*. Translated by E-Tu Zen Sun and Shiou-Chuan Sun. University Park: Pennsylvania State University Press.

Tilly, Charles. 1990. "Transplanted Networks." *Immigration Reconsidered: History, Sociology and Politics*. Virginia Yans-McLaughlin, ed. New York: Oxford University Press.

Timkowski, George. 1827. *Travels of the Russian Mission through Mongolia to China, and Residence in Peking, in the Years 1820–1821*. 2 vols. London: Longman, Rees, Orme, Brown, and Green.

Torbert, Preston M. 1977. *The Ch'ing Imperial Household Department: A Study of Its Organization and Principal Functions, 1662–1796*. Cambridge, MA: Harvard University Press.

Treadgold, Donald W. 1952. "Russian Expansion in the Light of Turner's Study of the American Frontier." *Agricultural History*, 26:147–52.

————. 1957. *The Great Siberian Migration: Government and Peasant in Resettlement from Emancipation to the First World War*. Princeton: Princeton University Press.

Tsao Lien-en. 1930. "The Method of Chinese Colonization in Manchuria." *Chinese Economic Journal* (August 1930), 7.2:831–52.

Turner, Frederick Jackson. 1963. *The Significance of the Frontier in American History*. Harold P. Simonson, ed. New York: Frederick Ungar Publishing Co.

U.S. Department of Agriculture. 1992. *Agricultural Statistics of the People's Republic of China, 1949–90*. W. Hunter Colby, ed. Washington, DC: Economic Research Service, Statistical Bulletin. Number 844.

Wakeman, Frederic, Jr. 1985. *The Great Enterprise: The Manchu Reconstruction of Imperial Order in Seventeenth-Century China*. 2 vols. Berkeley: University of California Press.

Walker, Brett L. 2001. *The Conquest of Ainu Lands: Ecology and Culture in Japanese Expansion, 1590–1800*. Berkeley: University of California Press.

Wang Gungwu. 1991. *China and the Chinese Overseas*. Singapore: Times Academic Press.

Wang, Yeh-chien. 1973. *Land Taxation in Imperial China, 1750–1911*. Cambridge, MA: Harvard University Press.

Weale, B. L. Putnam. 1904. *Manchu and Muscovite: Being Letters from Manchuria Written during the Autumn of 1903*. New York: Macmillan.

Webb, Walter Prescott. 1931. *The Great Plains*. Reprint: Lincoln, NE: Bison Books, 1981.

Weber, David J. and Jane M. Rausch. 1994. *Where Cultures Meet: Frontiers in Latin American History*. Wilmington: Scholarly Resources Books.

White, Richard. 1991. *The Middle Ground: Indians, Empires, and Republics in the Great Lakes Region, 1650–1815*. Cambridge: Cambridge University Press.

Wieczynski, Joseph L. 1976. *The Russian Frontier: The Impact of Borderlands upon the Course of Early Russian History.* Charlottesville: University Press of Virginia.

Will, Pierre-Etienne. 1990. *Bureaucracy and Famine in Eighteenth-Century China.* Translated by Elborg Forster. Stanford: Stanford University Press.

Williamson, Alexander. 1870. *Journeys in North China, Manchuria and Eastern Mongolia, with Some Account of Corea.* London: Smith, Elder & Co.

Wright, Mary C. 1957. *The Last Stand of Chinese Conservatism.* Stanford: Stanford University Press.

Wylie, J. A. 1893. "Journey Through Central Manchuria." *Geographical Journal,* 2:443–51.

Wyman, Mark. 1993. *Round-Trip to America: The Immigrants Return to Europe, 1880–1930.* Ithaca: Cornell University Press.

Wynne, Waller. 1958. *The Population of Manchuria.* U.S. Department of Commerce, Bureau of the Census. International Population Statistics Reports, Series P-90, No. 7. Washington: U.S. Government Printing Office.

Yang, Martin C. 1945. *A Chinese Village: Taitou, Shantung Province.* New York: Columbia University Press. Paperback edition, 1965.

Yang, Philip Q. 1999. "Sojourners or Settlers: Post-1965 Chinese Immigrants." *Journal of Asian American Studies,* 2.1:61–91.

Young, C. Walter. 1927A. "Chinese Labor Migration to Manchuria." *The Chinese Economic Journal* (July 1927), 1.7:613–33.

———. 1927B. "Economic Bases for New Railways in Manchuria." *The Chinese Economic Journal* (April 1927), 1.4:324–35.

———. 1928A. "Chinese Colonization in Manchuria." *The Far Eastern Review* (June 1928), 24.6:241–50; (July 1928), 24.7:296–303.

———. 1928B. "Manchuria, a New Homeland of the Chinese." *Current History,* 28:529–36.

———. 1932. "Chinese Immigration and Colonization in Manchuria." *Pioneer Settlement: Cooperative Studies by Twenty-Six Authors.* American Geographical Society. Special Publication No. 14. W. L. G. Joerg, ed. New York: American Geographical Society.

Younghusband, Francis Edward. 1898. *Among the Celestials: A Narrative of Travels in Manchuria, Across the Gobi Desert, Through the Himalayas to India.* London: John Murray, Albemarle Street.

———. 1904. *The Heart of a Continent: A Narrative of Travels in Manchuria, Across the Gobi Desert, Through the Himalayas, the Pamirs, and Hunza, 1884–1894.* New York: Charles Scribners Sons.

Yuan Chia-hua and Robert Payne, eds. and trans. 1946. *Contemporary Chinese Short Stories.* London: Noel Carrington.

Zhao Songqiao. 1986. *Physical Geography of China.* Beijing: Science Press. New York: John Wylye & Sons.

Zhu Hong, ed. and trans. 1988. *The Chinese Western: Short Fiction from Today's China.* New York: Ballantine Books.

Index

Italic page numbers indicate material in tables and illustrations.

Goldblatt, Howard, 256
Gorlos Banners, *44*, 50
Gottschang, Thomas, 98, 148
Great Britain, 206
Great Depression, 149, 240
Green Standard Forces, 89, 162
Guandi (god), 118
Guangdong, 49
Guangning, *10, 20,* 39
Guangxi, 49
Guantie (Chinese currency), 157
Guilds, 188, 192, 209
Guomindang, 149

Haicheng, *10, 20,* 39
Haijin (sea embargo), 178
Hailar, *10, 24,* 239
Hailong, 209
Hailun, *10,* 209
Hanjun, see Bannermen, Chinese
Harbin, *10, 44,* 107, 152, 156, 188, 209, 211, 215, 239, 255–58
Hebei (Zhili) Province, 117–18, 120, 130; source of migrants to Manchuria, 21, 68, 98–100, 125, 128, 145, 151, 224; land use in, 22, 22n, 46, 68, 106–10, 106n, 154, 154n, 231n; hardship in, 98–100, 106–10, 147
Heilongjiang Military Region, *82,* 99, 222; demography of, 2, 49–50, 77; government and organization in, 6, 24–27, 24n, 31, 34, 41, 73–74, 83; land use in, 29n, 38, 49–50, 58n, 79n, 105, 182–83; economy and finance of, 58, 72, 72n, 78, 175–76
Heilongjiang Province, *82,* 99, 113, *131,* 135, *222;* demography of, 97–98, 138, 145, 152, 152n; surveys of, 26, 106–7, 124, 224, 250; land use in, 106–7, 154, 158, 222, 231; economy and finance of, 211, 228, 238–39; Chinese writers in, 255, 258–59
Heilongjiang (Amur) River: Russians in, 6, 19, 24–25, 73, 87–88; natural conditions of, 9, *10,* 104, 113
Heilongjiangcheng, *see* Aihui
Ho, Franklin, 137–38, 148
Hong Huzi, see Red Beards
Hoshun (*khoshun*), 35

Hosie, Alexander, 116, 201
Howard, Harvey, 135–36
Huang, Philip, 9, 120, 228, 246–51
Huc, Abbe Evariste-Regis, 51
Hulan, *10,* 24, 77, 112, 142, 174–76, 209, 215, 255
Hulunbuir, 239
Hunchun, *10,* 24, 77, 112, 175–76

Imperial Household Department (*Neiwufu*), 31, 33, 74
Imperial Maritime Custom Service (IMCS), 98
Imperial Shengjing Gazetteer, 37
Inner Mongolia, 6, 45, 72, 79; geography of, 1–2, 261; land use in, 7, 27, 31, 58, 62, 68, 153, 160; migration and settlement in, 23–24, 37, 46, 50–54, 126, 128, 128n, 143; as border region, 85–88; comparison with Russia, 92–93, 116; trade in, 172–77, 174n, 239
Inspector General of Customs, 199

Jalait Banner, 44
James, Henry, 115, 120, 133–34, 143–44
Japan and Japanese, 2, 5, 17, 78, 98, 157, 222, 261; surveys and studies in Manchuria, 21–22, 106, 124, 151–53, 244–45; surveys and studies in Shandong, 120, 288; trade with Manchuria, 19th and early 20th century, 169–72, 187–89, 198–200, 200n; trade and transportation in Manchuria, 1930s, 114–15, 149–51, 204, 208–16, 231n, 239; Chinese resistance to, 255–57
Jardine, Matheson Company, 184
Jasagh (Mongol banner chief), 36
Jehol, 43, 44, 50, 105–7, 111, 137, 142, 178, 222, 222
Jesuits, 20, 26
Jilin City, *10,* 39, 44, 174, *191;* history of, 24–26, 113n, 175–76; roads through, 111–13, 113n, 186, 201; railroads in, 209, 215
Jilin Military Region, *82,* 99, *222;* government and organization in, 6, 24–25, 27, 31, 34, 37n, 39–41, 73–74, 75n; demography of, 26–27, 49, 67, 82, 105; land use in, 29n, 31, 37–38, 38n, 48–50, 56,